ISBN 0-8373-1936-6

C-1936
CAREER EXAMINATION SERIES

This is your
PASSBOOK® for...

Senior Clerk-Typist

Test Preparation Study Guide

Questions & Answers

NLC

NATIONAL LEARNING CORPORATION

PASSBOOK®

NOTICE

This book is SOLELY intended for, is sold ONLY to, and its use is RESTRICTED to *individual*, bona fide applicants or candidates who qualify by virtue of having seriously filed applications for appropriate license, certificate, professional and/or promotional advancement, higher school matriculation, scholarship, or other legitimate requirements of educational and/or governmental authorities.

This book is NOT intended for use, class instruction, tutoring, training, duplication, copying, reprinting, excerption, or adaptation, etc., by:

(1) Other publishers

(2) Proprietors and/or Instructors of "Coaching" and/or Preparatory Courses

(3) Personnel and/or Training Divisions of commercial, industrial, and governmental organizations

(4) Schools, colleges, or universities and/or their departments and staffs, including teachers and other personnel

(5) Testing Agencies or Bureaus

(6) Study groups which seek by the purchase of a single volume to copy and/or duplicate and/or adapt this material for use by the group as a whole without having purchased individual volumes for each of the members of the group

(7) Et al.

Such persons would be in violation of appropriate Federal and State statutes.

PROVISION OF LICENSING AGREEMENTS. — Recognized educational commercial, industrial, and governmental institutions and organizations, and others legitimately engaged in educational pursuits, including training, testing, and measurement activities, may address a request for a licensing agreement to the copyright owners, who will determine whether, and under what conditions, including fees and charges, the materials in this book may be used by them. In other words, a licensing facility exists for the legitimate use of the material in this book on other than an individual basis. However, it is asseverated and affirmed here that the material in this book *CANNOT* be used without the receipt of the express permission of such a licensing agreement from the Publishers.

NATIONAL LEARNING CORPORATION
212 Michael Drive
Syosset, New York 11791

Inquiries re licensing agreements should be addressed to:
The President
National Learning Corporation
212 Michael Drive
Syosset, New York 11791

PASSBOOK® SERIES

THE *PASSBOOK® SERIES* has been created to prepare applicants and candidates for the ultimate academic battlefield – the examination room.

At some time in our lives, each and every one of us may be required to take an examination – for validation, matriculation, admission, qualification, registration, certification, or licensure.

Based on the assumption that every applicant or candidate has met the basic formal educational standards, has taken the required number of courses, and read the necessary texts, the *PASSBOOK® SERIES* furnishes the one special preparation which may assure passing with confidence, instead of failing with insecurity. Examination questions – together with answers – are furnished as the basic vehicle for study so that the mysteries of the examination and its compounding difficulties may be eliminated or diminished by a sure method.

This book is meant to help you pass your examination provided that you qualify and are serious in your objective.

The entire field is reviewed through the huge store of content information which is succinctly presented through a provocative and challenging approach – the question-and-answer method.

A climate of success is established by furnishing the correct answers at the end of each test.

You soon learn to recognize types of questions, forms of questions, and patterns of questioning. You may even begin to anticipate expected outcomes.

You perceive that many questions are repeated or adapted so that you can gain acute insights, which may enable you to score many sure points.

You learn how to confront new questions, or types of questions, and to attack them confidently and work out the correct answers.

You note objectives and emphases, and recognize pitfalls and dangers, so that you may make positive educational adjustments.

Moreover, you are kept fully informed in relation to new concepts, methods, practices, and directions in the field.

You discover that you are actually taking the examination all the time: you are preparing for the examination by "taking" an examination, not by reading extraneous and/or supererogatory textbooks.

In short, this PASSBOOK®, used directedly, should be an important factor in helping you to pass your test.

SENIOR CLERK-TYPIST

DUTIES

Performs a wide variety of difficult and responsible clerical and typing functions requiring the application of independent judgment and clerical knowledge. Checks the accuracy and completeness of documents, applications, legal instruments, payment claims of vendors and contract claims. Composes routine letters and transcribes or types such items as reports, letters, statements, tabulations, vouchers and legal documents. Keeps perpetual inventory and consumption records. May supervise a small number of clerical personnel engaged in routine clerical duties. Does related work as required.

SCOPE OF THE EXAMINATION

The written test will cover knowledge, skills and/or abilities in such areas as:

1. **Spelling** - These questions test for the ability to spell words that are used in written business communications.

2. **Grammar, usage, punctuation** - The grammar and usage questions test for the ability to apply the basic rules of grammar and usage. The punctuation questions test for a knowledge of the correct placement of punctuation marks in sentences.

3. **Keyboarding practices** - These questions test for a knowledge of preferred practices in such areas as letter format, capitalization, hyphenation, plurals, possessives, word division, word and figure style for numbers, and common proofreading marks. In addition, you will be given a passage to proofread and asked questions about how to correct the errors in the passage.

4. **Office record keeping** - These questions evaluate your ability to perform common office record keeping tasks. The test consists of two or more "sets" of questions, each set concerning a different problem. Typical record keeping problems might involve the organization or collation of data from several sources; scheduling; maintaining a record system using running balances; or completion of a table summarizing data using totals, subtotals, averages and percents.

5. **Office practices** - These questions test for a knowledge of generally agreed-upon practices governing the handling of situations which stenographers, typists, and secretaries encounter in their work, as well as a knowledge of efficient and effective methods used to accomplish office tasks. The questions will cover such topics as planning work flow; setting priorities; dealing effectively with staff, visitors, and callers; filing and retrieving information; safeguarding confidentiality; using office equipment; and making procedural decisions and recommendations which contribute to a well-managed office.

HOW TO TAKE A TEST

I. YOU MUST PASS AN EXAMINATION

A. *WHAT EVERY CANDIDATE SHOULD KNOW*

Examination applicants often ask us for help in preparing for the written test. What can I study in advance? What kinds of questions will be asked? How will the test be given? How will the papers be graded?

As an applicant for a civil service examination, you may be wondering about some of these things. Our purpose here is to suggest effective methods of advance study and to describe civil service examinations.

Your chances for success on this examination can be increased if you know how to prepare. Those "pre-examination jitters" can be reduced if you know what to expect. You can even experience an adventure in good citizenship if you know why civil service exams are given.

B. *WHY ARE CIVIL SERVICE EXAMINATIONS GIVEN?*

Civil service examinations are important to you in two ways. As a citizen, you want public jobs filled by employees who know how to do their work. As a job seeker, you want a fair chance to compete for that job on an equal footing with other candidates. The best-known means of accomplishing this two-fold goal is the competitive examination.

Exams are widely publicized throughout the nation. They may be administered for jobs in federal, state, city, municipal, town or village governments or agencies.

Any citizen may apply, with some limitations, such as the age or residence of applicants. Your experience and education may be reviewed to see whether you meet the requirements for the particular examination. When these requirements exist, they are reasonable and applied consistently to all applicants. Thus, a competitive examination may cause you some uneasiness now, but it is your privilege and safeguard.

C. *HOW ARE CIVIL SERVICE EXAMS DEVELOPED?*

Examinations are carefully written by trained technicians who are specialists in the field known as "psychological measurement," in consultation with recognized authorities in the field of work that the test will cover. These experts recommend the subject matter areas or skills to be tested; only those knowledges or skills important to your success on the job are included. The most reliable books and source materials available are used as references. Together, the experts and technicians judge the difficulty level of the questions.

Test technicians know how to phrase questions so that the problem is clearly stated. Their ethics do not permit "trick" or "catch" questions. Questions may have been tried out on sample groups, or subjected to statistical analysis, to determine their usefulness.

Written tests are often used in combination with performance tests, ratings of training and experience, and oral interviews. All of these measures combine to form the best-known means of finding the right person for the right job.

II. HOW TO PASS THE WRITTEN TEST

A. NATURE OF THE EXAMINATION

To prepare intelligently for civil service examinations, you should know how they differ from school examinations you have taken. In school you were assigned certain definite pages to read or subjects to cover. The examination questions were quite detailed and usually emphasized memory. Civil service exams, on the other hand, try to discover your present ability to perform the duties of a position, plus your potentiality to learn these duties. In other words, a civil service exam attempts to predict how successful you will be. Questions cover such a broad area that they cannot be as minute and detailed as school exam questions.

In the public service similar kinds of work, or positions, are grouped together in one "class." This process is known as *position-classification*. All the positions in a class are paid according to the salary range for that class. One class title covers all of these positions, and they are all tested by the same examination.

B. FOUR BASIC STEPS

1) Study the announcement

How, then, can you know what subjects to study? Our best answer is: "Learn as much as possible about the class of positions for which you've applied." The exam will test the knowledge, skills and abilities needed to do the work.

Your most valuable source of information about the position you want is the official exam announcement. This announcement lists the training and experience qualifications. Check these standards and apply only if you come reasonably close to meeting them.

The brief description of the position in the examination announcement offers some clues to the subjects which will be tested. Think about the job itself. Review the duties in your mind. Can you perform them, or are there some in which you are rusty? Fill in the blank spots in your preparation.

Many jurisdictions preview the written test in the exam announcement by including a section called "Knowledge and Abilities Required," "Scope of the Examination," or some similar heading. Here you will find out specifically what fields will be tested.

2) Review your own background

Once you learn in general what the position is all about, and what you need to know to do the work, ask yourself which subjects you already know fairly well and which need improvement. You may wonder whether to concentrate on improving your strong areas or on building some background in your fields of weakness. When the announcement has specified "some knowledge" or "considerable knowledge," or has used adjectives like "beginning principles of..." or "advanced ... methods," you can get a clue as to the number and difficulty of questions to be asked in any given field. More questions, and hence broader coverage, would be included for those subjects which are more important in the work. Now weigh your strengths and weaknesses against the job requirements and prepare accordingly.

3) Determine the level of the position

Another way to tell how intensively you should prepare is to understand the level of the job for which you are applying. Is it the entering level? In other words, is this the position in which beginners in a field of work are hired? Or is it an intermediate or advanced level? Sometimes this is indicated by such words as "Junior" or "Senior" in the class title. Other jurisdictions use Roman numerals to designate the level – Clerk I, Clerk II, for example. The word "Supervisor" sometimes appears in the title. If the level is not indicated by the title, check the description of duties. Will you be working under very close supervision, or will you have responsibility for independent decisions in this work?

4) Choose appropriate study materials

Now that you know the subjects to be examined and the relative amount of each subject to be covered, you can choose suitable study materials. For beginning level jobs, or even advanced ones, if you have a pronounced weakness in some aspect of your training, read a modern, standard textbook in that field. Be sure it is up to date and has general coverage. Such books are normally available at your library, and the librarian will be glad to help you locate one. For entry-level positions, questions of appropriate difficulty are chosen – neither highly advanced questions, nor those too simple. Such questions require careful thought but not advanced training.

If the position for which you are applying is technical or advanced, you will read more advanced, specialized material. If you are already familiar with the basic principles of your field, elementary textbooks would waste your time. Concentrate on advanced textbooks and technical periodicals. Think through the concepts and review difficult problems in your field.

These are all general sources. You can get more ideas on your own initiative, following these leads. For example, training manuals and publications of the government agency which employs workers in your field can be useful, particularly for technical and professional positions. A letter or visit to the government department involved may result in more specific study suggestions, and certainly will provide you with a more definite idea of the exact nature of the position you are seeking.

III. KINDS OF TESTS

Tests are used for purposes other than measuring knowledge and ability to perform specified duties. For some positions, it is equally important to test ability to make adjustments to new situations or to profit from training. In others, basic mental abilities not dependent on information are essential. Questions which test these things may not appear as pertinent to the duties of the position as those which test for knowledge and information. Yet they are often highly important parts of a fair examination. For very general questions, it is almost impossible to help you direct your study efforts. What we can do is to point out some of the more common of these general abilities needed in public service positions and describe some typical questions.

1) General information

Broad, general information has been found useful for predicting job success in some kinds of work. This is tested in a variety of ways, from vocabulary lists to questions about current events. Basic background in some field of work, such as sociology or economics, may be sampled in a group of questions. Often these are principles which have become familiar to most persons through exposure rather than through formal training. It is difficult to advise you how to study for these questions; being alert to the world around you is our best suggestion.

2) Verbal ability

An example of an ability needed in many positions is verbal or language ability. Verbal ability is, in brief, the ability to use and understand words. Vocabulary and grammar tests are typical measures of this ability. Reading comprehension or paragraph interpretation questions are common in many kinds of civil service tests. You are given a paragraph of written material and asked to find its central meaning.

3) Numerical ability

Number skills can be tested by the familiar arithmetic problem, by checking paired lists of numbers to see which are alike and which are different, or by interpreting charts and graphs. In the latter test, a graph may be printed in the test booklet which you are asked to use as the basis for answering questions.

4) Observation

A popular test for law-enforcement positions is the observation test. A picture is shown to you for several minutes, then taken away. Questions about the picture test your ability to observe both details and larger elements.

5) Following directions

In many positions in the public service, the employee must be able to carry out written instructions dependably and accurately. You may be given a chart with several columns, each column listing a variety of information. The questions require you to carry out directions involving the information given in the chart.

6) Skills and aptitudes

Performance tests effectively measure some manual skills and aptitudes. When the skill is one in which you are trained, such as typing or shorthand, you can practice. These tests are often very much like those given in business school or high school courses. For many of the other skills and aptitudes, however, no short-time preparation can be made. Skills and abilities natural to you or that you have developed throughout your lifetime are being tested.

Many of the general questions just described provide all the data needed to answer the questions and ask you to use your reasoning ability to find the answers. Your best preparation for these tests, as well as for tests of facts and ideas, is to be at your physical and mental best. You, no doubt, have your own methods of getting into an exam-taking mood and keeping "in shape." The next section lists some ideas on this subject.

IV. KINDS OF QUESTIONS

Only rarely is the "essay" question, which you answer in narrative form, used in civil service tests. Civil service tests are usually of the short-answer type. Full instructions for answering these questions will be given to you at the examination. But in case this is your first experience with short-answer questions and separate answer sheets, here is what you need to know:

1) Multiple-choice Questions

Most popular of the short-answer questions is the "multiple choice" or "best answer" question. It can be used, for example, to test for factual knowledge, ability to solve problems or judgment in meeting situations found at work.

A multiple-choice question is normally one of three types—

- It can begin with an incomplete statement followed by several possible endings. You are to find the one ending which *best* completes the statement, although some of the others may not be entirely wrong.
- It can also be a complete statement in the form of a question which is answered by choosing one of the statements listed.

- It can be in the form of a problem – again you select the best answer.

Here is an example of a multiple-choice question with a discussion which should give you some clues as to the method for choosing the right answer:

When an employee has a complaint about his assignment, the action which will *best* help him overcome his difficulty is to
   A. discuss his difficulty with his coworkers
   B. take the problem to the head of the organization
   C. take the problem to the person who gave him the assignment
   D. say nothing to anyone about his complaint

In answering this question, you should study each of the choices to find which is best. Consider choice "A" – Certainly an employee may discuss his complaint with fellow employees, but no change or improvement can result, and the complaint remains unresolved. Choice "B" is a poor choice since the head of the organization probably does not know what assignment you have been given, and taking your problem to him is known as "going over the head" of the supervisor. The supervisor, or person who made the assignment, is the person who can clarify it or correct any injustice. Choice "C" is, therefore, correct. To say nothing, as in choice "D," is unwise. Supervisors have and interest in knowing the problems employees are facing, and the employee is seeking a solution to his problem.

2) True/False Questions

The "true/false" or "right/wrong" form of question is sometimes used. Here a complete statement is given. Your job is to decide whether the statement is right or wrong.

SAMPLE: A roaming cell-phone call to a nearby city costs less than a non-roaming call to a distant city.

This statement is wrong, or false, since roaming calls are more expensive.

This is not a complete list of all possible question forms, although most of the others are variations of these common types. You will always get complete directions for answering questions. Be sure you understand *how* to mark your answers – ask questions until you do.

V. RECORDING YOUR ANSWERS

Computer terminals are used more and more today for many different kinds of exams.

For an examination with very few applicants, you may be told to record your answers in the test booklet itself. Separate answer sheets are much more common. If this separate answer sheet is to be scored by machine – and this is often the case – it is highly important that you mark your answers correctly in order to get credit.

An electronic scoring machine is often used in civil service offices because of the speed with which papers can be scored. Machine-scored answer sheets must be marked with a pencil, which will be given to you. This pencil has a high graphite content which responds to the electronic scoring machine. As a matter of fact, stray dots may register as answers, so do not let your pencil rest on the answer sheet while you are pondering the correct answer. Also, if your pencil lead breaks or is otherwise defective, ask for another.

Since the answer sheet will be dropped in a slot in the scoring machine, be careful not to bend the corners or get the paper crumpled.

The answer sheet normally has five vertical columns of numbers, with 30 numbers to a column. These numbers correspond to the question numbers in your test booklet. After each number, going across the page are four or five pairs of dotted lines. These short dotted lines have small letters or numbers above them. The first two pairs may also have a "T" or "F" above the letters. This indicates that the first two pairs only are to be used if the questions are of the true-false type. If the questions are multiple choice, disregard the "T" and "F" and pay attention only to the small letters or numbers.

Answer your questions in the manner of the sample that follows:

32. The largest city in the United States is
    A. Washington, D.C.
    B. New York City
    C. Chicago
    D. Detroit
    E. San Francisco

1) Choose the answer you think is best. (New York City is the largest, so "B" is correct.)
2) Find the row of dotted lines numbered the same as the question you are answering. (Find row number 32)
3) Find the pair of dotted lines corresponding to the answer. (Find the pair of lines under the mark "B.")
4) Make a solid black mark between the dotted lines.

VI. BEFORE THE TEST

Common sense will help you find procedures to follow to get ready for an examination. Too many of us, however, overlook these sensible measures. Indeed, nervousness and fatigue have been found to be the most serious reasons why applicants fail to do their best on civil service tests. Here is a list of reminders:

- Begin your preparation early – Don't wait until the last minute to go scurrying around for books and materials or to find out what the position is all about.
- Prepare continuously – An hour a night for a week is better than an all-night cram session. This has been definitely established. What is more, a night a week for a month will return better dividends than crowding your study into a shorter period of time.
- Locate the place of the exam – You have been sent a notice telling you when and where to report for the examination. If the location is in a different town or otherwise unfamiliar to you, it would be well to inquire the best route and learn something about the building.
- Relax the night before the test – Allow your mind to rest. Do not study at all that night. Plan some mild recreation or diversion; then go to bed early and get a good night's sleep.
- Get up early enough to make a leisurely trip to the place for the test – This way unforeseen events, traffic snarls, unfamiliar buildings, etc. will not upset you.
- Dress comfortably – A written test is not a fashion show. You will be known by number and not by name, so wear something comfortable.

- Leave excess paraphernalia at home – Shopping bags and odd bundles will get in your way. You need bring only the items mentioned in the official notice you received; usually everything you need is provided. Do not bring reference books to the exam. They will only confuse those last minutes and be taken away from you when in the test room.
- Arrive somewhat ahead of time – If because of transportation schedules you must get there very early, bring a newspaper or magazine to take your mind off yourself while waiting.
- Locate the examination room – When you have found the proper room, you will be directed to the seat or part of the room where you will sit. Sometimes you are given a sheet of instructions to read while you are waiting. Do not fill out any forms until you are told to do so; just read them and be prepared.
- Relax and prepare to listen to the instructions
- If you have any physical problem that may keep you from doing your best, be sure to tell the test administrator. If you are sick or in poor health, you really cannot do your best on the exam. You can come back and take the test some other time.

VII. AT THE TEST

The day of the test is here and you have the test booklet in your hand. The temptation to get going is very strong. Caution! There is more to success than knowing the right answers. You must know how to identify your papers and understand variations in the type of short-answer question used in this particular examination. Follow these suggestions for maximum results from your efforts:

1) Cooperate with the monitor
The test administrator has a duty to create a situation in which you can be as much at ease as possible. He will give instructions, tell you when to begin, check to see that you are marking your answer sheet correctly, and so on. He is not there to guard you, although he will see that your competitors do not take unfair advantage. He wants to help you do your best.

2) Listen to all instructions
Don't jump the gun! Wait until you understand all directions. In most civil service tests you get more time than you need to answer the questions. So don't be in a hurry. Read each word of instructions until you clearly understand the meaning. Study the examples, listen to all announcements and follow directions. Ask questions if you do not understand what to do.

3) Identify your papers
Civil service exams are usually identified by number only. You will be assigned a number; you must not put your name on your test papers. Be sure to copy your number correctly. Since more than one exam may be given, copy your exact examination title.

4) Plan your time
Unless you are told that a test is a "speed" or "rate of work" test, speed itself is usually not important. Time enough to answer all the questions will be provided, but this does not mean that you have all day. An overall time limit has been set. Divide the total time (in minutes) by the number of questions to determine the approximate time you have for each question.

5) Do not linger over difficult questions

If you come across a difficult question, mark it with a paper clip (useful to have along) and come back to it when you have been through the booklet. One caution if you do this – be sure to skip a number on your answer sheet as well. Check often to be sure that you have not lost your place and that you are marking in the row numbered the same as the question you are answering.

6) Read the questions

Be sure you know what the question asks! Many capable people are unsuccessful because they failed to *read* the questions correctly.

7) Answer all questions

Unless you have been instructed that a penalty will be deducted for incorrect answers, it is better to guess than to omit a question.

8) Speed tests

It is often better NOT to guess on speed tests. It has been found that on timed tests people are tempted to spend the last few seconds before time is called in marking answers at random – without even reading them – in the hope of picking up a few extra points. To discourage this practice, the instructions may warn you that your score will be "corrected" for guessing. That is, a penalty will be applied. The incorrect answers will be deducted from the correct ones, or some other penalty formula will be used.

9) Review your answers

If you finish before time is called, go back to the questions you guessed or omitted to give them further thought. Review other answers if you have time.

10) Return your test materials

If you are ready to leave before others have finished or time is called, take ALL your materials to the monitor and leave quietly. Never take any test material with you. The monitor can discover whose papers are not complete, and taking a test booklet may be grounds for disqualification.

VIII. EXAMINATION TECHNIQUES

1) Read the general instructions carefully. These are usually printed on the first page of the exam booklet. As a rule, these instructions refer to the timing of the examination; the fact that you should not start work until the signal and must stop work at a signal, etc. If there are any *special* instructions, such as a choice of questions to be answered, make sure that you note this instruction carefully.

2) When you are ready to start work on the examination, that is as soon as the signal has been given, read the instructions to each question booklet, underline any key words or phrases, such as *least, best, outline, describe* and the like. In this way you will tend to answer as requested rather than discover on reviewing your paper that you *listed without describing*, that you selected the *worst* choice rather than the *best* choice, etc.

3) If the examination is of the objective or multiple-choice type – that is, each question will also give a series of possible answers: A, B, C or D, and you are called upon to select the best answer and write the letter next to that answer on your answer paper – it is advisable to start answering each question in turn. There may be anywhere from 50 to 100 such questions in the three or four hours allotted and you can see how much time would be taken if you read through all the questions before beginning to answer any. Furthermore, if you come across a question or group of questions which you know would be difficult to answer, it would undoubtedly affect your handling of all the other questions.

4) If the examination is of the essay type and contains but a few questions, it is a moot point as to whether you should read all the questions before starting to answer any one. Of course, if you are given a choice – say five out of seven and the like – then it is essential to read all the questions so you can eliminate the two that are most difficult. If, however, you are asked to answer all the questions, there may be danger in trying to answer the easiest one first because you may find that you will spend too much time on it. The best technique is to answer the first question, then proceed to the second, etc.

5) Time your answers. Before the exam begins, write down the time it started, then add the time allowed for the examination and write down the time it must be completed, then divide the time available somewhat as follows:
   - If 3-1/2 hours are allowed, that would be 210 minutes. If you have 80 objective-type questions, that would be an average of 2-1/2 minutes per question. Allow yourself no more than 2 minutes per question, or a total of 160 minutes, which will permit about 50 minutes to review.
   - If for the time allotment of 210 minutes there are 7 essay questions to answer, that would average about 30 minutes a question. Give yourself only 25 minutes per question so that you have about 35 minutes to review.

6) The most important instruction is to *read each question* and make sure you know what is wanted. The second most important instruction is to *time yourself properly* so that you answer every question. The third most important instruction is to *answer every question*. Guess if you have to but include something for each question. Remember that you will receive no credit for a blank and will probably receive some credit if you write something in answer to an essay question. If you guess a letter – say "B" for a multiple-choice question – you may have guessed right. If you leave a blank as an answer to a multiple-choice question, the examiners may respect your feelings but it will not add a point to your score. Some exams may penalize you for wrong answers, so in such cases *only*, you may not want to guess unless you have some basis for your answer.

7) Suggestions
   a. Objective-type questions
      1. Examine the question booklet for proper sequence of pages and questions
      2. Read all instructions carefully
      3. Skip any question which seems too difficult; return to it after all other questions have been answered
      4. Apportion your time properly; do not spend too much time on any single question or group of questions

5. Note and underline key words – *all, most, fewest, least, best, worst, same, opposite,* etc.
6. Pay particular attention to negatives
7. Note unusual option, e.g., unduly long, short, complex, different or similar in content to the body of the question
8. Observe the use of "hedging" words – *probably, may, most likely,* etc.
9. Make sure that your answer is put next to the same number as the question
10. Do not second-guess unless you have good reason to believe the second answer is definitely more correct
11. Cross out original answer if you decide another answer is more accurate; do not erase until you are ready to hand your paper in
12. Answer all questions; guess unless instructed otherwise
13. Leave time for review

b. Essay questions
1. Read each question carefully
2. Determine exactly what is wanted. Underline key words or phrases.
3. Decide on outline or paragraph answer
4. Include many different points and elements unless asked to develop any one or two points or elements
5. Show impartiality by giving pros and cons unless directed to select one side only
6. Make and write down any assumptions you find necessary to answer the questions
7. Watch your English, grammar, punctuation and choice of words
8. Time your answers; don't crowd material

8) Answering the essay question

Most essay questions can be answered by framing the specific response around several key words or ideas. Here are a few such key words or ideas:

M's: manpower, materials, methods, money, management
P's: purpose, program, policy, plan, procedure, practice, problems, pitfalls, personnel, public relations

a. Six basic steps in handling problems:
1. Preliminary plan and background development
2. Collect information, data and facts
3. Analyze and interpret information, data and facts
4. Analyze and develop solutions as well as make recommendations
5. Prepare report and sell recommendations
6. Install recommendations and follow up effectiveness

b. Pitfalls to avoid
1. *Taking things for granted* – A statement of the situation does not necessarily imply that each of the elements is necessarily true; for example, a complaint may be invalid and biased so that all that can be taken for granted is that a complaint has been registered

2. *Considering only one side of a situation* – Wherever possible, indicate several alternatives and then point out the reasons you selected the best one
3. *Failing to indicate follow up* – Whenever your answer indicates action on your part, make certain that you will take proper follow-up action to see how successful your recommendations, procedures or actions turn out to be
4. *Taking too long in answering any single question* – Remember to time your answers properly

IX. AFTER THE TEST

Scoring procedures differ in detail among civil service jurisdictions although the general principles are the same. Whether the papers are hand-scored or graded by machine we have described, they are nearly always graded by number. That is, the person who marks the paper knows only the number – never the name – of the applicant. Not until all the papers have been graded will they be matched with names. If other tests, such as training and experience or oral interview ratings have been given, scores will be combined. Different parts of the examination usually have different weights. For example, the written test might count 60 percent of the final grade, and a rating of training and experience 40 percent. In many jurisdictions, veterans will have a certain number of points added to their grades.

After the final grade has been determined, the names are placed in grade order and an eligible list is established. There are various methods for resolving ties between those who get the same final grade – probably the most common is to place first the name of the person whose application was received first. Job offers are made from the eligible list in the order the names appear on it. You will be notified of your grade and your rank as soon as all these computations have been made. This will be done as rapidly as possible.

People who are found to meet the requirements in the announcement are called "eligibles." Their names are put on a list of eligible candidates. An eligible's chances of getting a job depend on how high he stands on this list and how fast agencies are filling jobs from the list.

When a job is to be filled from a list of eligibles, the agency asks for the names of people on the list of eligibles for that job. When the civil service commission receives this request, it sends to the agency the names of the three people highest on this list. Or, if the job to be filled has specialized requirements, the office sends the agency the names of the top three persons who meet these requirements from the general list.

The appointing officer makes a choice from among the three people whose names were sent to him. If the selected person accepts the appointment, the names of the others are put back on the list to be considered for future openings.

That is the rule in hiring from all kinds of eligible lists, whether they are for typist, carpenter, chemist, or something else. For every vacancy, the appointing officer has his choice of any one of the top three eligibles on the list. This explains why the person whose name is on top of the list sometimes does not get an appointment when some of the persons lower on the list do. If the appointing officer chooses the second or third eligible, the No. 1 eligible does not get a job at once, but stays on the list until he is appointed or the list is terminated.

X. HOW TO PASS THE INTERVIEW TEST

The examination for which you applied requires an oral interview test. You have already taken the written test and you are now being called for the interview test – the final part of the formal examination.

You may think that it is not possible to prepare for an interview test and that there are no procedures to follow during an interview. Our purpose is to point out some things you can do in advance that will help you and some good rules to follow and pitfalls to avoid while you are being interviewed.

What is an interview supposed to test?

The written examination is designed to test the technical knowledge and competence of the candidate; the oral is designed to evaluate intangible qualities, not readily measured otherwise, and to establish a list showing the relative fitness of each candidate – as measured against his competitors – for the position sought. Scoring is not on the basis of "right" and "wrong," but on a sliding scale of values ranging from "not passable" to "outstanding." As a matter of fact, it is possible to achieve a relatively low score without a single "incorrect" answer because of evident weakness in the qualities being measured.

Occasionally, an examination may consist entirely of an oral test – either an individual or a group oral. In such cases, information is sought concerning the technical knowledges and abilities of the candidate, since there has been no written examination for this purpose. More commonly, however, an oral test is used to supplement a written examination.

Who conducts interviews?

The composition of oral boards varies among different jurisdictions. In nearly all, a representative of the personnel department serves as chairman. One of the members of the board may be a representative of the department in which the candidate would work. In some cases, "outside experts" are used, and, frequently, a businessman or some other representative of the general public is asked to serve. Labor and management or other special groups may be represented. The aim is to secure the services of experts in the appropriate field.

However the board is composed, it is a good idea (and not at all improper or unethical) to ascertain in advance of the interview who the members are and what groups they represent. When you are introduced to them, you will have some idea of their backgrounds and interests, and at least you will not stutter and stammer over their names.

What should be done before the interview?

While knowledge about the board members is useful and takes some of the surprise element out of the interview, there is other preparation which is more substantive. It *is* possible to prepare for an oral interview – in several ways:

1) Keep a copy of your application and review it carefully before the interview

This may be the only document before the oral board, and the starting point of the interview. Know what education and experience you have listed there, and the sequence and dates of all of it. Sometimes the board will ask you to review the highlights of your experience for them; you should not have to hem and haw doing it.

2) Study the class specification and the examination announcement

Usually, the oral board has one or both of these to guide them. The qualities, characteristics or knowledges required by the position sought are stated in these documents. They offer valuable clues as to the nature of the oral interview. For example, if the job involves supervisory responsibilities, the announcement will usually indicate that knowledge of modern supervisory methods and the qualifications of the candidate as a supervisor will be tested. If so, you can expect such questions, frequently in the form of a hypothetical situation which you are expected to solve. NEVER go into an oral without knowledge of the duties and responsibilities of the job you seek.

3) Think through each qualification required
Try to visualize the kind of questions you would ask if you were a board member. How well could you answer them? Try especially to appraise your own knowledge and background in each area, *measured against the job sought*, and identify any areas in which you are weak. Be critical and realistic – do not flatter yourself.

4) Do some general reading in areas in which you feel you may be weak
For example, if the job involves supervision and your past experience has NOT, some general reading in supervisory methods and practices, particularly in the field of human relations, might be useful. Do NOT study agency procedures or detailed manuals. The oral board will be testing your understanding and capacity, not your memory.

5) Get a good night's sleep and watch your general health and mental attitude
You will want a clear head at the interview. Take care of a cold or any other minor ailment, and of course, no hangovers.

What should be done on the day of the interview?
Now comes the day of the interview itself. Give yourself plenty of time to get there. Plan to arrive somewhat ahead of the scheduled time, particularly if your appointment is in the fore part of the day. If a previous candidate fails to appear, the board might be ready for you a bit early. By early afternoon an oral board is almost invariably behind schedule if there are many candidates, and you may have to wait. Take along a book or magazine to read, or your application to review, but leave any extraneous material in the waiting room when you go in for your interview. In any event, relax and compose yourself.

The matter of dress is important. The board is forming impressions about you – from your experience, your manners, your attitude, and your appearance. Give your personal appearance careful attention. Dress your best, but not your flashiest. Choose conservative, appropriate clothing, and be sure it is immaculate. This is a business interview, and your appearance should indicate that you regard it as such. Besides, being well groomed and properly dressed will help boost your confidence.

Sooner or later, someone will call your name and escort you into the interview room. *This is it.* From here on you are on your own. It is too late for any more preparation. But remember, you asked for this opportunity to prove your fitness, and you are here because your request was granted.

What happens when you go in?
The usual sequence of events will be as follows: The clerk (who is often the board stenographer) will introduce you to the chairman of the oral board, who will introduce you to the other members of the board. Acknowledge the introductions before you sit down. Do not be surprised if you find a microphone facing you or a stenotypist sitting by. Oral interviews are usually recorded in the event of an appeal or other review.

Usually the chairman of the board will open the interview by reviewing the highlights of your education and work experience from your application – primarily for the benefit of the other members of the board, as well as to get the material into the record. Do not interrupt or comment unless there is an error or significant misinterpretation; if that is the case, do not hesitate. But do not quibble about insignificant matters. Also, he will usually ask you some question about your education, experience or your present job – partly to get you to start talking and to establish the interviewing "rapport." He may start the actual questioning, or turn it over to one of the other members. Frequently, each member undertakes the questioning on a particular area, one in which he is perhaps most competent, so you can expect each member to participate in the examination. Because time is limited, you may also expect some rather abrupt switches in the direction the questioning takes, so do not be upset by it. Normally, a board member will not pursue a single line of questioning unless he discovers a particular strength or weakness.

After each member has participated, the chairman will usually ask whether any member has any further questions, then will ask you if you have anything you wish to add. Unless you are expecting this question, it may floor you. Worse, it may start you off on an extended, extemporaneous speech. The board is not usually seeking more information. The question is principally to offer you a last opportunity to present further qualifications or to indicate that you have nothing to add. So, if you feel that a significant qualification or characteristic has been overlooked, it is proper to point it out in a sentence or so. Do not compliment the board on the thoroughness of their examination – they have been sketchy, and you know it. If you wish, merely say, "No thank you, I have nothing further to add." This is a point where you can "talk yourself out" of a good impression or fail to present an important bit of information. Remember, *you close the interview yourself.*

The chairman will then say, "That is all, Mr. _____, thank you." Do not be startled; the interview is over, and quicker than you think. Thank him, gather your belongings and take your leave. Save your sigh of relief for the other side of the door.

How to put your best foot forward

Throughout this entire process, you may feel that the board individually and collectively is trying to pierce your defenses, seek out your hidden weaknesses and embarrass and confuse you. Actually, this is not true. They are obliged to make an appraisal of your qualifications for the job you are seeking, and they want to see you in your best light. Remember, they must interview all candidates and a non-cooperative candidate may become a failure in spite of their best efforts to bring out his qualifications. Here are 15 suggestions that will help you:

1) Be natural – Keep your attitude confident, not cocky

If you are not confident that you can do the job, do not expect the board to be. Do not apologize for your weaknesses, try to bring out your strong points. The board is interested in a positive, not negative, presentation. Cockiness will antagonize any board member and make him wonder if you are covering up a weakness by a false show of strength.

2) Get comfortable, but don't lounge or sprawl

Sit erectly but not stiffly. A careless posture may lead the board to conclude that you are careless in other things, or at least that you are not impressed by the importance of the occasion. Either conclusion is natural, even if incorrect. Do not fuss with your clothing, a pencil or an ashtray. Your hands may occasionally be useful to emphasize a point; do not let them become a point of distraction.

3) Do not wisecrack or make small talk

This is a serious situation, and your attitude should show that you consider it as such. Further, the time of the board is limited – they do not want to waste it, and neither should you.

4) Do not exaggerate your experience or abilities

In the first place, from information in the application or other interviews and sources, the board may know more about you than you think. Secondly, you probably will not get away with it. An experienced board is rather adept at spotting such a situation, so do not take the chance.

5) If you know a board member, do not make a point of it, yet do not hide it

Certainly you are not fooling him, and probably not the other members of the board. Do not try to take advantage of your acquaintanceship – it will probably do you little good.

6) Do not dominate the interview

Let the board do that. They will give you the clues – do not assume that you have to do all the talking. Realize that the board has a number of questions to ask you, and do not try to take up all the interview time by showing off your extensive knowledge of the answer to the first one.

7) Be attentive

You only have 20 minutes or so, and you should keep your attention at its sharpest throughout. When a member is addressing a problem or question to you, give him your undivided attention. Address your reply principally to him, but do not exclude the other board members.

8) Do not interrupt

A board member may be stating a problem for you to analyze. He will ask you a question when the time comes. Let him state the problem, and wait for the question.

9) Make sure you understand the question

Do not try to answer until you are sure what the question is. If it is not clear, restate it in your own words or ask the board member to clarify it for you. However, do not haggle about minor elements.

10) Reply promptly but not hastily

A common entry on oral board rating sheets is "candidate responded readily," or "candidate hesitated in replies." Respond as promptly and quickly as you can, but do not jump to a hasty, ill-considered answer.

11) Do not be peremptory in your answers

A brief answer is proper – but do not fire your answer back. That is a losing game from your point of view. The board member can probably ask questions much faster than you can answer them.

12) Do not try to create the answer you think the board member wants

He is interested in what kind of mind you have and how it works – not in playing games. Furthermore, he can usually spot this practice and will actually grade you down on it.

13) Do not switch sides in your reply merely to agree with a board member

Frequently, a member will take a contrary position merely to draw you out and to see if you are willing and able to defend your point of view. Do not start a debate, yet do not surrender a good position. If a position is worth taking, it is worth defending.

14) Do not be afraid to admit an error in judgment if you are shown to be wrong

The board knows that you are forced to reply without any opportunity for careful consideration. Your answer may be demonstrably wrong. If so, admit it and get on with the interview.

15) Do not dwell at length on your present job

The opening question may relate to your present assignment. Answer the question but do not go into an extended discussion. You are being examined for a *new* job, not your present one. As a matter of fact, try to phrase ALL your answers in terms of the job for which you are being examined.

Basis of Rating

Probably you will forget most of these "do's" and "don'ts" when you walk into the oral interview room. Even remembering them all will not ensure you a passing grade. Perhaps you did not have the qualifications in the first place. But remembering them will help you to put your best foot forward, without treading on the toes of the board members.

Rumor and popular opinion to the contrary notwithstanding, an oral board wants you to make the best appearance possible. They know you are under pressure – but they also want to see how you respond to it as a guide to what your reaction would be under the pressures of the job you seek. They will be influenced by the degree of poise you display, the personal traits you show and the manner in which you respond.

ABOUT THIS BOOK

This book contains tests divided into Examination Sections. Go through each test, answering every question in the margin. We have also attached a sample answer sheet at the back of the book that can be removed and used. At the end of each test look at the answer key and check your answers. On the ones you got wrong, look at the right answer choice and learn. Do not fill in the answers first. Do not memorize the questions and answers, but understand the answer and principles involved. On your test, the questions will likely be different from the samples. Questions are changed and new ones added. If you understand these past questions you should have success with any changes that arise. Tests may consist of several types of questions. We have additional books on each subject should more study be advisable or necessary for you. Finally, the more you study, the better prepared you will be. This book is intended to be the last thing you study before you walk into the examination room. Prior study of relevant texts is also recommended. NLC publishes some of these in our Fundamental Series. Knowledge and good sense are important factors in passing your exam. Good luck also helps. So now study this Passbook, absorb the material contained within and take that knowledge into the examination. Then do your best to pass that exam.

––––––––

EXAMINATION SECTION

EXAMINATION SECTION
TEST 1

DIRECTIONS: Each question or incomplete statement is followed by several suggested answers or completions. Select the one that BEST answers the question or completes the statement. *PRINT THE LETTER OF THE CORRECT ANSWER IN THE SPACE AT THE RIGHT.*

1. A push-button telephone with six buttons, one of which is a *hold* button, is often used when more than one outside line is needed.
   If you are talking on one line of this type of telephone when another call comes in, what is the procedure to follow if you want to answer the second call but keep the first call on the line? Push the

   A. *hold* button at the same time as you push the *pickup* button of the ringing line
   B. *hold* button and then push the *pickup* button of the ringing line
   C. *pickup* button of the ringing line and then push the *hold* button
   D. *pickup* button of the ringing line and push the *hold* button when you return to the original line

   1.____

2. Suppose that you are asked to prepare a petty cash statement for March. The original and one copy are to go to the personnel office. One copy is to go to the fiscal office, and another copy is to go to your supervisor. The last copy is for your files.
   In preparing the statement and the copies, how many sheets of copy paper should you use?

   A. 3   B. 4   C. 5   D. 8

   2.____

3. Which one of the following is the LEAST important advantage of putting the subject of a letter in the heading to the right of the address?
   It

   A. makes filing of the copy easier
   B. makes more space available in the body of the letter
   C. simplifies distribution of letters
   D. simplifies determination of the subject of the letter

   3.____

4. Of the following, the MOST efficient way to put 100 copies of a one-page letter into 9 1/2" x 4 1/8" envelopes for mailing is to fold _____ into an envelope.

   A. each letter and insert it immediately after folding
   B. each letter separately until all 100 are folded; then insert each one
   C. the 100 letters two at a time, then separate them and insert each one
   D. two letters together, slip them apart, and insert each one

   4.____

5. When preparing papers for filing, it is NOT desirable to

   A. smooth papers that are wrinkled
   B. use paper clips to keep related papers together in the files
   C. arrange the papers in the order in which they will be filed
   D. mend torn papers with cellophane tape

   5.____

6. Of the following, the BEST reason for a clerical unit to have its own duplicating machine   6.___
is that the unit

    A. uses many forms which it must reproduce internally
    B. must make two copies of each piece of incoming mail for a special file
    C. must make seven copies of each piece of outgoing mail
    D. must type 200 envelopes each month for distribution to the same offices

7. Several offices use the same photocopying machine.   7.___
If each office must pay its share of the cost of running this machine, the BEST way of
determining how much of this cost should be charged to each of these offices is to

    A. determine the monthly number of photocopies made by each office
    B. determine the monthly number of originals submitted for photocopying by each
       office
    C. determine the number of times per day each office uses the photocopy machine
    D. divide the total cost of running the photocopy machine by the total number of
       offices using the machine

8. Which one of the following would it be BEST to use to indicate that a file folder has been   8.___
removed from the files for temporary use in another office?
A(n)

    A. cross-reference card   B. tickler file marker
    C. aperture card   D. out guide

9. Which one of the following is the MOST important objective of filing?   9.___

    A. Giving a secretary something to do in her spare time
    B. Making it possible to locate information quickly
    C. Providing a place to store unneeded documents
    D. Keeping extra papers from accumulating on workers' desks

10. If a check has been made out for an incorrect amount, the BEST action for the writer of   10.___
the check to take is to

    A. erase the original amount and enter the correct amount
    B. cross out the original amount with a single line and enter the correct amount above
       it
    C. black out the original amount so that it cannot be read and enter the correct
       amount above it
    D. write a new check

11. Which one of the following BEST describes the usual arrangement of a tickler file?   11.___

    A. Alphabetical   B. Chronological
    C. Numerical   D. Geographical

12. Which one of the following is the LEAST desirable filing practice?   12.___

    A. Using staples to keep papers together
    B. Filing all material without regard to date
    C. Keeping a record of all materials removed from the files
    D. Writing filing instructions on each paper prior to filing

13. Assume that one of your duties is to keep records of the office supplies used by your unit for the purpose of ordering new supplies when the old supplies run out. The information that will be of MOST help in letting you know when to reorder supplies is the   13._____

    A. quantity issued   B. quantity received
    C. quantity on hand   D. stock number

Questions 14-19.

DIRECTIONS: Questions 14 through 19 consist of sets of names and addresses. In each question, the name and address in Column II should be an exact copy of the name and address in Column I. If there is:
        a mistake *only* in the name, mark your answer A;
        a mistake *only* in the address, mark your answer B;
        a mistake in *both* name and address, mark your answer C;
        no mistake in *either* name or address, mark your answer D.

SAMPLE QUESTION

Column I	Column II
Michael Filbert	Michael Filbert
456 Reade Street	645 Reade Street
New York, N.Y. 10013	New York, N.Y. 10013

Since there is a mistake only in the address (the street number should be 456 instead of 645), the answer to the sample question is B.

COLUMN I	COLUMN II	
14. Esta Wong 141 West 68 St. New York, N.Y. 10023	Esta Wang 141 West 68 St. New York, N.Y. 10023	14._____
15. Dr. Alberto Grosso 3475 12th Avenue Brooklyn, N.Y. 11218	Dr. Alberto Grosso 3475 12th Avenue Brooklyn, N.Y. 11218	15._____
16. Mrs. Ruth Bortlas 482 Theresa Ct. Far Rockaway, N.Y. 11691	Ms. Ruth Bortlas 482 Theresa Ct. Far Rockaway, N.Y. 11169	16._____
17. Mr. and Mrs. Howard Fox 2301 Sedgwick Ave. Bronx, N.Y. 10468	Mr. and Mrs. Howard Fox 231 Sedgwick Ave. Bronx, N.Y. 10468	17._____
18. Miss Marjorie Black 223 East 23 Street New York, N.Y. 10010	Miss Margorie Black 223 East 23 Street New York, N.Y. 10010	18._____
19. Michelle Herman 806 Valley Rd. Old Tappan, N.J. 07675	Michelle Hermann 806 Valley Dr. Old Tappan, N.J. 07675	19._____

Questions 20-25.

DIRECTIONS: Questions 20 through 25 are to be answered SOLELY on the basis of the information in the following passage.

Basic to every office is the need for proper lighting. Inadequate lighting is a familiar cause of fatigue and serves to create a somewhat dismal atmosphere in the office. One requirement of proper lighting is that it be of an appropriate intensity. Intensity is measured in foot-candles. According to the Illuminating Engineering Society of New York, for casual seeing tasks such as in reception rooms, inactive file rooms, and other service areas, it is recommended that the amount of light be 30 foot-candles. For ordinary seeing tasks such as reading and work in active file rooms and in mail rooms, the recommended lighting is 100 foot-candles. For very difficult seeing tasks such as accounting, transcribing, and business machine use, the recommended lighting is 150 foot-candles.

Lighting intensity is only one requirement. Shadows and glare are to be avoided. For example, the larger the proportion of a ceiling filled with lighting units, the more glare-free and comfortable the lighting will be. Natural lighting from windows is not too dependable because on dark wintry days, windows yield little usable light, and on sunny, summer afternoons, the glare from windows may be very distracting. Desks should not face the windows. Finally, the main lighting source ought to be overhead and to the left of the user.

20.   According to the above passage, insufficient light in the office may cause   20.___

A.   glare   B.   shadows
C.   tiredness   D.   distraction

21.   Based on the above passage, which of the following must be considered when planning   21.___
lighting arrangements?
The

A.   amount of natural light present
B.   amount of work to be done
C.   level of difficulty of work to be done
D.   type of activity to be carried out

22.   It can be inferred from the above passage that a well-coordinated lighting scheme is   22.___
LIKELY to result in

A.   greater employee productivity
B.   elimination of light reflection
C.   lower lighting cost
D.   more use of natural light

23.   Of the following, the BEST title for the above passage is   23.___

A.   Characteristics of Light
B.   Light Measurement Devices
C.   Factors to Consider When Planning Lighting Systems
D.   Comfort vs. Cost When Devising Lighting Arrangements

24. According to the above passage, a foot-candle is a measurement of the   24.____

    A. number of bulbs used
    B. strength of the light
    C. contrast between glare and shadow
    D. proportion of the ceiling filled with lighting units

25. According to the above passage, the number of foot-candles of light that would be   25.____
needed to copy figures onto a payroll is _____ foot-candles.

    A. less than 30   B. 30
    C. 100   D. 150

KEY (CORRECT ANSWERS)

1.	B	11.	B
2.	B	12.	B
3.	B	13.	C
4.	A	14.	A
5.	B	15.	D
6.	A	16.	C
7.	A	17.	B
8.	D	18.	A
9.	B	19.	C
10.	D	20.	C

21.	D
22.	A
23.	C
24.	B
25.	D

TEST 2

Each question or incomplete statement is followed by several suggested answers or completions. Select the one that BEST answers the question or completes the statement. *PRINT THE LETTER OF THE CORRECT ANSWER IN THE SPACE AT THE RIGHT.*

1. Assume that a supervisor has three subordinates who perform clerical tasks. One of the employees retires and is replaced by someone who is transferred from another unit in the agency. The transferred employee tells the supervisor that she has worked as a clerical employee for two years and understands clerical operations quite well. The supervisor then assigns the transferred employee to a desk, tells the employee to begin working, and returns to his own desk.
   The supervisor's action in this situation is

   A. *proper;* experienced clerical employees do not require training when they are transferred to new assignments
   B. *improper;* before the supervisor returns to his desk, he should tell the other two subordinates to watch the transferred employee perform the work
   C. *proper;* if the transferred employee makes any mistakes, she will bring them to the supervisor's attention
   D. *improper;* the supervisor should find out what clerical tasks the transferred employee has performed and give her instruction in those which are new or different

1.___

2. Assume that you are falling behind in completing your work assignments and you believe that your workload is too heavy.
   Of the following, the BEST course of action for you to take FIRST is to

   A. discuss the problem with your supervisor
   B. decide which of your assignments can be postponed
   C. try to get some of your co-workers to help you out
   D. plan to take some of the work home with you in order to catch up

2.___

3. Suppose that one of the clerks under your supervision is filling in monthly personnel forms. She asks you to explain a particular personnel regulation which is related to various items on the forms. You are not thoroughly familiar with the regulation.
   Of the following responses you may make, the one which will gain the MOST respect from the clerk and which is generally the MOST advisable is to

   A. tell the clerk to do the best she can and that you will check her work later
   B. inform the clerk that you are not sure of a correct explanation but suggest a procedure for her to follow
   C. give the clerk a suitable interpretation so that she will think you are familiar with all regulations
   D. tell the clerk that you will have to read the regulation more thoroughly before you can give her an explanation

3.___

4. Charging out records until a specified due date, with prompt follow-up if they are not returned, is a

4.___

A. *good* idea; it may prevent the records from being kept needlessly on someone's desk for long periods of time
B. *good* idea; it will indicate the extent of your authority to other departments
C. *poor* idea; the person borrowing the material may make an error because of the pressure put upon him to return the records
D. *poor* idea; other departments will feel that you do not trust them with the records and they will be resentful

Questions 5-9.

DIRECTIONS: Questions 5 through 9 consist of three lines of code letters and numbers. The numbers on each line should correspond with the code letters on the same line in accordance with the table below.

Code Letter	P	L	I	J	B	0	H	U	C	G
Corresponding Number	0	1	2	3	4	5	6	7	8	9

On some of the lines, an error exists in the coding. Compare the letters and numbers in each question carefully. If you find an error or errors on
only *one* of the lines in the question, mark your answer A;
any *two* lines in the question, mark your answer B;
all *three* lines in the question, mark your answer C;
none of the lines in the question, mark your answer D.

SAMPLE QUESTION

JHOILCP   3652180
BICLGUP   4286970
UCIBHLJ   5824613

In the above sample, the first line is correct since each code letter listed has the correct corresponding number. On the second line, an error exists because code letter L should have the number 1 instead of the number 6. On the third line, an error exists because the code letter U should have the number 7 instead of the number 5. Since there are errors on two of the three lines, the correct answer is B.

5. BULJCIP   4713920   5._____
    HIGPOUL   6290571
    OCUHJBI   5876342

6. CUBLOIJ   8741023   6._____
    LCLGCLB   1818914
    JPUHIOC   3076158

7. OIJGCBPO   52398405   7._____
    UHPBLIOP   76041250
    CLUIPGPC   81720908

8. BPCOUOJI   40875732   8.___
    UOHCIPLB   75682014
    GLHUUCBJ   92677843

9. HOIOHJLH   65256361   9.___
    IOJJHHBP   25536640
    OJHBJOPI   53642502

Questions 10-13.

DIRECTIONS: Questions 10 through 13 are to be answered SOLELY on the basis of the information given in the following passage.

The mental attitude of the employee toward safety is exceedingly important in preventing accidents. All efforts designed to keep safety on the employee's mind and to keep accident prevention a live subject in the office will help substantially in a safety program. Although it may seem strange, it is common for people to be careless. Therefore, safety education is a continuous process.

Safety rules should be explained, and the reasons for their rigid enforcement should be given to employees. Telling employees to be careful or giving similar general safety warnings and slogans is probably of little value. Employees should be informed of basic safety fundamentals. This can be done through staff meetings, informal suggestions to employees, movies, and safety instruction cards. Safety instruction cards provide the employees with specific suggestions about safety and serve as a series of timely reminders helping to keep safety on the minds of employees. Pictures, posters, and cartoon sketches on bulletin boards that are located in areas continually used by employees arouse the employees' interest in safety. It is usually good to supplement this type of safety promotion with intensive individual follow-up.

10. The above passage implies that the LEAST effective of the following safety measures is 10.___

  A. rigid enforcement of safety rules
  B. getting employees to think in terms of safety
  C. elimination of unsafe conditions in the office
  D. telling employees to stay alert at all times

11. The reason given by the passage for maintaining ongoing safety education is that 11.___

  A. people are often careless
  B. office tasks are often dangerous
  C. the value of safety slogans increases with repetition
  D. safety rules change frequently

12. Which one of the following safety aids is MOST likely to be preferred by the passage? 12.___
A

  A. cartoon of a man tripping over a carton and yelling, *Keep aisles clear!*
  B. poster with a large number one and a caption saying, *Safety First*
  C. photograph of a very neatly arranged office
  D. large sign with the word *THINK* in capital letters

13. Of the following, the BEST title for the above passage is   13.____

    A. Basic Safety Fundamentals
    B. Enforcing Safety Among Careless Employees
    C. Attitudes Toward Safety
    D. Making Employees Aware of Safety

Questions 14-21.

DIRECTIONS: Questions 14 through 21 are to be answered SOLELY on the basis of the information and the chart given below.

    The following chart shows expenses in five selected categories for a one-year period, expressed as percentages of these same expenses during the previous year. The chart compares two different offices. In Office T (represented by ▨▨▨), a cost reduction program has been tested for the past year. The other office, Office Q (represented by ▨▨▨), served as a control, in that no special effort was made' to reduce costs during the past year.

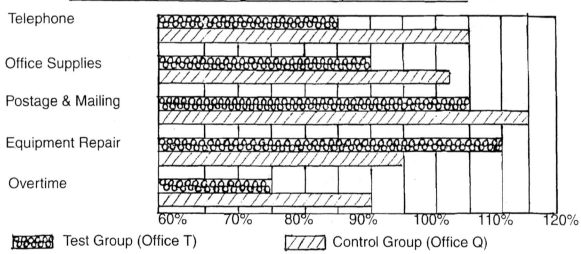

RESULTS OF OFFICE COST REDUCTION PROGRAM

Expenses of Test and Control Groups for 2009
Expressed as Percentages of Same Expenses for 2008

▨▨▨ Test Group (Office T)   ▨▨▨ Control Group (Office Q)

14. In Office T, which category of expense showed the greatest percentage REDUCTION   14.____
    from 2008 to 2009?

    A. Telephone   B. Office Supplies
    C. Postage & Mailing   D. Overtime ,

15. In which expense category did Office T show the BEST results in percentage terms   15.____
    when compared to Office Q?

    A. Telephone   B. Office Supplies
    C. Postage & Mailing   D. Overtime

16. According to the above chart, the cost reduction program was LEAST effective for the   16.___
    expense category of

    A. Office Supplies   B. Postage & Mailing
    C. Equipment Repair   D. Overtime

17. Office T's telephone costs went down during 2009 by approximately how many percent-   17.___
    age points?

    A. 15   B. 20   C. 85   D. 105

18. Which of the following changes occurred in expenses for Office Supplies in Office Q in   18.___
    the year 2009 as compared with the year 2008?
    They

    A. increased by more than 100%
    B. remained the same
    C. decreased by a few percentage points
    D. increased by a few percentage points

19. For which of the following expense categories do the results in Office T and the results in   19.___
    Office Q differ MOST NEARLY by 10 percentage points?

    A. Telephone   B. Postage & Mailing
    C. Equipment Repair   D. Overtime

20. In which expense category did Office Q's costs show the GREATEST percentage   20.___
    increase in 2009?

    A. Telephone   B. Office Supplies
    C. Postage & Mailing   D. Equipment Repair

21. In Office T, by approximately what percentage did overtime expense change during the   21.___
    past year?
    It

    A. *increased* by 15%   B. *increased* by 75%
    C. *decreased* by 10%   D. *decreased* by 25%

22. In a particular agency, there were 160 accidents in 2007. Of these accidents, 75% were   22.___
    due to unsafe acts and the rest were due to unsafe conditions. In the following year, a
    special safety program was established. The number of accidents in 2009 due to unsafe
    acts was reduced to 35% of what it had been in 2007.
    How many accidents due to unsafe acts were there in 2009?

    A. 20   B. 36   C. 42   D. 56

23. At the end of every month, the petty cash fund of Agency A is reimbursed for payments   23.___
    made from the fund during the month. During the month of February, the amounts paid
    from the fund were entered on receipts as follows: 10 bus fares of 35¢ each and one taxi
    fare of $3.50.
    At the end of the month, the money left in the fund was in the following denominations:
    15 one dollar bills, 4 quarters, 10 dimes, and 20 nickels.
    If the petty cash fund is reduced by 20% for the following month, how much money will
    there be available in the petty cash fund for March?

    A. $11.00   B. $20.00   C. $21.50   D. $25.00

24. The one of the following records which it would be MOST advisable to keep in alphabeti-   24.____
cal order is a

    A. continuous listing of phone messages, including time and caller, for your supervi-
sor
    B. listing of individuals currently employed by your agency in a particular title
    C. record of purchases paid for by the petty cash fund
    D. dated record of employees who have borrowed material from the files in your office

25. Assume that you have been asked to copy by hand a column of numbers with two deci-   25.____
mal places from one record to another. Each number consists of three, four, and five dig-
its.
In order to copy them quickly and accurately, you should copy

    A. each number exactly, making sure that the column of digits farthest to the right is in
a straight line and all other columns are lined up
    B. the column of digits farthest to the right and then copy the next column of digits
moving from right to left
    C. the column of digits farthest to the left and then copy the next column of digits mov-
ing from left to right
    D. the digits to the right of each decimal point and then copy the digits to the left of
each decimal point

———

KEY (CORRECT ANSWERS)

1.	D		11.	A
2.	A		12.	A
3.	D		13.	D
4.	A		14.	D
5.	A		15.	A
6.	C		16.	C
7.	D		17.	A
8.	B		18.	D
9.	C		19.	B
10.	D		20.	C

21.	D
22.	C
23.	B
24.	B
25.	A

———

EXAMINATION SECTION
TEST 1

DIRECTIONS: Each question or incomplete statement is followed by several suggested answers or completions. Select the one that BEST answers the question or completes the statement. *PRINT THE LETTER OF THE CORRECT ANSWER IN THE SPACE AT THE RIGHT.*

1. A coworker has e-mailed a file containing a spreadsheet for your review. Which of the following programs will open the file?   1.____

    A. Adobe Reader
    B. Microsoft Excel
    C. Microsoft PowerPoint
    D. Adobe Illustrator

2. A report needs to be forwarded immediately to a supervisor in another office. Which of the following is the LEAST effective way of giving the supervisor the report?   2.____

    A. scanning the report and e-mailing the file
    B. faxing it to the supervisor's office
    C. uploading it to the office network and informing the supervisor
    D. waiting for the supervisor to come to your office and giving it to him/her then

3. Suppose your supervisor is on the telephone in his office and an applicant arrives for a scheduled interview with him.   3.____
Of the following, the BEST procedure to follow ordinarily is to

    A. informally chat with the applicant in your office until your supervisor has finished his phone conversation
    B. escort him directly into your supervisor's office and have him wait for him there
    C. inform your supervisor of the applicant's arrival and try to make the applicant feel comfortable while waiting
    D. have him hang up his coat and tell him to go directly in to see your supervisor

Questions 4-9.

DIRECTIONS: Questions 4 through 9 each consist of a sentence which may or may not be an example of good English usage. Consider grammar, punctuation, spelling, capitalization, awkwardness, etc. Examine each sentence, and then choose the correct statement about it from the four choices below it. If the English usage in the sentence given is better than any of the changes suggested in options B, C, or D, choose option A. Do not choose an option that will change the meaning of the sentence.

4. The report, along with the accompanying documents, were submitted for review.   4.____

    A. This is an example of acceptable writing.
    B. The words *were submitted* should be changed to *was submitted.*
    C. The word *accompanying* should be spelled *accompaning.*
    D. The comma after the word *report* should be taken out.

5. If others must use your files, be certain that they understand how the system works, but insist that you do all the filing and refiling.   5.___

   A. This is an example of acceptable writing.
   B. There should be a period after the word *works*, and the word *but* should start a new sentence.
   C. The words *filing* and *refiling* should be spelled *fileing* and *refileing*.
   D. There should be a comma after the word *but*.

6. The appeal was not considered because of its late arrival.   6.___

   A. This is an example of acceptable writing.
   B. The word *its* should be changed to *it's*.
   C. The word *its* should be changed to *the*.
   D. The words *late arrival* should be changed to *arrival late*.

7. The letter must be read carefuly to determine under which subject it should be filed.   7.___

   A. This is an example of acceptable writing.
   B. The word *under* should be changed to *at*.
   C. The word *determine* should be spelled *determin*.
   D. The word *carefuly* should be spelled *carefully*.

8. He showed potential as an office manager, but he lacked skill in delegating work.   8.___

   A. This is an example of acceptable writing.
   B. The word *delegating* should be spelled *delagating*.
   C. The word *potential* should be spelled *potencial*.
   D. The words *lie lacked* should be changed to *was lacking*.

9. His supervisor told him that it would be all right to receive personal mail at the office.   9.___

   A. This is an example of acceptable writing.
   B. The words *all right* should be changed to *alright*.
   C. The word *personal* should be spelled *personel*.
   D. The word *mail* should be changed to *letters*.

Questions 10-13.

DIRECTIONS: Questions 10 through 13 are to be answered SOLELY on the basis of the information given in the following passage.

Typed pages can reflect the simplicity of modern art in a machine age. Lightness and evenness can be achieved by proper layout and balance of typed lines and white space. Instead of solid, cramped masses of uneven, crowded typing, there should be a pleasing balance up and down as well as horizontal.

To have real balance, your page must have a center. The eyes see the center of the sheet slightly above the real center. This is the way both you and the reader see it. Try imagining a line down the center of the page that divides the paper in equal halves. On either side of your paper, white space and blocks of typing need to be similar in size and shape. Although left and right margins should be equal, top and bottom margins need not be as exact. It looks better to hold a bottom border wider than a top margin, so that your typing rests *upon a cushion of white space. To add interest to the appearance of the page, try making one paragraph between one-half and two-thirds the size of an adjacent paragraph.*

Thus, by taking full advantage of your typewriter, the pages that you type will not only be accurate but will also be attractive.

10. It can be inferred from the passage that the BASIC importance of proper balancing on a typed page is that proper balancing

   A. makes a typed page a work of modern art
   B. provides exercise in proper positioning of a typewriter
   C. increases the amount of typed copy on the paper
   D. draws greater attention and interest to the page

10.____

11. A reader will tend to see the center of a typed page

   A. somewhat higher than the true center
   B. somewhat lower than the true center
   C. on either side of the true center
   D. about two-thirds of an inch above the true center

11.____

12. Which of the following suggestions is NOT given by the passage?

   A. Bottom margins may be wider than top borders.
   B. Keep all paragraphs approximately the same size.
   C. Divide your page with an imaginary line down the middle.
   D. Side margins should be equalized.

12.____

13. Of the following, the BEST title for this passage is:

   A. INCREASING THE ACCURACY OF THE TYPED PAGE
   B. DETERMINATION OF MARGINS FOR TYPED COPY
   C. LAYOUT AND BALANCE OF THE TYPED PAGE
   D. HOW TO TAKE FULL ADVANTAGE OF THE TYPEWRITER

13.____

14. In order to type addresses on a large number of envelopes MOST efficiently, you should

   A. insert another envelope into the typewriter before removing each typed envelope
   B. take each typed envelope out of the machine before starting the next envelope
   C. insert several envelopes into the machine at one time, keeping all top and bottom edges even
   D. insert several envelopes into the machine at one time, keeping the top edge of each envelope two inches below the top edge of the one beneath it

14.____

15. A senior typist has completed copying a statistical report from a rough draft.
Of the following, the BEST way to be sure that her typing is correct is for the typist to

   A. fold the rough draft, line it up with the typed copy, compare one-half of the columns with the original, and have a co-worker compare the other half
   B. check each line of the report as it is typed and then have a co-worker check each line again after the entire report is finished

15.____

C. have a co-worker add each column and check the totals on the typed copy with the totals on the original

D. have a co-worker read aloud from the rough draft while the typist checks the typed copy and then have the typist read while the co-worker checks

16. In order to center a heading when typing a report, you should 16.___

A. measure your typing paper with a ruler and begin the heading one-third of the way in from the left margin

B. begin the heading at the point on the typewriter scale which is 50 minus the number of letters in the heading

C. multiply the number of characters in the heading by two and begin the heading that number of spaces in from the left margin

D. begin the heading at the point on the scale which is equal to the center point of your paper minus one-half the number of characters and spaces in the heading

17. Which of the following recommendations concerning the use of copy paper for making typewritten copies should NOT be followed? 17.___

A. Copy papers should be checked for wrinkles before being used.

B. Legal-size copy paper may be folded if it is too large to fit into a convenient drawer space.

C. When several sheets of paper are being used, they should be fastened with a paper clip at the top after insertion in the typewriter.

D. For making many copies, paper of the same weight and brightness should be used.

18. Assume that a new typist, Norma Garcia, has been assigned to work under your supervision and is reporting to work for the first time. You formally introduce Norma to her co-workers and suggest that a few of the other typists explain the office procedures and typing formats to her. The practice of instructing Norma in her duties in this manner is 18.___

A. *good* because she will be made to feel at home

B. *good* because she will learn more about routine office tasks from co-workers than from you

C. *poor* because her co-workers will resent the extra work

D. *poor* because you will not have enough control over her training

19. Suppose that Jean Brown, a typist, is typing a letter following the same format that she has always used. However, she notices that the other two typists in her office are also typing letters, but are using a different format. Jean is concerned that she might not have been informed of a change in format.
Of the following, the FIRST action that Jean should take is to 19.___

A. seek advice from her supervisor as to which format to use

B. ask the other typists whether she should use a new format for typing letters

C. disregard the format that the other typists are using and continue to type in the format she had been using

D. use the format that the other typists are using, assuming that it is a newly accepted method

20. Suppose that the new office to which you have been assigned has put up Christmas dec-   20.____
    orations, and a Christmas party is being planned by the city agency in which you work.
    However, nothing has been said about Christmas gifts.
    It would be CORRECT for you to assume that

    A. you are expected to give a gift to your supervisor
    B. your supervisor will give you a gift
    C. you are expected to give gifts only to your subordinates
    D. you will neither receive gifts nor will you be expected to give any

---

KEY (CORRECT ANSWERS)

1.	B	11.	A
2.	D	12.	B
3.	C	13.	C
4.	B	14.	A
5.	A	15.	D
6.	A	16.	D
7.	D	17.	B
8.	A	18.	D
9.	A	19.	A
10.	D	20.	D

TEST 2

DIRECTIONS: Each question or incomplete statement is followed by several suggested answers or completions. Select the one that BEST answers the question or completes the statement. *PRINT THE LETTER OF THE CORRECT ANSWER IN THE SPACE AT THE RIGHT.*

1. The supervisor you assist is under great pressure to meet certain target dates. He has scheduled an emergency meeting to take place in a few days, and he asks you to send out notices immediately. As you begin to prepare the notices, however, you realize he has scheduled the meeting for a Saturday, which is not a working day. Also, you sense that your supervisor is not in a good mood.
Which of the following is the MOST effective method of handling this situation?

    A. Change the meeting date to the first working day after that Saturday and send out the notices.
    B. Change the meeting date to a working day on which his calendar is clear and send out the notices.
    C. Point out to your supervisor that the date is a Saturday.
    D. Send out the notices as they are since you have received specific instructions.

1.___

Questions 2-7.

DIRECTIONS: Questions 2 through 7 each consist of a sentence which may or may not be an example of good English usage. Consider grammar, punctuation, spelling, capitalization, awkwardness, etc. Examine each sentence, and then choose the correct statement about it from the four choices below it. If the English usage in the sentence given is better than any of the changes suggested in options B, C, or D, choose option A. Do not choose an option that will change the meaning of the sentence.

2. The typist used an extention cord in order to connect her typewriter to the outlet nearest to her desk.

    A. This is an example of acceptable writing.
    B. A period should be placed after the word *cord,* and the word *in* should have a capital I.
    C. A comma should be placed after the word *typewriter.*
    D. The word *extention* should be spelled *extension.*

2.___

3. He would have went to the conference if he had received an invitation.

    A. This is an example of acceptable writing.
    B. The word *went* should be replaced by the word *gone.*
    C. The word *had* should be replaced by *would have.*
    D. The word *conference* should be spelled *conferance.*

3.___

4. In order to make the report neater, he spent many hours rewriting it.

    A. This is an example of acceptable writing.
    B. The word *more* should be inserted before the word *neater.*
    C. There should be a colon after the word *neater.*
    D. The word *spent* should be changed to *have spent.*

4.___

5. His supervisor told him that he should of read the memorandum more carefully.   5.____

    A. This is an example of acceptable writing.
    B. The word *memorandum* should be spelled *memorandom*.
    C. The word *of* should be replaced by the word *have*.
    D. The word *carefully* should be replaced by the word *careful*.

6. It was decided that two separate reports should be written.   6.____

    A. This is an example of acceptable writing.
    B. A comma should be inserted after the word *decided*.
    C. The word *be* should be replaced by the word *been*.
    D. A colon should be inserted after the word *that*.

7. She don't seem to understand that the work must be done as soon as possible.   7.____

    A. This is an example of acceptable writing.
    B. The word *doesn't* should replace the word *don't*.
    C. The word *why* should replace the word *that*.
    D. The word *as* before the word *soon* should be eliminated.

Questions 8-11.

DIRECTIONS: Questions 8 through 11 are to be answered SOLELY on the basis of the following passage.

There is nothing that will take the place of good sense on the part of the stenographer. You may be perfect in transcribing exactly what the dictator says and your speed may be adequate; but without an understanding of the dictator's intent as well as his words, you are likely to be a mediocre secretary.

A serious error that is made when taking dictation is putting down something that does not make sense. Most people who dictate material would rather be asked to repeat and explain than to receive transcribed material which has errors due to inattention or doubt. Many dictators request that their grammar be corrected by their secretaries; but unless specifically asked to do so, secretaries should not do it without first checking with the dictator. Secretaries should be aware that, in some cases, dictators may use incorrect grammar or slang expressions to create a particular effect.

Some people dictate commas, periods, and paragraphs, while others expect the stenographer to know when, where, and how to punctuate. A well-trained secretary should be able to indicate the proper punctuation by listening to the pauses and tones of the dictator's voice.

A stenographer who has taken dictation from the same person for a period of time should be able to understand him under most conditions. By increasing her tact, alertness, and efficiency, a secretary can become more competent.

8. According to the passage, which of the following statements concerning the dictation of punctuation is CORRECT?   8.____
   A

    A. dictator may use incorrect punctuation to create a desired style

B. dictator should indicate all punctuation
C. stenographer should know how to punctuate based on the pauses and tones of the dictator
D. stenographer should not type any punctuation if it has not been dictated to her

9. According to the passage, how should secretaries handle grammatical errors in a dictation?
Secretaries should

    9.___

A. *not correct* grammatical errors unless the dictator is aware that this is being done
B. *correct* grammatical errors by having the dictator repeat the line with proper pauses
C. *correct* grammatical errors if they have checked the correctness in a grammar book
D. *correct* grammatical errors based on their own good sense

10. If a stenographer is confused about the method of spacing and indenting of a report which has just been dictated to her, she GENERALLY should

    10.___

A. do the best she can
B. ask the dictator to explain what she should do
C. try to improve her ability to understand dictated material
D. accept the fact that her stenographic ability is not adequate

11. In the last line of the first paragraph, the word *mediocre* means MOST NEARLY

    11.___

A. superior
C. respected

B. disregarded
D. second-rate

12. Assume that is is your responsibility to schedule meetings for your supervisor, who believes in starting these meetings strictly on time. He has told you to schedule separate meetings with Mr. Smith and Ms. Jones, which will last approximately 20 minutes each. You have told Mr. Smith to arrive at 10:00 A.M. and Ms. Jones at 10:30 A.M. Your supervisor will have an hour of free time at 11:00 A.M. At 10:25 A.M., Mr. Smith arrives and states that there was a train delay, and he is sorry that he is late. Ms. Jones has not yet arrived. You do not know who Mr. Smith and Ms. Jones are or what the meetings will be about.
Of the following, the BEST course of action for you to take is to

    12.___

A. send Mr. Smith in to see your supervisor; and when Ms. Jones arrives, tell her that your supervisor's first meeting will take more time than he expected
B. tell Mr. Smith that your supervisor has a meeting at 10:30 A.M. and that you will have to reschedule his meeting for another day
C. check with your supervisor to find out if he would prefer to see Mr. Smith immediately or at 11:00 A.M.
D. encourage your supervisor to meet with Mr. Smith immediately because Mr. Smith's late arrival was not intentional

13. Assume that you have been told by your boss not to let anyone disturb him for the rest of the afternoon unless absolutely necessary since he has to complete some urgent work. His supervisor, who is the bureau chief, telephones and asks to speak to him.
The BEST course of action for you to take is to

    13.___

A. ask the bureau chief if he can leave a message
B. ask your boss if he can take the call
C. tell the bureau chief that your boss is out
D. tell your boss that his instructions will get you into trouble

14. Which one of the following is the MOST advisable procedure for a stenographer to follow when a dictator asks her to make extra copies of dictated material?   14.____

    A. Note the number of copies required at the beginning of the notes.
    B. Note the number of copies required at the end of the notes.
    C. Make a mental note of the number of copies required to be made.
    D. Make a checkmark beside the notes to serve as a reminder that extra copies are required.

15. Suppose that, as you are taking shorthand notes, the dictator tells you that the sentence he has just dictated is to be deleted.   15.____
Of the following, the BEST thing for you to do is to

    A. place the correction in the left-hand margin next to the deleted sentence
    B. write the word *delete* over the sentence and place the correction on a separate page for corrections
    C. erase the sentence and use that available space for the correction
    D. draw a line through the sentence and begin the correction on the next available line

16. Assume that your supervisor, who normally dictates at a relatively slow rate, begins dictating to you very rapidly. You find it very difficult to keep up at this speed. Which one of the following is the BEST action to take in this situation?   16.____

    A. Ask your supervisor to dictate more slowly since you are having difficulty.
    B. Continue to take the dictation at the fast speed and fill in the blanks later.
    C. Interrupt your supervisor with a question about the dictation, hoping that when she begins again it will be slower.
    D. Refuse to take the dictation unless given at the speed indicated in your job description.

17. Assume that you have been asked to put a heading on the second, third, and fourth pages of a four-page letter to make sure they can be identified in case they are separated from the first page.   17.____
Which of the following is it LEAST important to include in such a heading?

    A. Date of the letter
    B. Initials of the typist
    C. Name of the person to whom the letter is addressed
    D. Number of the page

18. Which one of the following is NOT generally accepted when dividing words at the end of a line?   18.____
Dividing

    A. a hyphenated word at the hyphen
    B. a word immediately after the prefix
    C. a word immediately before the suffix
    D. proper names between syllables

19. In the preparation of a business letter which has two enclosures, the MOST generally accepted of the following procedures to follow is to type

    A. *See Attached Items* one line below the last line of the body of the letter
    B. *See Attached Enclosures* to the left of the signature
    C. *Enclosures 2* at the left margin below the signature line
    D. nothing on the letter to indicate enclosures since it will be obvious to the reader that there are enclosures in the envelope

19.___

20. Standard rules for typing spacing have developed through usage. According to these rules, one space is left AFTER

    A. a comma   B. every sentence
    C. a colon   D. an opening parenthesis

20.___

KEY (CORRECT ANSWERS)

1.	C	11.	D
2.	D	12.	C
3.	B	13.	B
4.	A	14.	A
5.	C	15.	D
6.	A	16.	A
7.	B	17.	B
8.	C	18.	D
9.	A	19.	C
10.	B	20.	A

EXAMINATION SECTION
TEST 1

DIRECTIONS: Each question or incomplete statement is followed by several suggested
answers or completions. Select the one that BEST answers the question or
completes the statement. *PRINT THE LETTER OF THE CORRECT ANSWER
IN THE SPACE AT THE RIGHT.*

Questions 1-2.

DIRECTIONS: Questions 1 and 2 are to be answered on the basis of the following conditions.

*Assume that you work for Department A, which occupies several floors in one building.
There is a reception office on each floor. All visitors (persons not employed in the department) are required to go to the reception office on the same floor as the office of the person
they want to see. They sign a register, their presence is announced by the receptionist, and
they wait in the reception room for the person they are visiting.*

1.   As you are walking in the corridor of your department on your way to a meeting in Room   1.____
     314, a visitor approaches you and asks you to direct her to Room 312. She says that she
     is delivering some papers to Mr. Crane in that office. The MOST APPROPRIATE action
     for you to take is to

     A.   offer to deliver the papers to Mr. Crane since you will be passing his office
     B.   suggest that she come with you since you will be passing Room 312
     C.   direct her to the reception office where Mr. Crane will be contacted for her
     D.   take her to the reception office and contact Mr. Crane for her

2.   You are acting as receptionist in the reception office on the second floor. A man enters,   2.____
     stating that he is an accountant from another department and that he has an appoint-
     ment with Mr. Prince, who is located in Room 102 on the first floor.
     The BEST action for you to take is to

     A.   phone the reception office on the first floor and ask the receptionist to contact Mr.
          Prince
     B.   advise the man to go to the reception office on the first floor where he will be fur-
          ther assisted
     C.   contact Mr. Prince for him and ask that he come to your office where his visitor is
          waiting
     D.   send him directly to Room 102 where he can see Mr. Prince

3.   One of the employees whom you supervise complains to you that you give her more   3.____
     work than the other employees and that she cannot finish these assignments by the time
     you expect them to be completed.
     Of the following, the FIRST action you should then take is to

     A.   tell the employee that you expect more work from her because the other employ-
          ees do not have her capabilities
     B.   assure the employee that you always divide the work equally among your subordi-
          nates

C.   review the employee's recent assignments in order to determine whether her complaint is justified
D.   ask the employee if there are any personal problems which are interfering with the completion of the assignments

4.   Assume that a staff regulation exists which requires an employee to inform his supervisor   4._____
if the employee will be absent on a particular day.
If an employee fails to follow this regulation, the FIRST action his supervisor should take is to

A.   inform his own supervisor of the situation and ask for further instructions
B.   ask the employee to explain his failure to follow the regulation
C.   tell the employee that another breach of the regulation will lead to disciplinary action
D.   reprimand the employee for failing to follow the regulation

5.   An employee tells his supervisor that he submitted an idea to the employees' suggestion   5._____
program by mail over two months ago and still has not received an indication that the suggestion is being considered. The employee states that when one of his co-workers sent in a suggestion, he received a response within one week. The employee then asks his supervisor what he should do.
Which of the following is the BEST response for the supervisor to make?

A.   "Next time you have a suggestion, see me about it first and I will make sure that it is properly handled."
B.   "I'll try to find out whether your suggestion was received by the program and whether a response was sent."
C.   "Your suggestion probably wasn't that good so there's no sense in pursuing the matter any further."
D.   "Let's get together and submit the suggestion jointly so that it will carry more weight."

6.   Assume that you have been trying to teach a newly appointed employee the filing proce-   6._____
dures used in your office. The employee seems to be having difficulty learning the procedures even though you consider them relatively simple and you originally learned them in less time than you have already spent trying to teach the new employee.
Before you spend any time trying to teach him any new filing procedures, which of the following actions should you take FIRST?

A.   Try to teach him some other aspect of your office's work.
B.   Tell him that you had little difficulty learning the procedures and ask him why he finds them so hard to learn.
C.   Review with him those procedures you have tried to teach him and determine whether he understands them.
D.   Report to your supervisor that the new employee is unsuited for the work performed in your office.

7.   There is a rule in your office that all employees must sign in and out for lunch. You notice   7._____
that a new employee who is under your direct supervision has not signed in or out for lunch for the past three days. Of the following, the MOST effective action to take is to

A. immediately report this matter to your supervisor
B. note this infraction of rules on the employee's personnel record
C. remind the employee that she must sign in and out for lunch every day
D. send around a memorandum to all employees in the office telling them they must sign in and out for lunch every day

Questions 8-15.

DIRECTIONS: Questions 8 through 15 each show in Column I names written on four cards (lettered w, x, y, z) which have to be filed. You are to choose the option (lettered A, B, C, or D) in Column II which BEST represents the proper order of filing according to the rules and sample question given below. The cards are to be filed according to the following Rules for Alphabetical Filing.

RULES FOR ALPHABETICAL FILING

Names of Individuals

1. The names of individuals are filed in strict alphabetical order, first according to the last name, then according to first name or initial, and finally according to middle name or initial. For example: George Allen precedes Edward Bell and Leonard Reston precedes Lucille Reston.

2. When last names are the same, for example, A. Green and Agnes Green, the one with the initial comes before the one with the name written out when the first initials are identical.

3. When first and last names are the same, a name without a middle initial comes before one with a middle initial. For example: Ralph Simon comes before both Ralph A. Simon and Ralph Adam Simon.

4. When first and last names are the same, a name with a middle initial comes before one with a middle name beginning with the same initial. For example: Sam P. Rogers comes before Sam Paul Rogers.

5. Prefixes such as De , O', Mac, Mc, and Van are filed as written and are treated as part of the names to which they are connected. For example: Gladys McTeaque is filed before Frances Meadows.

6. Abbreviated names are treated as if they were spelled out. For example: Chas. is filed as Charles and Thos. is filed as Thomas.

7. Titles and designations such as Dr., Mr., and Prof, are ignored in filing.

Names of Organizations

1. The names of business organizations are filed according to the order in which each word in the name appears. When an organization name bears the name of a person, it is filed according to the rules for filing names of people as given above. Vivian Quinn Boutique would, therefore, come before Security Locks Inc. because Quinn comes before Security.

2. *When numerals occur in a name, they are treated as if they were spelled out. For example: 4th Street Thrift Shop is filed as Fourth Street Thrift Shop.*

3. *When the following words are part of the name of an organization, they are ignored: on, the, of, and.*

<u>SAMPLE</u>

	<u>Column I</u>	<u>Column II</u>	The correct way to file the cards is:
w.	Jane Earl	A. w, y, z, x	y. James Earl
x.	James A. Earle	B. y, w, z, x	w. Jane Earl
y.	James Earl	C. x, y, w, z	z. J. Earle
z.	J. Earle	D. x, w, y, z	x. James A. Earle

The correct filing order is shown by the letters, y, w, z, x (in that sequence). Since, in Column II, B appears in front of the letters, y, w, z, x (in that sequence), B is the correct answer to the sample question.

Now answer the following questions using that same procedure.

<u>Column I</u> <u>Column II</u>

8.　w.　James Rothschild
　　x.　Julius B. Rothchild
　　y.　B. Rothstein
　　z.　Brian Joel Rothenstein

　　A.　x, z, w, y
　　B.　x, w, z, y
　　C.　z, y, w, x
　　D.　z, w, x, y

8.___

9.　w.　George S. Wise
　　x.　S. G. Wise
　　y.　Geo. Stuart Wise
　　z.　Prof. Diana Wise

　　A.　w, y, z, x
　　B.　x , w , y , z
　　C.　y, x, w, z
　　D.　z, w, y, x

9.___

10.　w.　10th Street Bus Terminal
　　x.　Buckingham Travel Agency
　　y.　The Buckingham Theater
　　z.　Burt Tompkins Studio

　　A.　x, z, w, y
　　B.　y, x, w, z
　　C.　w, z, y, x
　　D.　x, w, y, z

10.___

11.　w.　National Council of American Importers
　　x.　National Chain Co. of Providence
　　y.　National Council on Alcoholism
　　z.　National Chain Co.

　　A.　w, y, x, z
　　B.　x, z, w, y
　　C.　z, x, w, y
　　D.　z, x, y, w

11.___

12.　w.　Dr. Herbert Alvary
　　x.　Mr. Victor Alvarado
　　y.　Alvar Industries
　　z.　V. Alvarado

　　A.　w, y, x, z
　　B.　z, w, x, y
　　C.　y, z, x, w
　　D.　w, z, x, y

12.___

	Column I		Column II	
13.	w. Joan MacBride x. Wm. Mackey y. Roslyn McKenzie z. Winifred Mackey	A. w, x, z, y B. w, y, z, x C. w, z, x, y D. w, y , x, z		13.____

	Column I		Column II	
14.	w. 3 Way Trucking Co. x. 3rd Street Bakery y. 380 Realty Corp. z. Three Lions Pub	A. y, x, z, w B. y, z, w, x C. x, y, z, w D. x, y, w, z		14.____
15.	w. Miss Rose Leonard x. Rev. Leonard Lucas y. Sylvia Leonard Linen Shop z. Rose S. Leonard	A. z, w, x, y B. w, z, y, x C. w, x, z, y D. z, w, y, x		15.____

Questions 16-19.

DIRECTIONS: Answer Questions 16 through 19 ONLY on the basis of the information given in the following passage.

Work measurement concerns accomplishment or productivity. It has to do with results; it does not deal with the amount of energy used up, although in many cases this may be in direct proportion to the work output. Work measurement not only helps a manager to distribute work loads fairly, but it also enables him to define work sueeess in actual units, evaluate employee performance, and determine where corrective help is needed. Work measurement is accomplished by measuring the amount produced, measuring the time spent to produce it, and relating the two. To illustrate, it is common to speak of so many orders processed within a given time. The number of orders processed becomes meaningful when related to the amount of time taken.

Much of the work in an office can be measured fairly accurately and inexpensively. The extent of wo.rk measurement possible in any given case will depend upon the particular type of office tasks performed, but usually from two-thirds to three-fourths of all work in an office can be measured. It is true that difficulty in work measurement is encountered, for example, when the office work is irregular and not repeated often, or when the work is primarily mental rather than manual. These are problems, but they are used as excuses for doing no work measurement far more frequently than is justified.

16. According to the above passage, which of the following BEST illustrates the type of information obtained as a result of work measurement? A   16.____

    A. clerk takes one hour to file 150 folders
    B. typist types five letters
    C. stenographer works harder typing from shorthand notes than she does typing from a typed draft
    D. clerk keeps track of employees' time by computing sick leave, annual leave, and overtime leave

17. The above passage does NOT indicate that work measurement can be used to help a supervisor to determine 17.__

    A. why an employee is performing poorly on the job
    B. who are the fast and slow workers in the unit
    C. how the work in the unit should be divided up
    D. how long it should take to perform a certain task

18. According to the above passage, the kind of work that would be MOST difficult to measure would be such work as 18.__

    A. sorting mail
    B. designing a form for a new procedure
    C. photocopying various materials
    D. answering inquiries with form letters

19. The excuses mentioned in the above passage for failure to perform work measurement can be BEST summarized as the 19.__

    A. repetitive nature of office work
    B. costs involved in carrying out accurate work measurement
    C. inability to properly use the results obtained from work measurement
    D. difficulty involved in measuring certain types of work

Questions 20-24.

DIRECTIONS: In each of Questions 20 through 24, there is a sentence containing one underlined word. Choose the word (lettered A, B, C, or D) which means MOST NEARLY the same as the underlined word as it is used in the sentence.

20. Mr. Warren could not attend the luncheon because he had a prior appointment. 20.__

    A. conflicting   B. official
    C. previous   D. important

21. The time allowed to complete the task was not adequate. 21.__

    A. long   B. enough   C. excessive   D. required

22. The investigation unit began an extensive search for the information. 22.__

    A. complicated   B. superficial
    C. thorough   D. leisurely

23. The secretary answered the telephone in a courteous manner. 23.__

    A. businesslike   B. friendly
    C. formal   D. polite

24. The recipient of the money checked the total amount. 24.__

    A. receiver   B. carrier   C. borrower   D. giver

25. You receive a telephone call from an employee in another agency requesting information 25.____
about a project being carried out by a division other than your own. You know little about
the work being done, but you would like to help the caller.
Of the following, the BEST action for you to take is to

    A. ask the caller exactly what he would like to know and then tell him all you know
       about the work being done
    B. ask the caller to tell you exactly what he would like to know so that you can get the
       information while he waits
    C. tell the caller that you will have the call transferred to the division working on the
       project
    D. request that the caller write to you so that you can send him the necessary infor-
       mation

_____

KEY (CORRECT ANSWERS)

1.	C		11.	D
2.	B		12.	C
3.	C		13.	A
4.	B		14.	C
5.	B		15.	B
6.	C		16.	A
7.	C		17.	A
8.	A		18.	B
9.	D		19.	D
10.	B		20.	C

21.	B
22.	C
23.	D
24.	A
25.	C

_____

TEST 2

DIRECTIONS: Each question or incomplete statement is followed by several suggested answers or completions. Select the one that BEST answers the question or completes the statement. *PRINT THE LETTER OF THE CORRECT ANSWER IN THE SPACE AT THE RIGHT.*

1. Which of the following actions by a supervisor is LEAST likely to result in an increase in morale or productivity?   1.__

    A. Delegating additional responsibility but not authority to his subordinates
    B. Spending more time than his subordinates in planning and organizing the office's work
    C. Giving positive rather than negative orders to his subordinates
    D. Keeping his subordinates informed about changes in rules or policies which affect their work

Questions 2-8.

DIRECTIONS: Questions 2 through 8 are based SOLELY on the information and the form given below.

The following form is a *Weekly Summary of New Employees* and lists all employees appointed to Department F in the week indicated. In addition to the starting date and name, the form includes each new employee's time card number, title, status, work location and supervisor 's name.

DEPARTMENT F						
Weekly Summary of New Employees					Week Starting March 25	
Start-ing Date	Name Last, First	Time Card No.	Title	Status	Work Location	Supervisor
3/25	Astaire, Hannah	361	Typist	Prov.	Rm. 312	Merrill, Judy
3/25	Silber, Arthur	545	Clerk	Perm.	Rm. 532	Rizzo, Joe
3/26	Vecchio, Robert	620	Accountant	Perm.	Rm. 620	Harper, Ruth
3/26	Goldberg, Sally	373	Stenographer	Prov .	Rm. 308	Merrill, Judy
3/26	Yee, Bruce	555	Accountant	Perm.	Rm. 530	Rizzo, Joe
3/27	Dunning, Betty	469	Typist	Perm.	Rm. 411	Miller, Tony
3/28	Goldman, Sara	576	Stenographer	Prov .	Rm. 532	Rizzo, Joe
3/29	Vesquez, Roy	624	Accountant	Perm.	Rm. 622	Harper, Ruth
3/29	Browning, David	464	Typist	Perm.	Rm. 411	Miller, Tony

2. On which one of the following dates did two employees *in the same title* begin work?   2.____

    A. 3/25   B. 3/26   C. 3/27   D. 3/29

3. To which one of the following supervisors was ONE typist assigned?   3.____

    A. Judy Merrill   B. Tony Miller
    C. Ruth Harper   D. Joe Rizzo

4. Which one of the following supervisors was assigned the GREATEST number of new   4.____
employees during the week of March 25?

    A. Ruth Harper   B. Judy Merrill
    C. Tony Miller   D. Joe Rizzo

5. Which one of the following employees was assigned *three days after another employee*   5.____
to the same job location?

    A. Sara Goldman   B. David Browning
    C. Bruce Yee   D. Roy Vesquez

6. The title in which BOTH provisional and permanent appointments were made is   6.____

    A. accountant   B. clerk   C. stenographer   D. typist

7. The employee who started work on the SAME day and have the SAME status but DIF-   7.____
FERENT titles are

    A. Arthur Silber and Hannah Astaire
    B. Robert Vecchio and Bruce Yee
    C. Sally Goldberg and Sara Goldman
    D. Roy Vesquez and David Browning

8. On the basis of the information given on the form, which one of the following conclusions   8.____
regarding time card numbers appears to be CORRECT?

    A. The first digit of the time card number is coded according to the assigned title.
    B. The middle digit of the time card number is coded according to the assigned title.
    C. The first digit of the time card number is coded according to the employees' floor
        locations.
    D. Time card numbers are randomly assigned.

9. Assume that a caller arrives at your desk and states that she is your supervisor's daugh-   9.____
ter and that she would like to see her father. You have been under the impression that
your supervisor has only a two-year-old son.
Of the following, the BEST way to deal with this visitor is to

    A. offer her a seat and advise your supervisor of the visitor
    B. tell her to go right in to her father's office
    C. ask her for some proof to show that she is your supervisor's daughter
    D. escort her into your supervisor's office and ask him if the visitor is his daughter

10. Assume that you answer the telephone and the caller says that he is a police officer and   10.____
asks for personal information about one of your co-workers.
Of the following, the BEST course of action for you to take is to

A. give the caller the information he has requested
B. ask the caller for the telephone number of the phone he is using, call him back, and then give him the information
C. refuse to give him any information and offer to transfer the call to your supervisor
D. ask the caller for his name and badge number before giving him the information

Questions 11-16.

DIRECTIONS: Questions 11 through 16 each consist of a sentence which may or may not be an example of good English usage. Consider grammar, punctuation, spelling, capitalization, awkwardness, etc. Examine each sentence, and then choose the correct statement about it from the four choices below it. If the English usage in the sentence given is better than it would be with any of the changes suggested in Options B, C, or D, choose Option A. Do not choose an option that will change the meaning of the sentence.

11. The recruiting officer said, *"There are many different goverment jobs available."*   11.____

   A. This is an example of acceptable writing.
   B. The word *There* should not be capitalized.
   C. The word *goverment* should be spelled *government*.
   D. The comma after the word *said* should be removed.

12. He can recommend a mechanic whose work is reliable.   12.____

   A. This is an example of acceptable writing.
   B. The word *reliable* should be spelled *relyable.*
   C. The word *whose* should be spelled *who's.*
   D. The word *mechanic* should be spelled *mecanic.*

13. She typed quickly; like someone who had not a moment to lose.   13.____

   A. This is an example of acceptable writing.
   B. The word *not* should be removed.
   C. The semicolon should be changed to a comma.
   D. The word *quickly* should be placed before instead of after the word *typed.*

14. She insisted that she had to much work to do.   14.____

   A. This is an example of acceptable writing.
   B. The word *insisted* should be spelled *incisted.*
   C. The word *to* used in front of *much* should be spelled *too.*
   D. The word *do* should be changed to *be done.*

15. He excepted praise from his supervisor for a job well done.   15.____

   A. This is an example of acceptable writing.
   B. The word *excepted* should be spelled *accepted.*
   C. The order of the words *well done* should be changed to *done well.*
   D. There should be a comma after the word,*supervisor*

16. What appears to be intentional errors in grammar occur several times in the passage.   16.____

    A. This is an example of acceptable writing.
    B. The word *occur* should be spelled *occurr*.
    C. The word *appears* should be changed to *appear*.
    D. The phrase *several times* should be changed to *from time to time*.

17. The daily compensation to be paid to each consultant hired in a certain agency is computed by dividing his professional earnings in the previous year by 250. The maximum daily compensation they can receive is $200 each. Four consultants who were hired to work on a special project had the following professional earnings in the previous year: $37,500, $44,000, $46,500, and $61,100.   17.____
What will be the TOTAL DAILY COST to the agency for these four consultants?

    A. $932   B. $824   C. $756   D. $712

18. In a typing and stenographic pool consisting of 30 employees, 2/5 of them are typists, 1/3 of them are senior typists and senior stenographers, and the rest are stenographers. If there are 5 more stenographers than senior stenographers, how many senior stenographers are in the typing and stenographic pool?   18.____

    A. 3   B. 5   C. 8   D. 10

19. There are 3330 copies of a three-page report to be collated. One clerk starts collating at 9:00 A.M. and is joined 15 minutes later by two other clerks. It takes 15 minutes for each of these clerks to collate 90 copies of the report.   19.____
At what time should the job be completed if ALL three clerks continue working at the SAME rate without breaks?

    A. 12:00 Noon   B. 12:15 P.M.   C. 1:00 P.M.   D. 1:15 P.M.

20. By the end of last year, membership in the blood credit program in a certain agency had increased from the year before by 500, bringing the total to 2500.   20.____
If the membership increased by the same percentage this year, the TOTAL number of members in the blood credit program for this agency by the end of this year should be

    A. 2625   B. 3000   C. 3125   D. 3250

21. During this year, an agency suggestion program put into practice suggestions from 24 employees, thereby saving the agency 40 times the amount of money it paid in awards. If 1/3 of the employees were awarded $50 each, 1/2 of the employees were awarded $25 each, and the rest were awarded $10 each, how much money did the agency SAVE by using the suggestions?   21.____

    A. $18,760   B. $29,600   C. $32,400   D. $46,740

22. Which of the following actions should a supervisor generally find MOST effective as a method of determining whether subordinates need additional training in performing their work?   22.____

    A. Compiling a list of absences and latenesses of subordinates
    B. Observing the manner in which his subordinates carry out their various tasks
    C. Reviewing the grievances submitted by subordinates
    D. Reminding his subordinates to consult him if they experience difficulty in completing an assignment

23. Of the following types of letters, the MOST difficult to trace if lost after mailing is the _____ letter.   23.__

    A. special delivery   B. registered
    C. insured   D. certified

24. Suppose that you are looking over a few incoming letters that have been put in your mail basket. You see that one has a return address on the envelope but not on the letter itself. Of the following, the BEST way to make sure there is a correct record of the return address is to   24.__

    A. return the letter to the sender and ask him to fill in his address on his own letter
    B. put the letter back into the envelope and close the opening with a paper clip
    C. copy the address onto a 3"x5" index card and throw away the envelope
    D. copy the address onto the letter and staple the envelope to the letter

25. Although most incoming mail that you receive in an office will pertain to business matters, there are times when a letter may be delivered for your supervisor that is marked *Personal.*
    Of the following, the BEST way for you to handle this type of mail is to   25.__

    A. open the letter but do not read it, and route it along with the other mail
    B. read the letter to see if it really is personal
    C. have the letter forwarded unopened to your supervisor's home address
    D. deliver the letter to your supervisor's desk unopened

KEY (CORRECT ANSWERS)

1.	A		11.	C
2.	B		12.	A
3.	A		13.	C
4.	D		14.	C
5.	A		15.	B
6.	D		16.	C
7.	D		17.	D
8.	C		18.	A
9.	A		19.	B
10.	C		20.	C

21.	B
22.	B
23.	D
24.	D
25.	D

EXAMINATION SECTION
TEST 1

DIRECTIONS: Each question or incomplete statement is followed by several suggested answers or completions. Select the one that BEST answers the question or completes the statement. *PRINT THE LETTER OF THE CORRECT ANSWER IN THE SPACE AT THE RIGHT.*

Questions 1-4.

DIRECTIONS: Answer Questions 1 through 4 SOLELY on the basis of the following passage.

Job analysis combined with performance appraisal is an excellent method of determining training needs of individuals. The steps in this method are to determine the specific duties of the job, to evaluate the adequacy with which the employee performs each of these duties, and finally to determine what significant improvements can be made by training.

The list of duties can be obtained in a number of ways: asking the employee, asking the supervisor, observing the employee, etc. Adequacy of performance can be estimated by the employee, but the supervisor's evaluation must also be obtained. This evaluation will usually be based on observation.

What does the supervisor observe? The employee, while he is working; the employee's work relationships; the ease, speed, and sureness of the employee's actions; the way he applies himself to the job; the accuracy and amount of completed work; its conformity with established procedures and standards; the appearance of the work; the soundness of judgment it shows; and, finally, signs of good or poor communication, understanding, and cooperation among employees.

Such observation is a normal and inseparable part of the everyday job of supervision. Systematically, recorded, evaluated, and summarized, it highlights both general and individual training needs.

1. According to the passage, job analysis may be used by the supervisor in   1.____

    A. increasing his own understanding of tasks performed in his unit
    B. increasing efficiency of communication within the organization
    C. assisting personnel experts in the classification of positions
    D. determining in which areas an employee needs more instruction

2. According to the passage, the FIRST step in determining the training needs of employees is to   2.____

    A. locate the significant improvements that can be made by training
    B. determine the specific duties required in a job
    C. evaluate the employee's performance
    D. motivate the employee to want to improve himself

3. On the basis of the above passage, which of the following is the BEST way for a supervisor to determine the adequacy of employee performance?   3.____

    A. Check the accuracy and amount of completed work
    B. Ask the training officer
    C. Observe all aspects of the employee's work
    D. Obtain the employee's own estimate

4. Which of the following is NOT mentioned by the passage as a factor to be taken into consideration in judging the adequacy of employee performance?

    A. Accuracy of completed work
    B. Appearance of completed work
    C. Cooperation among employees
    D. Attitude of the employee toward his supervisor

4.___

5. In indexing names of business firms and other organizations, ONE of the rules to be followed is:

    A. The word *and* is considered an indexing unit
    B. When a firm name includes the full name of a person who is not well-known, the person's first name is considered as the first indexing unit
    C. Usually the units in a firm name are indexed in the order in which they are written
    D. When a firm's name is made up of single letters (such as ABC Corp.), the letters taken together are considered more than one indexing unit

5.___

6. Assume that people often come to your office with complaints of errors in your agency's handling of their clients. The employees in your office have the job of listening to these complaints and investigating them. One day, when it is almost closing time, a person comes into your office, apparently very angry, and demands that you take care of his complaint at once.
Your IMMEDIATE reaction should be to

    A. suggest that he return the following day
    B. find out his name and the nature of his complaint
    C. tell him to write a letter
    D. call over your superior

6.___

7. Assume that part of your job is to notify people concerning whether their applications for a certain program have been approved or disapproved. However, you do not actually make the decision on approval or disapproval. One day, you answer a telephone call from a woman who states that she has not yet received any word on her application. She goes on to tell you her qualifications for the program. From what she has said, you know that persons with such qualifications are usually approved.
Of the following, which one is the BEST thing for you to say to her?

    A. "You probably will be accepted, but wait until you receive a letter before trying to join the program."
    B. "Since you seem well qualified, I am sure that your application will be approved."
    C. "If you can write us a letter emphasizing your qualifications, it may speed up the process."
    D. "You will be notified of the results of your application as soon as a decision has been made."

7.___

8. Suppose that one of your duties includes answering specific telephone inquiries. Your superior refers a call to you from an irate person who claims that your agency is inefficient and is wasting taxpayers' money.
Of the following, the BEST way to handle such a call is to

    A. listen briefly and then hang up without answering
    B. note the caller's comments and tell him that you will transmit them to your superiors

8.___

C. connect the caller with the head of your agency
D. discuss your own opinions with the caller

9. An employee has been assigned to open her division head's mail and place it on his desk. One day, the employee opens a letter which she then notices is marked *Personal*. Of the following, the BEST action for her to take is to

    9.____

A. write *Personal* on the letter and staple the envelope to the back of the letter
B. ignore the matter and treat the letter the same way as the others
C. give it to another division head to hold until her own division head comes into the office
D. leave the letter in the envelope and write *Sorry opened by mistake* on the envelope and initial it

Questions 10-14.

DIRECTIONS: Questions 10 through 14 each consist of a quotation which contains one word that is incorrectly used because it is not in keeping with the meaning that the quotation is evidently intended to convey. Of the words underlined in each quotation, determine which word is incorrectly used. Then select from among the words lettered A, B, C, and D the word which, when substituted for the incorrectly used word, would BEST help to convey the meaning of the quotation. (Do NOT indicate a change for an underlined word unless the underlined word is incorrectly used.)

10. Unless reasonable managerial supervision is <u>exercised</u> over office supplies, it is certain that there will be extravagance, <u>rejected</u> items out of stock, <u>excessive</u> prices paid for certain items, and <u>obsolete</u> material in the stockroom.

    10.____

A. overlooked   B. immoderate
C. needed   D. instituted

11. Since <u>office</u> supplies are in such <u>common</u> use, an attitude of indifference about their handling is not <u>unusual</u>. Their importance is often recognized only when they are <u>utilized</u> or out of stock, for office employees must have proper supplies if maximum productivity is to be <u>attained</u>.

    11.____

A. plentiful   B. unavailable
C. reduced   D. expected

12. Anyone <u>effected</u> by paperwork, <u>interested</u> in or engaged in office work, or desiring to improve <u>informational</u> activities can find materials <u>keyed</u> to his needs.

    12.____

A. attentive   B. available   C. affected   D. ambitious

13. Information is <u>homogeneous</u> and must therefore be properly classified so that each type may be <u>employed</u> in ways <u>appropriate</u> to its <u>own peculiar</u> properties.

    13.____

A. apparent   B. heterogeneous
C. consistent   D. idiosyncratic

14. <u>Intellectual</u> training may seem a <u>formidable</u> phrase, but it means nothing more than the <u>deliberate</u> cultivation of the ability to think, and there is no <u>dark</u> contrast between the intellectual and the practical.

    14.____

A. subjective   B. objective
C. sharp   D. vocational

15. The MOST important reason for having a filing system is to   15.___

     A. get papers out of the way
     B. have a record of everything that has happened
     C. retain information to justify your actions
     D. enable rapid retrieval of information

16. The system of filing which is used MOST frequently is called _____ filing.   16.___

     A. alphabetic   B. alphanumeric
     C. geographic   D. numeric

17. One of the clerks under your supervision has been telephoning frequently to tell you that   17.___
he was taking the day off. Unless there is a real need for it, taking leave which is not
scheduled is frowned upon because it upsets the work schedule.
Under these circumstances, which of the following reasons for taking the day off is
MOST acceptable?

     A. "I can't work when my arthritis bothers me."
     B. "I've been pressured with work from my night job and needed the extra time to
        catch up."
     C. "My family just moved to a new house, and I needed the time to start the repairs."
     D. "Work here has not been challenging, and I've been looking for another job."

18. One of the employees under your supervision, previously a very satisfactory worker, has   18.___
begun arriving late one or two mornings each week. No explanation has been offered for
this change. You call her to your office for a conference. As you are explaining the purpose of the conference and your need to understand this sudden lateness problem, she
becomes angry and states that you have no right to question her.
Of the following, the BEST course of action for you to take at this point is to

     A. inform her in your most authoritarian tone that you are the supervisor and that you
        have every right to question her
     B. end the conference and advise the employee that you will have no further discus-
        sion with her until she controls her temper
     C. remain calm, try to calm her down, and when she has quieted, explain the reasons
        for your questions and the need for answers
     D. hold your temper; when she has calmed down, tell her that you will not have a
        tardy worker in your unit and will have her transferred at once

19. Assume that, in the branch of the agency for which you work, you are the only clerical   19.___
person on the staff with a supervisory title and, in addition, that you are the office manager. On a particular day when all members of the professional staff are away from the
building attending an important meeting, an urgent call comes through requesting some
confidential information ordinarily released only by professional staff.
Of the following, the MOST reasonable action for you to take is to

     A. decline to give the information because you are not a member of the professional
        staff
     B. offer to call back after you get permission from the agency director at the main
        office

C. advise the caller that you will supply the information as soon as your chief returns
D. supply the information requested and inform your chief when she returns

20. As a supervisor, you are scheduled to attend an important conference with your superior.   20._____
However, that day you learn that your very capable assistant is ill and unable to come to
work. Several highly sensitive tasks are scheduled for completion on this day.
Of the following, the BEST way to handle this situation is to

    A. tell your supervisor you cannot attend the meeting and ask that it be postponed
    B. assign one of your staff to see that the jobs are completed and turned in
    C. advise your supervisor of the situation and ask what you should do
    D. call the departments for which the work is being done and ask for an extension of
       time

21. When a decision needs to be made which is likely to affect units other than his own, a   21._____
supervisor should USUALLY

    A. make such a decision quickly and then discuss it with his supervisor
    B. make such a decision only after careful consultation with his subordinates
    C. discuss the problem with his immediate superior before making such a decision
    D. have his subordinates arrive at such a decision in conference with the subordi-
       nates in the other units

22. Assume that, as a supervisor in Division X, you are training Ms. Y, a new employee, to   22._____
answer the telephone properly.
You should explain that the BEST way to answer is to pick up the receiver and say:

    A. "What is your name, please?"
    B. "May I help you?"
    C. "Ms. Y speaking."
    D. "Division X, Ms. Y speaking."

Questions 23-25.

DIRECTIONS: Questions 23 through 25 consist of sentences in which two words are missing.
Examine each sentence, and then choose from below it the words which
should be inserted in the blank spaces in order to create a coherent and well-
written sentence.

23. Human behavior is far _____ variable, and therefore _____ predictable, than that of   23._____
any other species.

    A. less; as   B. less; not
    C. more; not   D. more; less

24. The _____ limitation of this method is that the results are based _____ a narrow sam-   24._____
ple.

    A. chief; with   B. chief; on
    C. only; for   D. only; to

25. Although there _____ a standard procedure for handling these problems, each case   25._____
often has _____ own unique features.

    A. are; its   B. are; their
    C. is; its   D. is; their

KEY (CORRECT ANSWERS)

1.	D	11.	B
2.	B	12.	C
3.	C	13.	B
4.	D	14.	C
5.	C	15.	D
6.	B	16.	A
7.	D	17.	A
8.	B	18.	C
9.	D	19.	B
10.	C	20.	C

21.	C
22.	D
23.	D
24.	B
25.	C

TEST 2

DIRECTIONS: Each question or incomplete statement is followed by several suggested answers or completions. Select the one that BEST answers your question or completes the statement. *PRINT THE LETTER OF THE CORRECT ANSWER IN THE SPACE AT THE RIGHT.*

Questions 1-3.

DIRECTIONS: Questions 1 through 3 each consist of a group of four sentences. Read each sentence carefully, and select the one of the four in each group which represents the BEST English usage for business letters and reports.

1. A. The chairman himself, rather than his aides, hasreviewed the report.   1.____
   B. The chairman himself, rather than his aides, have reviewed the report.
   C. The chairmen, not the aide, has reviewed the report.
   D. The aide, not the chairmen, have reviewed the report.

2. A. Various proposals were submitted but the decision is not been made.   2.____
   B. Various proposals has been submitted but the decision has not been made.
   C. Various proposals were submitted but the decision is not been made.
   D. Various proposals have been submitted but the decision has not been made.

3. A. Everyone were rewarded for his successful attempt.   3.____
   B. They were successful in their attempts and each of them was rewarded.
   C. Each of them are rewarded for their successful attempts.
   D. The reward for their successful attempts were made to each of them.

4. Which of the following is MOST suited to arrangement in chronological order?   4.____

   A. Applications for various types and levels of jobs
   B. Issues of a weekly publication
   C. Weekly time cards for all employees for the week of April 21
   D. Personnel records for all employees

5. Words that are *synonymous* with a given word ALWAYS   5.____

   A. have the same meaning as the given word
   B. have the same pronunciation as the given word
   C. have the opposite meaning of the given word
   D. can be rhymed with the given word

Questions 6-11.

DIRECTIONS: Answer Questions 6 through 11 on the basis of the following chart showing numbers of errors made by four clerks in one work unit for a half-year period.

	Allan	Barry	Cary	David
July	5	4	1	7
Aug.	8	3	9	8
Sept.	7	8	7	5
Oct.	3	6	5	3
Nov .	2	4	4	6
Dec.	5	2	8	4

6. The clerk with the HIGHEST number of errors for the six-month period was   6.___

   A. Allan   B. Barry   C. Cary   D. David

7. If the number of errors made by Allan in the six months shown represented one-eighth of   7.___
the total errors made by the unit during the entire year, what was the TOTAL number of
errors made by the unit for the year?

   A. 124   B. 180   C. 240   D. 360

8. The number of errors made by David in November was what FRACTION of the total   8.___
errors made in November?

   A. 1/3   B. 1/6   C. 3/8   D. 3/16

9. The average number of errors made per month per clerk was MOST NEARLY   9.___

   A. 4   B. 5   C. 6   D. 7

10. Of the total number of errors made during the six-month period, the percentage made in   10.___
August was MOST NEARLY

   A. 2%   B. 4%   C. 23%   D. 44%

11. If the number of errors in the unit were to decrease in the next six months by 30%, what   11.___
would be MOST NEARLY the total number of errors for the unit for the next six months?

   A. 87   B. 94   C. 120   D. 137

12. The arithmetic mean salary for five employees earning $18,500, $18,300, $18,600,   12.___
$18,400, and $18,500, respectively, is

   A. $18,450   B. $18,460   C. $18,475   D. $18,500

13. Last year, a city department which is responsible for purchasing supplies ordered bond   13.___
paper in equal quantities from 22 different companies. The price was exactly the same
for each company, and the total cost for the 22 orders was $693,113.
Assuming prices did not change during the year, the cost of EACH order was MOST
NEARLY

   A. $31,490   B. $31,495   C. $31,500   D. $31,505

14. A city agency engaged in repair work uses a small part which the city purchases for 14?   14.___
each. Assume that, in a certain year, the total expenditure of the city for this part was
$700.
How MANY of these parts were purchased that year?

   A. 50   B. 200   C. 2,000   D. 5,000

15. The work unit which you supervise is responsible for processing fifteen reports per month.
If your unit has four clerks and the best worker completes 40% of the reports himself, how many reports would each of the other clerks have to complete if they all do an equal number?

    A. 1   B. 2   C. 3   D. 4

  15.____

16. Assume that the work unit in which you work has 24 clerks and 18 stenographers. In order to change the ratio of stenographers to clerks so that there is one stenographer for every four clerks, it would be necessary to REDUCE the number of stenographers by

    A. 3   B. 6   C. 9   D. 12

  16.____

17. Assume that your office is responsible for opening and distributing all the mail of the division. After opening a letter, one of your subordinates notices that it states that there should be an enclosure in the envelope. However, there is no enclosure in the envelope. Of the following, the BEST instruction that you can give the clerk is to

    A. call the sender to obtain the enclosure
    B. call the addressee to inform him that the enclosure is missing
    C. note the omission in the margin of the letter
    D. forward the letter without taking any action

  17.____

18. While opening the envelope containing official correspondence, you accidentally cut the enclosed letter.
Of the following, the BEST action for you to take is to

    A. leave the material as it is
    B. put it together by using transparent mending tape
    C. keep it together by putting it back in the envelope
    D. keep it together by using paper clips

  18.____

19. Suppose your supervisor is on the telephone in his office and an applicant arrives for a scheduled interview with him.
Of the following, the BEST procedure to follow ordinarily is to

    A. informally chat with the applicant in your office until your supervisor has finished his phone conversation
    B. escort him directly into your supervisor's office and have him wait for him there
    C. inform your supervisor of the applicant's arrival and try to make the applicant feel comfortable while waiting
    D. have him hang up his coat and tell him to go directly in to see your supervisor

  19.____

20. The length of time that files should be kept is GENERALLY

    A. considered to be seven years
    B. dependent upon how much new material has accumulated in the files
    C. directly proportionate to the number of years the office has been in operation
    D. dependent upon the type and nature of the material in the files

  20.____

21. Cross-referencing a document when you file it means 21.____
   A. making a copy of the document and putting the copy into a related file
   B. indicating on the front of the document the name of the person who wrote it, the date it was written, and for what purpose
   C. putting a special sheet or card in a related file to indicate where the document is filed
   D. indicating on the document where it is to be filed

22. Unnecessary handling and recording of incoming mail could be eliminated by 22.____
   A. having the person who opens it initial it
   B. indicating on the piece of mail the names of all the individuals who should see it
   C. sending all incoming mail to more than one central location
   D. making a photocopy of each piece of incoming mail

23. Of the following, the office tasks which lend themselves MOST readily to planning and study are 23.____
   A. repetitive, occur in volume, and extend over a period of time
   B. cyclical in nature, have small volume, and extend over a short period of time
   C. tasks which occur only once in a great while not according to any schedule, and have large volume
   D. special tasks which occur only once, regardless of their volume and length of time

24. A good recordkeeping system includes all of the following procedures EXCEPT the 24.____
   A. filing of useless records
   B. destruction of certain files
   C. transferring of records from one type of file to another
   D. creation of inactive files

25. Assume that, as a supervisor, you are responsible for orienting and training new employ- 25.____
   ees in your unit. Which of the following can MOST properly be omitted from your discus-
   sions with a new employee?
   A. The purpose of commonly used office forms
   B. Time and leave regulations
   C. Procedures for required handling of routine business calls
   D. The reason the last employee was fired

KEY (CORRECT ANSWERS)

1.	A		11.	A
2.	D		12.	B
3.	B		13.	D
4.	B		14.	D
5.	A		15.	C
6.	C		16.	D
7.	C		17.	C
8.	C		18.	B
9.	B		19.	C
10.	C		20.	D

21.	C
22.	B
23.	A
24.	A
25.	D

EXAMINATION SECTION

TEST 1

DIRECTIONS: Each question or incomplete statement is followed by several suggested answers or completions. Select the one that BEST answers the question or completes the statement. *PRINT THE LETTER OF THE CORRECT ANSWER IN THE SPACE AT THE RIGHT.*

1. The one of the following that is MOST advisable to do before transcribing your dictation notes is to
   A. check the syllabification of long words for typing purposes
   B. edit your notes
   C. number the pages of dictation
   D. sort them by the kind of typing format required

1._____

2. As a secretary, the one of the following which is LEAST important in writing a letter under your own signature is
   A. the accuracy of the information
   B. the appropriateness of the language
   C. the reason for the letter
   D. your supervisor's approval of the final copy

2._____

3. In a typed letter, the reference line is used
   A. for identification purposes on typed pages of more than one page
   B. to indicate under what heading the copy of the letter should be filed
   C. to indicate who dictated the letter and who typed it
   D. to make the subject of the letter prominent by typing it a single space below the salutation

3._____

Questions 4-5:

DIRECTIONS: For questions 4 and 5, choose the letter of the sentence that BEST and MOST clearly expresses its meaning.

4. A. It has always been the practice of this office to effectuate recruitment of prospective employees from other departments.
   B. This office has always made a practice of recruiting prospective employees from other departments.
   C. Recruitment of prospective employees from other departments has always been a practice which has been implemented by this office.
   D. Implementation of the policy of recruitment of prospective employees from other departments has always been a practice of this office.

4._____

5.   A. These employees are assigned to the level of work evidenced by   5._____
         their efforts and skills during the training period.
      B. The level of work to which these employees is assigned is
         decided upon on the basis of the efforts and skills evidenced by
         them during the period in which they were trained.
      C. Assignment of these employees is made on the basis of the level
         of work their efforts and skills during the training period has
         evidenced.
      D. These employees are assigned to a level of work their efforts and
         skills during the training period have evidenced.

6. An office assistant was asked to mail a duplicated report of 100 pages to   6._____
   a professor in an out-of-town university. The professor sending the report
   dictated a short letter that he wanted to mail with the report.
   Of the following, the MOST inexpensive proper means of sending these
   two items would be to send the report
      A. and the letter first class
      B. by parcel post and the letter separately by air mail
      C. and the letter by parcel post
      D. by parcel post and attach to the package an envelope with first-
         class postage in which is enclosed the letter

7. Plans are underway to determine the productivity of the typists who work   7._____
   in a central office. Of the procedures listed, the one generally considered
   the MOST accurate for finding out the typists' output is to
      A. keep a record of how much typing is done over specified periods
         of time
      B. ask each typist how fast she types when she is doing a great deal
         of word processing
      C. give each typist a timed test during a specified period
      D. ask the supervisor to estimate the typing speed of each
         subordinate

8. Assume that an executive regularly receives the four types of mail listed   8._____
   below.
   As a general rule, the executive's secretary should arrange the mail from
   top to bottom so that the top items are
      A. advertisements
      B. airmail letters
      C. business letters
      D. unopened personal letters

9. An office assistant in transcribing reports and letters from dictation should MOST generally assume that

9._____

    A. the transcript should be exactly what was dictated so there is little need to check any details

    B. the dictated material is merely an idea of what the dictator wanted to say so changes should be made to improve any part of the dictation

    C. there may be some slight changes, but essentially the transcription is to be a faithful copy of what was dictated

    D. the transcript is merely a very rough draft and should be typed quickly so that the dictator can review it and make changes preliminary to having the final copy typed

10. The one of the following which generally is the CHIEF disadvantage of using office machines in place of human workers in office work is that the machines are

10._____

    A. slower   B. less accurate

    C. more costly   D. less flexible

11. An office assistant in a New York City college is asked to place a call to a prospective visiting professor in Los Angeles. It is 1 p.m. in New York (EST). The time in Los Angeles is

11._____

    A. 9 a.m.   B. 10 a.m.   C. 4 p.m.   D. 5 p.m.

12. An office assistant is instructed to send a copy of a report to a professor located in a building across campus. The fastest and most efficient way for this report to reach the professor is by

12._____

    A. sending a messenger to hand-deliver it to the professor's office

    B. sending it via fax to the main office of the professor's department

    C. e-mailing it to the professor

    D. dictating the contents of the report to the professor over the phone

13. An office assistant is in the process of typing the forms for recommendation for promotion for a member of the faculty who is away for a week. She notes that two books of which he is the author are listed without dates.

13._____

Of the following, the procedure she should BEST follow at this point generally is to

    A. postpone doing the job until the professor returns to campus the following week

    B. type the material omitting the books

    C. check the professor's office for copies of the books and obtain the correct data

    D. call the professor's wife and ask her when the books were published

14. An office has introduced work standards for all of the employees.　　　　14._____
Of the following, it is MOST likely that use of such standards would tend
to
    A. make it more difficult to determine numbers of employees needed
    B. lead to a substantial drop in morale among all of the employees
    C. reduce the possibility of planning to meet emergencies
    D. reduce uncertainty about the costs of doing tasks

15. Of the following clerical errors, the one which probably is LEAST　　　　15._____
important is
    A. adding 543 instead of 548 to a bookkeeping account
    B. putting the wrong code on a data processing card
    C. recording a transaction on the record of Henry Smith instead of on
       the record of Harry Smith
    D. writing John Murpfy instead of John Murphy when addressing an
       envelope

16. Of the following errors, the one which probably is MOST important is　　　16._____
    A. writing "they're" instead of "their" in an office memo
    B. misplacing a decimal point on a sales invoice
    C. forgetting to write the date on a note for a supervisor
    D. sending an e-mail to a misspelled e-mail address

17. The chairman of an academic department tells an office assistant that a　　17._____
meeting of the faculty is to be held four weeks from the current date.
Of the following responsibilities, the office assistant is MOST frequently
held responsible for
    A. planning the agenda of the meeting
    B. presiding over the conduct of the meeting
    C. reserving the meeting room and notifying the members
    D. initiating all formal resolutions

18. Of the following, a centralized filing system is LEAST suitable for filing　　18._____
    A. material which is confidential in nature
    B. routine correspondence
    C. periodic reports of the divisions of the department
    D. material used by several divisions of the department

19. A misplaced record is a lost record.　　　　19._____
Of the following, the MOST valid implication of this statement in regard to
office work is that
    A. all records in an office should be filed in strict alphabetical order
    B. accuracy in filing is essential
    C. only one method of filing should be used throughout the office
    D. files should be locked when not in use

20. When typing names or titles on a roll of folder labels, the one of the
    following which is MOST important to do is to type the caption
    A. as it appears on the papers to be placed in the folder
    B. in capital letters
    C. in exact indexing or filing order
    D. so that it appears near the bottom of the folder tab when the label
       is attached

20._____

21. A professor at a Boston university asks an office assistant to place a call
    to a fellow professor in San Francisco. The MOST appropriate local time
    for the assistant to place the call to the professor in California, given the
    time difference, would be
    A. 8:30 a.m.   B. 10:00 a.m.   C. 11:30 a.m.   D. 1:30 p.m.

21._____

22. When typing the rough draft of a report, the computer application you
    would use is
    A. Excel   B. Word
    C. PowerPoint   D. Internet Explorer

22._____

23. Which of the following is the BEST and most appropriate way to
    proofread and edit a report before submitting it to a supervisor for review?
    A. Scan the report with the program's spell check feature
    B. Proof the report yourself, then ask another office assistant to read
       the report over as well until it is finished
    C. Give the report to another office assistant who is more skilled at
       proofreading
    D. Use the spell checker, then scan the report yourself as many
       times as needed in order to pick up any additional errors

23._____

24. The one of the following situations in which it would be MOST justifiable
    for an office to use standard or form paragraphs in its business letters is
    when
    A. a large number of similar letters is to be sent
    B. the letters are to be uniform in length and appearance
    C. it is desired to reduce typing errors in correspondence
    D. the office is to carry on a lengthy correspondence with an
       individual

24._____

25. Of the following, the MOST important factor in determining whether or not
    an office filing system is effective is that the
    A. information in the files is legible
    B. records in the files are used frequently
    C. information in the files is accurate
    D. records in the files can be located readily

25._____

KEY (CORRECT ANSWERS)

1. B	11. B	21. D
2. D	12. C	22. B
3. C	13. C	23. D
4. B	14. D	24. A
5. A	15. D	25. D
6. D	16. B	
7. A	17. C	
8. D	18. A	
9. C	19. B	
10. D	20. C	

TEST 2

DIRECTIONS: Each question or incomplete statement is followed by several suggested answers or completions. Select the one that BEST answers the question or completes the statement. *PRINT THE LETTER OF THE CORRECT ANSWER IN THE SPACE AT THE RIGHT.*

1. For the office assistant whose duties include frequent recording and transcription of minutes of formal meetings, the one of the following reference works generally considered to be MOST useful is
   A. *Robert's Rules of Order*
   B. *Bartlett's Familiar Quotations*
   C. *World Almanac and Book of Facts*
   D. *Conway's Reference*

1._____

2. Of the following statements about the numeric system of filing, the one which is CORRECT is that it
   A. is the least accurate of all methods of filing
   B. eliminates the need for cross-referencing
   C. allows for very limited expansion
   D. requires a separate index

2._____

3. When more than one name or subject is involved in a piece of correspondence to be filed, the office assistant should GENERALLY
   A. prepare a cross-reference sheet
   B. establish a geographical filing system
   C. prepare out-guides
   D. establish a separate index card file for noting such correspondence

3._____

4. A tickler file is MOST generally used for
   A. identification of material contained in a numeric file
   B. maintenance of a current listing of telephone numbers
   C. follow-up of matters requiring future attention
   D. control of records borrowed or otherwise removed from the files

4._____

5. In filing, the name Ms. *Ann Catalana-Moss* should GENERALLY be indexed as
   A. Moss, Catalana, Ann (Ms.)
   B. Catalana-Moss, Ann (Ms.)
   C. Ann Catalana-Moss (Ms.)
   D. Moss-Catalana, Ann (Ms.)

5._____

6. An office assistant has a set of four cards, each of which contains one of   6._____
   the following names.
   In alphabetic filing, the FIRST of the cards to be filed is
      A. Ms. Alma John
      B. Mrs. John (Patricia) Edwards
      C. John-Edward School Supplies, Inc.
      D. John H. Edwards

7. Generally, of the following, the name to be filed FIRST in an alphabetical   7._____
   filing system is
      A. Diane Maestro   B. Diana McElroy
      C. James Mackell   D. James McKell

8. After checking several times, you are unable to locate a student record in   8._____
   its proper file drawer. The file drawer in question is used constantly by
   many members of the staff.
   In this situation, the NEXT step you should take in locating the missing
   record is to
      A. ask another worker to look through the file drawer
      B. determine if there is another copy of the record filed in a different
         place
      C. find out if the record has been removed by another staff member
      D. wait a day or two and see if the record turns up

9. It is MOST important that an enclosure which is to be mailed with a letter   9._____
   should be put in an envelope so that
      A. any printing on the enclosure will not be visible through the
         address side of the envelope
      B. it is obvious that there is an enclosure inside the envelope
      C. the enclosure takes up less space than the letter
      D. the person who opens the envelope will pull out both the letter and
         the enclosure

10. Suppose that one of the student aides with whom you work suggests a   10._____
    change in the filing procedure. He is sure the change will result in
    increased rates of filing among the other employees.
    The one of the following which you should do FIRST is to
       A. ask him to demonstrate his method in order to determine if he files
          more quickly than the other employees
       B. ask your supervisor if you may make a change in the filing
          procedure
       C. ignore the aide's suggestion since he is not a filing expert
       D. tell him to show his method to the other employees and to
          encourage them to use it

11. It is generally advisable to leave at least six inches of working space in a
     file drawer. This procedure is MOST useful in

     A. decreasing the number of filing errors
     B. facilitating the sorting of documents and folders
     C. maintaining a regular program of removing inactive records
     D. preventing folders and papers from being torn

11._____

12. Assume that a dictator is briefly interrupted because of a telephone call or
     other similar matter (no more than three minutes).
     Of the following tasks, the person taking the dictation should NORMALLY
     use the time to

     A. re-read notes already recorded
     B. tidy the dictator's desk
     C. check the accuracy of the dictator's desk files
     D. return to her own desk to type the dictated material

12._____

13. When typing a preliminary draft of a report, the one of the following which
     you should generally NOT do is

     A. erase typing errors and deletions rather than cross them out
     B. leave plenty of room at the top, bottom and sides of each page
     C. make only the number of copies that you are asked to make
     D. type double or triple space

13._____

14. The BEST way for a receptionist to deal with a situation in which she
     must leave her desk for a long time is to

     A. ask someone to take her place while she is away
     B. leave a note or sign on her desk which indicates the time she will
        return
     C. take a chance that no one will arrive while she is gone and leave
        her desk unattended
     D. tell a coworker to ask any visitors that arrive to wait until she
        returns

14._____

15. Suppose that two individuals come up to your desk at the same time.
     One of them asks you for the location of the nearest public phone. After
     you answer the question, you turn to the second person who asks you the
     same question.
     The one of the following actions that would be BEST for you to take in this
     situation is to

     A. ignore the second person since he obviously overheard your first
        answer
     B. point out that you just answered the same question and quickly
        repeat the information
     C. politely repeat the information to the second individual
     D. tell the second person to follow the first to the public telephone

15._____

16. Which of the following names should be filed FIRST in an alphabetical filing system?
    A. Anthony Aarvedsen
    B. William Aaron
    C. Denise Aron
    D. A.J. Arrington

16._____

17. New material added to a file folder should USUALLY be inserted
    A. in the order of importance (the most important in front)
    B. in the order of importance (the most important in back)
    C. chronologically (most recent in front)
    D. chronologically (most recent in back)

17._____

18. An individual is looking for a name in the White Pages of a telephone directory.
Which of the following BEST describes the system of filing found there?
    A. alphabetic
    B. sequential
    C. locator
    D. index

18._____

19. The MAIN purpose of a tickler file is to
    A. help prevent overlooking matters that require future attention
    B. check on adequacy of past performance
    C. pinpoint responsibility for recurring daily tasks
    D. reduce the volume of material kept in general files

19._____

20. Which of the following BEST describes the process of *reconciling* a bank statement?
    A. Analyzing the nature of the expenditures made by the office during the preceding month
    B. Comparing the statement of the bank with the banking records maintained in the office
    C. Determining the liquidity position by reading the bank statement carefully
    D. Checking the service charges noted on the bank statement

20._____

21. From the viewpoint of preserving agency or institutional funds, the LEAST acceptable method for making a payment is a check made out to
    A. cash
    B. a company
    C. an individual
    D. a partnership

21._____

22. Listed below are four of the steps in the process of preparing correspondence for filing.
If they were to be put in logical sequence, the SECOND step would be
    A. preparing cross-reference sheets or cards
    B. coding the correspondence using a classification system
    C. sorting the correspondence in the order to be filed
    D. checking for follow-up action required and preparing a follow-up slip

22._____

23. The process of *justifying* typed copy involves laying out the copy so that 23._____
    A. each paragraph appears to be approximately the same size
    B. no long words are broken up at the end of a line
    C. the right and left hand margins are even
    D. there is enough room to enter proofreading marks at the end of each line

24. The MOST important reason for a person in charge of a petty cash fund 24._____
    to obtain receipts for payments is that this practice would tend to
    A. decrease robberies by delivery personnel
    B. eliminate the need to keep a record of petty cash expenditures
    C. prove that the fund has been used properly
    D. provide a record of the need for cash in the daily operations of the office

25. You should GENERALLY replenish a petty cash fund 25._____
    A. at regularly established intervals
    B. each time you withdraw a sum
    C. when the amount of cash gets below a certain specified amount
    D. when the fund is completely empty

KEY (CORRECT ANSWERS)

1. A	11. D	21. A
2. D	12. A	22. A
3. A	13. A	23. C
4. C	14. A	24. C
5. B	15. C	25. C
6. D	16. B	
7. C	17. C	
8. C	18. A	
9. D	19. A	
10. A	20. B	

READING COMPREHENSION
UNDERSTANDING AND INTERPRETING WRITTEN MATERIAL
EXAMINATION SECTION
TEST 1

DIRECTIONS: Each question or incomplete statement is followed by several suggested answers or completions. Select the one that BEST answers the question or completes the statement. *PRINT THE LETTER OF THE CORRECT ANSWER IN THE SPACE AT THE RIGHT.*

Questions 1-6.

DIRECTIONS: Questions 1 through 6 are to be answered SOLELY on the basis of the information contained in the following passage.

Duplicating is the process of making a number of identical copies of letters, documents, etc from an original. Some duplicating processes make copies directly from the original document. Other duplicating processes require the preparation of a special master, and copies are then made from the master. Four of the most common duplicating processes are stencil, fluid, offset, and xerox.

In the stencil process, the typewriter is used to cut the words into a master called a stencil. Drawings, charts, or graphs can be cut into the stencil using a stylus. As many as 3,500 good-quality copies can be reproduced from one stencil. Various grades of finished paper from inexpensive mimeograph to expensive bond can be used.

The fluid process is a good method of copying from 50 to 125 good-quality copies from a master, which is prepared with a special dye. The master is placed on the duplicator, and special paper with a hard finish is moistened and then passed through the duplicator. Some of the dye on the master is dissolved, creating an impression on the paper. The impression becomes lighter as more copies are made; and once the dye on the master is used up, a new master must be made.

The offset process is the most adaptable office duplicating process because this process can be used for making a few copies or many copies. Masters can be made on paper or plastic for a few hundred copies, or on metal plates for as many as 75,000 copies. By using a special technique called photo-offset, charts, photographs, illustrations, or graphs can be reproduced on the master plate. The offset process is capable of producing large quantities of fine, top-quality copies on all types of finished paper.

The xerox process reproduces an exact duplicate from an original. It is the fastest duplicating method because the original material is placed directly on the duplicator, eliminating the need to make a special master. Any kind of paper can be used. The xerox process is the most expensive duplicating process; however, it is the best method of reproducing small quantities of good-quality copies of reports, letters, official documents, memos, or contracts.

1. Of the following, the MOST efficient method of reproducing 5,000 copies of a graph is   1.___

    A. stencil   B. fluid
    C. offset   D. Xerox

2. The offset process is the MOST adaptable office duplicating process because   2.___

    A. it is the quickest duplicating method
    B. it is the least expensive duplicating method
    C. it can produce a small number or large number of copies
    D. a softer master can be used over and over again

3. Which one of the following duplicating processes uses moistened paper?   3.___

    A. Stencil   B. Fluid
    C. Offset   D. Xerox

4. The fluid process would be the BEST process to use for reproducing   4.___

    A. five copies of a school transcript
    B. fifty copies of a memo
    C. five hundred copies of a form letter
    D. five thousand copies of a chart

5. Which one of the following duplicating processes does NOT require a special master?   5.___

    A. Fluid   B. Xerox
    C. Offset   D. Stencil

6. Xerox is NOT used for all duplicating jobs because   6.___

    A. it produces poor-quality copies
    B. the process is too expensive
    C. preparing the master is too time-consuming
    D. it cannot produce written reports

Questions 7-10.

DIRECTIONS: Questions 7 through 10 are to be answered SOLELY on the basis of the information contained in the following passage.

City government is committed to providing a safe and healthy work environment for all city employees. An effective agency safety program reduces accidents by educating employees about the types of careless acts which can cause accidents. Even in an office, accidents can happen. If each employee is aware of possible safety hazards, the number of accidents on the job can be reduced.

Careless use of office equipment can cause accidents and injuries. For example, file cabinet drawers which are filled with papers can be so heavy that the entire cabinet could tip over from the weight of one open drawer.

The bottom drawers of desks and file cabinets should never be left open since employees could easily trip over open drawers and injure themselves.

When reaching for objects on a high shelf, an employee should use a strong, sturdy object such as a step stool to stand on. Makeshift platforms made out of books, papers, or boxes can easily collapse. Even chairs can slide out from under foot, causing serious injury.

Even at an employee's desk, safety hazards can occur. Frayed or cut wires should be repaired or replaced immediately. Typewriters which are not firmly anchored to the desk or table could fall, causing injury.

Smoking is one of the major causes of fires in the office. A lighted match or improperly extinguished cigarette thrown into a wastebasket filled with paper could cause a major fire with possible loss of life. Where smoking is permitted, ashtrays should be used. Smoking is particularly dangerous in offices where flammable chemicals are used.

7. The goal of an effective safety program is to 　　　　　　　　　　　　　　　　7._____

    A. reduce office accidents
    B. stop employees from smoking on the job
    C. encourage employees to continue their education
    D. eliminate high shelves in offices

8. Desks and file cabinets can become safety hazards when 　　　　　　　　　　8._____

    A. their drawers are left open
    B. they are used as wastebaskets
    C. they are makeshift
    D. they are not anchored securely to the floor

9. Smoking is especially hazardous when it occurs 　　　　　　　　　　　　　　9._____

    A. near exposed wires
    B. in a crowded office
    C. in an area where flammable chemicals are used
    D. where books and papers are stored

10. Accidents are likely to occur when 　　　　　　　　　　　　　　　　　　　10._____

    A. employees' desks are cluttered with books and papers
    B. employees are not aware of safety hazards
    C. employees close desk drawers
    D. step stools are used to reach high objects

Questions 11-18.

DIRECTIONS:　Questions 11 through 18 are to be answered SOLELY on the basis of the information contained in the following passage.

The telephone directory is made up of two books. The first book consists of the introductory section and the alphabetical listing of names section. The second book is the classified directory (also known as the yellow pages). Many people who are familiar with one book do not realize how useful the other can be. The efficient office worker should become familiar with both books in order to make the best use of this important source of information.

The introductory section gives general instructions for finding numbers in the alphabetical listing and classified directory. This section also explains how to use the telephone company's many services, including the operator and information services, gives examples of charges for local and long distance calls, and lists area codes for the entire country. In addition, this section provides a useful postal zip code map.

The alphabetical listing of names section lists the names, addresses, and telephone numbers of subscribers in an area. Guide names, or *telltales*, are on the top corner of each page. These guide names indicate the first and last name to be found on that page. *Telltales* help locate any particular name quickly. A cross-reference spelling is also given to help locate names which are spelled several different ways. City, state, and federal government agencies are listed under the major government heading. For example, an agency of the federal government would be listed under *United States Government.*

The classified directory, or yellow pages, is a separate book. In this section are advertising services, public transportation line maps, shopping guides, and listings of businesses arranged by the type of product or services they offer. This book is most useful when looking for the name or phone number of a business when all that is known is the type of product offered and the address, or when trying to locate a particular type of business in an area. Businesses listed in the classified directory can usually be found in the alphabetical listing of names section. When the name of the business is known, you will find the address or phone number more quickly in the alphabetical listing of names section.

11. The introductory section provides 11.___

    A. shopping guides   B. government listings
    C. business listings   D. information services

12. Advertising services would be found in the 12.___

    A. introductory section
    B. alphabetical listing of names section
    C. classified directory
    D. information services

13. According to the information in the above passage for locating government agencies, the 13.___
Information Office of the Department of Consumer Affairs of New York City government
would be alphabetically listed FIRST under

    A. *I* for Information Offices
    B. *D* for Department of Consumer Affairs
    C. *N* for New York City
    D. *G* for government

14. When the name of a business is known, the QUICKEST way to find the phone number is 14.___
to look in the

    A. classified directory
    B. introductory section
    C. alphabetical listing of names section
    D. advertising service section

15. The QUICKEST way to find the phone number of a business when the type of service a business offers and its address is known is to look in the   15.____

    A. classified directory
    B. alphabetical listing of names section
    C. introductory section
    D. information service

16. What is a *telltale*?   16.____
    A(n)

    A. alphabetical listing   B. guide name
    C. map   D. cross-reference listing

17. The BEST way to find a postal zip code is to look in the   17.____

    A. classified directory
    B. introductory section
    C. alphabetical listing of names section
    D. government heading

18. To help find names which have several different spellings, the telephone directory provides   18.____

    A. cross-reference spelling
    B. *tell tales*
    C. spelling guides
    D. advertising services

Questions 19-24.

DIRECTIONS: Questions 19 through 24 are to be answered on the basis of the information contained in the following instructions on

SWEEPING

    All sweeping must be done with damp sawdust, which is used to prevent the raising of dust when sweeping platforms and mezzanines. Soak sawdust thoroughly in a bucket of water for two to three hours before use. Drain before use so that no stains are left on concrete from excess water. In order to keep sawdust moist while being used, spread for an area of 120 feet in advance of actual sweeping. Never sweep sawdust over drains. To assure good footing, do not spread it on stairways or on damp or wet floor areas.

19. Dampened sawdust should be used when   19.____

    A. scrapping   B. dusting
    C. sweeping   D. mopping

20. Of the following procedures, which is the CORRECT order to be followed when sweeping with sawdust?   20.____

    A. Soak, drain, and spread   B. Spread, drain, and soak
    C. Spread, soak, and drain   D. Drain, spread, and soak

21. Of the following, it is MOST correct to soak the sawdust in a bucket of water for _____ hour(s).

    A. a half-hour to an   B. one to two
    C. two to three   D. three to four

21.___

22. The water should be drained from the bucket of sawdust so that excess water does NOT

    A. cause passengers to lose their footing
    B. stain the concrete
    C. flood the tracks
    D. slow down the sweeping

22.___

23. Sawdust is dampened in order to

    A. assure good footing on stairways
    B. prevent the raising of dust when sweeping
    C. prevent the staining of concrete
    D. cool off platforms

23.___

24. The dampened sawdust may be spread on

    A. wet floors   B. drains
    C. stairways   D. mezzanines

24.___

Questions 25-27.

DIRECTIONS: Questions 25 through 27 are to be answered on the basis of the information contained in the following paragraph.

Whether a main lobby or upper corridor requires scrubbing or mopping and whether it should be done nightly or less frequently depends on the nature of the floor surface and the amount of traffic. In a building with heavy traffic, it may be desirable every night to scrub the main lobby and to mop the upper floor corridors. In such cases, it may also be found desirable to scrub the upper floors once a week. If traffic is light, it may be only necessary to mop the main lobby every other night and to mop the upper floor corridors once a week. If there is any traffic or usage at all, it will be necessary to at least sweep the corridors nightly.

25. According to the above paragraph, in a building with light traffic, the upper floor corridors should be

    A. swept every other night
    B. mopped every night
    C. swept nightly
    D. mopped every other night

25.___

26. According to the above paragraph, the number of times a floor is cleaned depends

    A. mainly on the type of floor surface
    B. mainly on the type of traffic
    C. only on the amount of traffic
    D. on both the floor surface and amount of traffic

26.___

27. According to the above paragraph, it may be DESIRABLE to have a heavily used main   27.____
lobby swept

    A. daily and scrubbed weekly
    B. daily and mopped weekly
    C. and mopped weekly
    D. and scrubbed daily

Questions 28-30.

DIRECTIONS: Questions 28 through 30 are to be answered SOLELY on the basis of the information contained in the passage below.

SENIOR CITIZEN AND HANDICAPPED PASSENGER REDUCED FARE PROGRAM

Upon display of his or her Medicare Card, Senior Citizen Reduced Fare Card, or Handicapped Photo I.D. Card to the Railroad Clerk on duty, and upon purchase of a token or evidence of having a token, a passenger will be issued a free return trip ticket. The passenger
will then be directed to deposit full fare in a turnstile and enter the controlled area. Return trip
tickets are valid 24 hours a day, 7 days a week, for the day of purchase and the following two
(2) calendar days.

Each return trip ticket will be stamped with the station name and the date only at the time
of issuing to a properly identified senior citizen or handicapped passenger. Overstamping of
tickets is not allowed. Return trip tickets issued from 2300 hours will be stamped with the date
of the following day.

On the return trip, the Railroad Clerk on duty will direct the passenger to enter the controlled area via the exit gate upon the passenger turning in the return trip ticket and displaying
his/her Medicare Card, Senior Citizen Reduced Fare Card, or Handicapped Photo I.D. Card.

28. A Railroad Clerk issued a free return ticket to a senior citizen who displayed a birth certif-   28.____
icate and a token. The Railroad Clerk's action was

    A. *proper* because the Railroad Clerk had proof of the senior citizen's age
    B. *improper* because the senior citizen did not display a Medicare Card, Senior Citi-
        zen Reduced Fare Card, or Handicapped Photo I.D. Card
    C. *proper* because it is inconvenient for many senior citizens to obtain a Medicare
        Card, Senior Citizen Reduced Fare Card, or Handicapped Photo I.D. Card
    D. *improper* because the senior citizen did not buy a token from the Railroad Clerk

29. The return trip ticket issued to a senior citizen is valid for ONLY   29.____

    A. 24 hours
    B. the day of purchase
    C. two days
    D. the day of purchase and the following two calendar days

30. A Railroad Clerk denied entry to the controlled area via the exit gate to an 18 year-old   30.___
handicapped passenger who turned in a correctly stamped return trip ticket, but did not
display any type of identification card. The Railroad Clerk's action was

   A. *proper* because the passenger should have displayed his Handicapped Photo I.D.
Card
   B. *improper* because the passenger turned in a correctly stamped return trip ticket
   C. *proper* because the passenger should have displayed either his Handicapped
Photo I.D. Card or Social Security Card
   D. *improper* because it should have been obvious to the Railroad Clerk that the pas-
senger was handicapped

———

KEY (CORRECT ANSWERS)

1.	C	16.	B
2.	C	17.	B
3.	B	18.	A
4.	B	19.	C
5.	B	20.	A
6.	A	21.	C
7.	A	22.	B
8.	A	23.	B
9.	C	24.	D
10.	B	25.	C
11.	D	26.	D
12.	C	27.	D
13.	C	28.	B
14.	C	29.	D
15.	A	30.	A

———

TEST 2

Questions 1-2.

DIRECTIONS: Questions 1 and 2 are to be answered on the basis of the information given in the following passage.

The Commissioner of Investigation shall have general responsibility for the investigation and elimination of corrupt or other criminal activity, conflicts of interest, unethical conduct, misconduct, and incompetence by city agencies, by city officers and employees, and by persons regulated by, doing business with, or receiving funds directly or indirectly from the city, with respect to their dealings with the city. All agency heads shall be responsible for establishing, subject to review for completeness and inter-agency consistency by the Commissioner of Investigation, written standards of conduct for the officials and employees of their respective agencies, and fair and efficient disciplinary systems to maintain those standards of conduct. All agencies shall have an Inspector General who shall report directly to the respective agency head and to the Commissioner of Investigation and be responsible for maintaining standards of conduct as may be established in such agency under this Order. Inspectors General shall be responsible for the investigation and elimination of corrupt or other criminal activity, conflicts of interest, unethical conduct, misconduct, and incompetence within their respective agencies. Except to the extent otherwise provided by law, the employment or continued employment of all existing and prospective Inspectors General and members of their staffs shall be subject to complete background investigations and approval by the Department of Investigation.

1. According to the above passage, establishing written standards of conduct for each agency is the responsibility of the

    A. agency head
    B. Commissioner of Investigation
    C. Department of Investigation
    D. Inspector General

1.____

2. According to the above passage, maintaining standards of conduct within each agency is the responsibility of the

    A. agency head
    B. Commissioner of Investigation
    C. Department of Investigation
    D. Inspector General

2.____

Questions 3-6.

DIRECTIONS: Questions 3 through 6 are to be answered on the basis of the following information.

Assume that Warehouse X uses the following procedures for receiving stock. When a delivery is received, the stock handler who receives the delivery should immediately unpack and check the delivery. This check is to ensure that the quantity and kinds of stock items delivered match those on the purchase order which had been sent to the vendor. After the delivery is checked, a receiving report is prepared by the same stock handler. This receiving report should include the name of the shipper, the purchase order number, the description of the item, and the actual count or weight of the item. The receiving report, along with the packing slip, should then be checked by the stores clerk against the purchase order to make sure that the quantity received is correct. This is necessary before credit can be obtained from the vendor for any items that are missing or damaged. After the checking is completed, the stock items can be moved to the stockroom.

3. According to the procedures described above, the stock person who receives the delivery should   3.___

    A.   place the unopened delivery in a secure area for checking at a later date
    B.   notify the stores clerk that the delivery has arrived and is ready for checking
    C.   unpack the delivery and check the quantity and types of stock items against the purchase order
    D.   closely examine the outside of the delivery containers for dents and damages

4. According to the procedures described above, credit can be obtained from the vendor   4.___

    A.   *before* the stock handler checks the delivery of stock items
    B.   *after* the stock handler checks the delivery of stock items
    C.   *before* the stores clerk checks the receiving report against the purchase order
    D.   *after* the stores clerk checks the receiving report against the purchase order

5. According to the procedures described above, all of the following information should be included when filling out a receiving report EXCEPT the   5.___

    A.   purchase order number
    B.   name of the shipper
    C.   count or weight of the item
    D.   unit cost per item

6. According to the procedures described above, after the stores clerk has checked the receiving report against the purchase order, the NEXT step is to   6.___

    A.   move the stock items to the stockroom
    B.   return the stock items received to the vendor
    C.   give the stock items to the stock handler for final checking
    D.   file the packing slip for inventory purposes

Questions 7-9.

DIRECTIONS: Questions 7 through 9 are to be answered on the basis of the information given in the following passage.

A filing system for requisition forms used in a warehouse will be of maximum benefit only if it provides ready access to information needed and is not too complex. How effective the system will be depends largely on how well the filing system is organized. A well-organized system usually results in a smooth-running operation.

When setting up a system for filing requisition forms, one effective method would be to first make an alphabetical listing of all the authorized requisitioning agencies. Then file folders should be prepared for each of these agencies and arranged alphabetically in file cabinets. Following this, each agency should be assigned a series of numbers corresponding to those on the blank requisition forms with which they will be supplied. When an agency then submits a requisition and it is filled, the form should be filed in numerical order in the designated agency folder. By using this system, any individual requisition form which is missing from its folder can be easily detected. Regardless of the filing system used, simplicity is essential if the filing system is to be successful.

7. According to the above passage, a filing system is MOST likely to be successful if it is   7.____

    A. alphabetical   B. uncomplicated
    C. numerical   D. reliable

8. According to the above passage, the reason numbers are assigned to each agency is to   8.____

    A. simplify stock issuing procedures
    B. keep a count of all incoming requisition forms
    C. be able to know when a form is missing from its folder
    D. eliminate the need for an alphabetical filing system

9. According to the above passage, which one of the following is an ACCURATE statement   9.____
regarding the establishment of a well-organized filing system?

    A. Requisitioned stock items will be issued at a faster rate.
    B. Stock items will be stored in storage areas alphabetically arranged.
    C. Information concerning ordered stock items will be easily obtainable.
    D. Maximum productivity can be expected from each employee.

Questions 10-13.

DIRECTIONS: Questions 10 through 13 are to be answered SOLELY on the basis of the information in the following paragraph.

On Tuesday, October 21, Protection Agent Williams, on duty at the Jamaica Depot, observed a man jump over the fence and into the parking lot at 2:12 P.M. and run to a car that was parked with the engine running. The man, who limped slightly, opened the car door, jumped into the car, and sped out of the yard. The car was a 1991 gray Buick Electra, license plate 563-JYN, with parking decal No. 6043. The man was white, about 6 feet tall, about 175 pounds, in his mid-20's, with a scar on his left cheek. He wore a blue sportcoat, tan slacks, a white shirt open at the neck with no tie, and brown loafers.

10. What was the color of the car?   10.____

    A. White   B. Blue
    C. Two-tone brown and tan   D. Gray

11. What were the distinguishing personal features of the man who jumped over the fence?　　11.__

    A. A scar on the left cheek
    B. Pockmarks on his face
    C. A cast on his left wrist
    D. Bushy eyebrows

12. What was the number on the car's parking decal?　　12.__

    A. 1991　　　　　　　　　　　B. 673-JYN
    C. 6043　　　　　　　　　　　D. 175

13. On what day of the week did the incident occur?　　13.__

    A. Monday　　　　　　　　　　B. Tuesday
    C. Wednesday　　　　　　　　D. Sunday

14. *It is a violation of rules for a Protection Agent to carry a firearm while on Transit Authority*　　14.__
property. The possession of such a weapon, whether carried on the person, in a per-
sonal vehicle, or stored in a locker, can result in charges being filed against the Agent.
According to the above information, the carrying of a firearm

    A. on Authority property by any employee is prohibited
    B. anywhere by an Agent is prohibited under all circumstances
    C. on Authority property by an Agent is prohibited under all circumstances
    D. anywhere by an Authority employee may be reason for charges being filed against that employee

15. *News reporters may enter Authority property if they have the written authorization of a*　　15.__
Public Affairs Department official. The Agent on duty must get permission from the Prop-
erty Protection Control Desk before admitting to the property a news person who has no
such written authorization.
If a reporter tells a Protection Agent that she has received permission from the Authority President to enter the property, what is the FIRST thing the Agent should do?

    A. Call the Authority police.
    B. Admit the reporter immediately.
    C. Call the Authority President's office.
    D. Call the Property Protection Control Desk.

Questions 16-20.

DIRECTIONS: Questions 16 through 20 are to be answered SOLELY on the basis of the information in the paragraphs below.

FIRES AND EXTINGUISHERS

There are four classes of fires.

Trash fires, paper fires, cloth fires, wood fires, etc. are classified as Class A fires. Water or
a water-base solution should be used to extinguish Class A fires. They also can be extinguished by covering the combustibles with a multi-purpose dry chemical.

Burning liquids, gasoline, oil, paint, tar, etc. are considered Class B fires. Such fires can be extinguished by smothering or blanketing them. Extinguishers used for Class B fires are Halon, CO_2, or multi-purpose dry chemical. Water tends to spread such fires and should not be used.

Fires in electrical equipment and switchboards are classified as Class C fires. When live electrical equipment is involved, a non-conducting extinguishing agent like CO_2, a multi-purpose dry chemical, or Halon should always be used. Soda-acid or other water-type extinguishers should not be used.

Class D fires consist of burning metals in finely-divided forms like chips, turnings, and shavings. Specially-designed extinguishing agents that provide a smothering blanket or coating should be used to extinguish Class D fires. Multipurpose dry-powder extinguishants are such agents.

16. The ONLY type of extinguishing agent that can be used on any type of fire is   16.____

    A. a multi-purpose, dry-chemical extinguishing agent
    B. soda-acid
    C. water
    D. carbon dioxide

17. A fire in litter swept from a subway car in a yard is MOST likely to be a Class _____ fire.   17.____

    A. A   B. B
    C. C   D. D

18. Fire coming from the underbody of a subway car is MOST likely to be a Class _____ fire.   18.____

    A. A   B. B
    C. C   D. D

19. Which of the following extinguishing agents should NOT be used in fighting a Class C fire involving live electrical equipment?   19.____

    A. Halon
    B. Carbon dioxide
    C. A multi-purpose dry chemical
    D. Soda-acid

20. Water is NOT recommended for use on Class B fires because water   20.____

    A. would cool the fire   B. evaporates too quickly
    C. might spread the fire   D. would smother the fire

Questions 21-24.

DIRECTIONS: Questions 21 through 24 are to be answered SOLELY on the basis of the information in the paragraph below.

Protection Agent Brown, working the midnight to 8:00 A.M. tour at the Flushing Bus Depot, discovered a fire at 2:17 A.M. in Bus No. 4651, which was parked in the southeast portion of the depot yard. He turned in an alarm to the Fire Department from Box 3297 on the nearby street at 2:18 A.M. At 2:20 A.M., he called the Property Protection Control Desk and reported the fire and his action to Line Supervisor Wilson. Line Supervisor Wilson instructed Agent Brown to lock his booth and go to the fire alarm box to direct the fire companies. The first arriving companies were Engine 307 and Ladder 154. Brown directed them to the burning bus. Two minutes later, at 2:23 A.M. Battalion Chief Welsh arrived from Battalion 14. The fire had made little headway. It was extinguished in about two minutes. Brown then wrote a fire report for submittal to Line Supervisor Wilson.

21. What was the FIRST thing Protection Agent Brown did after observing the fire? 21.___
He

   A. called Battalion Chief Welsh
   B. called the Fire Dispatcher
   C. transmitted an alarm from a nearby alarm box
   D. called 911

22. In what part of the yard was the burning bus? 22.___

   A. Northeast section   B. Southwest end
   C. Northwest part   D. Southeast portion

23. What time did Agent Brown call Line Supervisor Wilson? 23.___

   A. 2:18 PM   B. 2:20 AM
   C. 2:29 AM   D. 2:36 AM

24. Which of the following CORRECTLY describes the sequence of Agent Brown's actions? 24.___
He

   A. saw the fire, turned in an alarm, called the Property Protection Control Desk, directed the fire companies to the fire, and wrote a report
   B. called the Property Protection Control Desk, directed the fire apparatus, directed Chief Welsh, and wrote a report
   C. called Line Supervisor Wilson, turned in an alarm, waited by the burning bus, and directed the fire companies
   D. called Line Supervisor Wilson, directed the firefighters, waited for instructions from Line Supervisor Wilson, and wrote a report

Questions 25-26.

DIRECTIONS: Questions 25 and 26 are to be answered SOLELY on the basis of the following paragraph and rule.

Protection Agents may admit to Transit Authority headquarters only persons with Transit Authority passes, persons with job appointment letters, and persons who have permission to enter from Transit Authority officials.

During his tour in the Authority's headquarters lobby, Protection Agent Williams admitted to the building 326 persons with Authority passes and 41 persons with job appointment letters. He telephoned authorized officials for permission to admit 14 others, 13 of whom were granted permission and entered and one of whom was denied permission. He also turned away two persons who wanted to enter to sell to employees merchandise for their personal use, and one person who appeared inebriated.

25. How many persons did Agent Williams admit to the building?   25.____

    A. 326   B. 367
    C. 380   D. 382

26. To how many persons did Agent Williams refuse admittance?   26.____

    A. 4   B. 13
    C. 14   D. 41

Questions 27-30.

DIRECTIONS: Questions 27 through 30 are to be answered on the basis of the information contained in the following instructions on LOST PROPERTY.

<u>LOST PROPERTY</u>

All inquiries for information regarding lost property will be referred to the Lost Property Office. Any Station Department employee finding a lost article, of any description, will immediately hand it over to the railroad clerk in the nearest 24-hour booth of the station where the article is found. The clerk must give the employee a receipt for the article. Should a passenger hand over a lost article to a cleaner, the cleaner will offer to escort the passenger to the nearest 24-hour booth in order that a receipt may be given by the railroad clerk there. If the passenger declines, the cleaner will accept the lost article without giving a receipt and proceed as described above. Each employee who receives lost property will be held responsible for it unless he produces a receipt for it from another employee. Should any lost property disappear, the last employee who signed for it will be held strictly accountable.

27. If a cleaner turns in a lost article to a railroad clerk in the nearest 24-hour booth, he should make sure that he   27.____

    A. gets a receipt for the article
    B. notifies his supervisor about the lost article
    C. finds out the name of the owner of the article
    D. writes a report on the incident

28. If a lost article disappears after a cleaner has properly turned it in to the railroad clerk in the nearest 24-hour booth, the one who will be held accountable is the   28.____

    A. person who found the lost article
    B. cleaner who turned in the article
    C. supervisor in charge of the station
    D. last employee to sign a receipt for the article

29. A passenger finds a lost article and gives it to a cleaner. The cleaner gives the passenger a receipt. The cleaner's action was

    A. *proper* because the passenger was relieved of any responsibility for the lost article
    B. *improper* because the cleaner should have offered to escort the passenger to the nearest 24-hour booth
    C. *proper* because the cleaner is required to give the passenger a receipt
    D. *improper* because the cleaner should have sent the passenger to the Lost Property Office

29.__

30. A cleaner finds a five dollar bill on a crowded station platform. Three passengers who see him pick it up rush up and claim the money. The first passenger said he had just taken a roll of bills out of his pocket and must have dropped it. The second said he had just given two five dollar bills to his wife, and she had dropped one of them. The third said he had a hole in his pocket and the bill fell out of it. The cleaner should

    A. give the five dollar bill to the second passenger because he had his wife as a witness
    B. give the five dollar bill to the third passenger because he had a hole in his pocket
    C. keep the five dollar bill
    D. bring the five dollar bill to the railroad clerk in the nearest 24-hour booth

30.__

KEY (CORRECT ANSWERS)

1.	A	16.	A
2.	D	17.	A
3.	C	18.	C
4.	D	19.	D
5.	D	20.	C
6.	A	21.	C
7.	B	22.	D
8.	C	23.	B
9.	C	24.	A
10.	D	25.	C
11.	A	26.	A
12.	C	27.	A
13.	B	28.	D
14.	C	29.	B
15.	D	30.	D

PREPARING WRITTEN MATERIAL

PARAGRAPH REARRANGEMENT
COMMENTARY

The sentences which follow are in scrambled order. You are to rearrange them in proper order and indicate the letter choice containing the correct answer at the space at the right.

Each group of sentences in this section is actually a paragraph presented in scrambled order. Each sentence in the group has a place in that paragraph; no sentence is to be left out. You are to read each group of sentences and decide upon the best order in which to put the sentences so as to form as well-organized paragraph.

The questions in this section measure the ability to solve a problem when all the facts relevant to its solution are not given.

More specifically, certain positions of responsibility and authority require the employee to discover connections between events sometimes, apparently, unrelated. In order to do this, the employee will find it necessary to correctly infer that unspecified events have probably occurred or are likely to occur. This ability becomes especially important when action must be taken on incomplete information.

Accordingly, these questions require competitors to choose among several suggested alternatives, each of which presents a different sequential arrangement of the events. Competitors must choose the MOST logical of the suggested sequences.

In order to do so, they may be required to draw on general knowledge to infer missing concepts or events that are essential to sequencing the given events. Competitors should be careful to infer only what is essential to the sequence. The plausibility of the wrong alternatives will always require the inclusion of unlikely events or of additional chains of events which are NOT essential to sequencing the given events.

It's very important to remember that you are looking for the best of the four possible choices, and that the best choice of all may not even be one of the answers you're given to choose from.

There is no one right way to these problems. Many people have found it helpful to first write out the order of the sentences, as they would have arranged them, on their scrap paper before looking at the possible answers. If their optimum answer is there, this can save them some time. If it isn't, this method can still give insight into solving the problem. Others find it most helpful to just go through each of the possible choices, contrasting each as they go along. You should use whatever method feels comfortable, and works, for you.

While most of these types of questions are not that difficult, we've added a higher percentage of the difficult type, just to give you more practice. Usually there are only one or two questions on this section that contain such subtle distinctions that you're unable to answer confidently, and you then may find yourself stuck deciding between two possible choices, neither of which you're sure about.

EXAMINATION SECTION
TEST 1

DIRECTIONS: The following groups of sentences need to be arranged in an order that makes sense. Select the letter preceding the sequence that represents the BEST sentence order. *PRINT THE LETTER OF THE CORRECT ANSWER IN THE SPACE AT THE RIGHT.*

1.   I.   The keyboard was purposely designed to be a little awkward to slow typists down.   1._____
      II.   The arrangement of letters on the keyboard of a typewriter was not designed for the convenience of the typist.
      III. Fortunately, no one is suggesting that a new keyboard be designed right away.
      IV.   If one were, we would have to learn to type all over again.
      V.   The reason was that the early machines were slower than the typists and would jam easily.

      A. I, III, IV, II, V   B. II, V, I, IV, III
      C. V, I, II, III, IV   D. II, I, V, III, IV

2.   I.   The majority of the new service jobs are part-time or low-paying.   2._____
      II.   According to the U.S. Bureau of Labor Statistics, jobs in the service sector constitute 72% of all jobs in this country.
      III. If more and more workers receive less and less money, who will buy the goods and services needed to keep the economy going?
      IV.   The service sector is by far the fastest growing part of the United States economy.
      V.   Some economists look upon this trend with great concern.

      A. II, IV, I, V, III   B. II, III, IV, I, V
      C. V, IV, II, III, I   D. III, I, II, IV, V

3.   I.   They can also affect one's endurance.   3._____
      II.   This can stabilize blood sugar levels, and ensure that the brain is receiving a steady, constant supply of glucose, so that one is *hitting on all cylinders* while taking the test.
      III. By food, we mean real food, not junk food or unhealthy snacks.
      IV.   For this reason, it is important not to skip a meal, and to bring food with you to the exam.
      V.   One's blood sugar levels can affect how clearly one is able to think and concentrate during an exam.

      A. V, IV, II, III, I   B. V, II, I, IV, III
      C. V, I, IV, III, II   D. V, IV, I, III, II

4.   I.   Those who are the embodiment of desire are absorbed in material quests, and those who are the embodiment of feeling are warriors who value power more than possession.   4._____
      II.   These qualities are in everyone, but in different degrees.
      III. But those who value understanding yearn not for goods or victory, but for knowledge.
      IV.   According to Plato, human behavior flows from three main sources: desire, emotion, and knowledge,

V. In the perfect state, the industrial forces would produce but not rule, the military would protect but not rule, and the forces of knowledge, the philosopher kings, would reign.

A. IV, V, I, II, III
B. V, I, II, III, IV
C. IV, III, II, I, V
D. IV, II, I, III, V

5.
I. Of the more than 26,000 tons of garbage produced daily in New York City, 12,000 tons arrive daily at Fresh Kills.
II. In a month, enough garbage accumulates there to fill the Empire State Building.
III. In 1937, the Supreme Court halted the practice of dumping the trash of New York City into the sea.
IV. Although the garbage is compacted, in a few years the mounds of garbage at Fresh Kills will be the highest points south of Maine's Mount Desert Island on the Eastern Seaboard.
V. Instead, tugboats now pull barges of much of the trash to Staten Island and the largest landfill in the world, Fresh Kills.

A. III, V, IV, I, II
B. III, V, II, IV, I
C. III, V, I, II, IV
D. III, II, V, IV, I

5.___

6.
I. Communists rank equality very high, but freedom very low.
II. Unlike communists, conservatives place a high value on freedom and a very low value on equality.
III. A recent study demonstrated that one way to classify people's political beliefs is to look at the importance placed on two words: freedom and equality.
IV. Thus, by demonstrating how members of these groups feel about the two words, the study has proved to be useful for political analysts in several European countries.
V. According to the study, socialists and liberals rank both freedom and equality very high, while fascists rate both very low.

A. III, V, I, II, IV
B. III, IV, V, I, II
C. III, V, IV, II, I
D. III, I, II, IV, V

6.___

7.
I. "Can there be anything more amazing than this?"
II. If the riddle is successfully answered, his dead brothers will be brought back to life.
III. "Even though man sees those around him dying every day," says Dharmaraj, "he still believes and acts as if he were immortal."
IV. "What is the cause of ceaseless wonder?" asks the Lord of the Lake.
V. In the ancient epic, The Mahabharata, a riddle is asked of one of the Pandava brothers.

A. V, II, I, IV, III
B. V, IV, III, I, II
C. V, II, IV, III, I
D. V, II, IV, I, III

7.___

8. I.   On the contrary, the two main theories — the cooperative (neoclassical) theory and the radical (labor theory) — clearly rest on very different assumptions, which have very different ethical overtones.
    II. The distribution of income is the primary factor in determining the relative levels of material well-being that different groups or individuals attain.
    III. Of all issues in economics, the distribution of income is one of the most controversial.
    IV. The neoclassical theory tends to support the existing income distribution (or minor changes), while the labor theory tends to support substantial changes in the way income is distributed.
    V.   The intensity of the controversy reflects the fact that different economic theories are not purely neutral, *detached* theories with no ethical or moral implications.

8.____

    A. II, I, V, IV, III
    B. III, II, V, I, IV
    C. III, V, II, I, IV
    D. III, V, IV, I, II

9. I.   The pool acts as a broker and ensures that the cheapest power gets used first.
    II. Every six seconds, the pool's computer monitors all of the generating stations in the state and decides which to ask for more power and which to cut back.
    III. The buying and selling of electrical power is handled by the New York Power Pool in Guilderland, New York.
    IV. This is to the advantage of both the buying and selling utilities.
    V.   The pool began operation in 1970, and consists of the state's eight electric utilities.

9.____

    A. V, I, II, III, IV
    B. IV, II, I, III, V
    C. III, V, I, IV, II
    D. V, III, IV, II, I

10. I.   Modern English is much simpler grammatically than Old English.
    II. Finnish grammar is very complicated; there are some fifteen cases, for example.
    III. Chinese, a very old language, may seem to be the exception, but it is the great number of characters/ words that must be mastered that makes it so
    IV. difficult to learn, not its grammar.
    V.   The newest literary language — that is, written as well as spoken — is Finnish, whose literary roots go back only to about the middle of the nineteenth century.
    VI. Contrary to popular belief, the longer a language is been in use the simpler its grammar — not the reverse.

10.____

    A. IV, I, II, III, V
    B. V, I, IV, II, III
    C. I, II, IV, III, V
    D. IV, II, III, I, V

———

KEY (CORRECT ANSWERS)

1.	D	6.	A
2.	A	7.	C
3.	C	8.	B
4.	D	9.	C
5.	C	10.	B

———

TEST 2

DIRECTIONS: This type of question tests your ability to recognize accurate paraphrasing, well-constructed paragraphs, and appropriate style and tone. It is important that the answer you select contains only the facts or concepts given in the original sentences. It is also important that you be aware of incomplete sentences, inappropriate transitions, unsupported opinions, incorrect usage, and illogical sentence order. Paragraphs that do not include all the necessary facts and concepts, that distort them, or that add new ones are not considered correct.

The format for this section may vary. Sometimes, long paragraphs are given, and emphasis is placed on style and organization. Our first five questions are of this type. Other times, the paragraphs are shorter, and there is less emphasis on style and more emphasis on accurate representation of information. Our second group of five questions are of this nature.

For each of Questions 1 through 10, select the paragraph that BEST expresses the ideas contained in the sentences above it. *PRINT THE LETTER OF THE CORRECT ANSWER IN THE SPACE AT THE RIGHT.*

1.
   I.   Listening skills are very important for managers.
  II. Listening skills are not usually emphasized.
 III. Whenever managers are depicted in books, manuals or the media, they are always talking, never listening.
 IV. We'd like you to read the enclosed handout on listening skills and to try to consciously apply them this week.
  V. We guarantee they will improve the quality of your interactions.

  A. Unfortunately, listening skills are not usually emphasized for managers. Managers are always depicted as talking, never listening. We'd like you to read the enclosed handout on listening skills. Please try to apply these principles this week. If you do, we guarantee they will improve the quality of your interactions.
  B. The enclosed handout on listening skills will be important improving the quality of your interactions. We guarantee it. All you have to do is take some time this week to read it and to consciously try to apply the principles. Listening skills are very important for managers, but they are not usually emphasized. Whenever managers are depicted in books, manuals or the media, they are always talking, never listening.
  C. Listening well is one of the most important skills a manager can have, yet it's not usually given much attention. Think about any representation of managers in books, manuals, or in the media that you may have seen. They're always talking, never listening. We'd like you to read the enclosed handout on listening skills and consciously try to apply them the rest of the week. We guarantee you will see a difference in the quality of your interactions.
  D. Effective listening, one very important tool in the effective manager's arsenal, is usually not emphasized enough. The usual depiction of managers in books, manuals or the media is one in which they are always talking, never listening. We'd like you to read the enclosed handout and consciously try to apply the information contained therein throughout the rest of the week. We feel sure that you will see a marked difference in the quality of your interactions.

1.___

2.   I.   Chekhov wrote three dramatic masterpieces which share certain themes and for-   2.____
       mats: <u>Uncle Vanya</u>, <u>The Cherry Orchard</u>, and <u>The Three Sisters</u>.
   II.   They are primarily concerned with the passage of time and how this erodes
       human aspirations.
  III.   The plays are haunted by the ghosts of the wasted life.
  IV.   The characters are concerned with life's lesser problems; however, such as the
       inability to make decisions, loyalty to the wrong cause, and the inability to be
       clear.
   V.   This results in a sweet, almost aching, type of a sadness referred to as Chek-
       hovian.

   A.   Chekhov wrote three dramatic masterpieces: Uncle <u>Vanya</u>, <u>The Cherry Orchard,</u>
       and <u>The Three Sisters</u>. These masterpieces share certain themes and formats: the
       passage of time, how time erodes human aspirations, and the ghosts of wasted
       life. Each masterpiece is characterized by a sweet, almost aching, type of sadness
       that has become known as Chekhovian. The sweetness of this sadness hinges on
       the fact that it is not the great tragedies of life which are destroying these charac-
       ters, but their minor flaws: indecisiveness, misplaced loyalty, unclarity.
   B.   <u>The Cherry Orchard</u>, <u>Uncle Vanya</u>, and <u>The Three Sisters</u> are three dramatic mas-
       terpieces written by Chekhov that use similar formats to explore a common theme.
       Each is primarily concerned with the way that passing time wears down human
       aspirations, and each is haunted by the ghosts of the wasted life. The characters
       are shown struggling futilely with the lesser problems of life: indecisiveness, loyalty
       to the wrong cause, and the inability to be clear. These struggles create a mood of
       sweet, almost aching, sadness that has become known as Chekhovian.
   C.   Chekhov's dramatic masterpieces are, along with <u>The Cherry Orchard</u>, <u>Uncle</u>
       <u>Vanya</u>, and The Three Sisters. These plays share certain thematic and formal simi-
       larities. They are concerned most of all with the passage of time and the way in
       which time erodes human aspirations. Each play is haunted by the specter of the
       wasted life. Chekhov's characters are caught, however, by life's lesser snares:
       indecisiveness, loyalty to the wrong cause, and unclarity. The characteristic mood
       is a sweet, almost aching type of sadness that has come to be known as Chek-
       hovian.
   D.   A Chekhovian mood is characterized by sweet, almost aching, sadness. The term
       comes from three dramatic tragedies by Chekhov which revolve around the sad-
       ness of a wasted life. The three masterpieces (<u>Uncle Vanya</u>, <u>The Three Sisters</u>,
       and <u>The Cherry Orchard)</u> share the same theme and format. The plays are con-
       cerned with how the passage of time erodes human aspirations. They are peopled
       with characters who are struggling with life's lesser problems. These are people
       who are indecisive, loyal to the wrong causes, or are unable to make themselves
       clear.

3. I. Movie previews have often helped producers decide what parts of movies they should take out or leave in.

II. The first 1933 preview of <u>King Kong</u> was very helpful to the producers because many people ran screaming from the theater and would not return when four men first attacked by Kong were eaten by giant spiders.

III. The 1950 premiere of Sunset Boulevard resulted in the filming of an entirely new beginning, and a delay of six months in the film's release.

IV. In the original opening scene, William Holden was in a morgue talking with thirty-six other "corpses" about the ways some of them had died.

V. When he began to tell them of his life with Gloria Swanson, the audience found this hilarious, instead of taking the scene seriously.

A. Movie previews have often helped producers decide what parts of movies they should leave in or take out. For example, the first preview of <u>King Kong</u> in 1933 was very helpful. In one scene, four men were first attacked by Kong and then eaten by giant spiders. Many members of the audience ran screaming from the theater and would not return. The premiere of the 1950 film <u>Sunset Boulevard</u> was also very helpful. In the original opening scene, William Holden was in a morgue with thirty-six other "corpses," discussing the ways some of them had died. When he began to tell them of his life with Gloria Swanson, the audience found this hilarious. They were supposed to take the scene seriously. The result was a delay of six months in the release of the film while a new beginning was added.

B. Movie previews have often helped producers decide whether they should change various parts of a movie. After the 1933 preview of <u>King Kong,</u> a scene in which four men who had been attacked by Kong were eaten by giant spiders was taken out as many people ran screaming from the theater and would not return. The 1950 premiere of <u>Sunset Boulevard</u> also led to some changes. In the original opening scene, William Holden was in a morgue talking with thirty-six other "corpses" about the ways some of them had died. When he began to tell them of his life with Gloria Swanson, the audience found this hilarious, instead of taking the scene seriously.

C. What do <u>Sunset Boulevard</u> and <u>King Kong</u> have in common? Both show the value of using movie previews to test audience reaction. The first 1933 preview of <u>King Kong</u> showed that a scene showing four men being eaten by giant spiders after having been attacked by Kong was too frightening for many people. They ran screaming from the theater and couldn't be coaxed back. The 1950 premiere of <u>Sunset Boulevard</u> was also a scream, but not the kind the producers intended. The movie opens with William Holden lying in a morgue discussing the ways they had died with thirty-six other "corpses." When he began to tell them of his life with Gloria Swanson, the audience couldn't take him seriously. Their laughter caused a six-month delay while the beginning was rewritten.

D. Producers very often use movie previews to decide if changes are needed. The premiere of <u>Sunset Boulevard</u> in 1950 led to a new beginning and a six-month delay in film release. At the beginning, William Holden and thirty-six other "corpses" discuss the ways some of them died. Rather than taking this seriously, the audience thought it was hilarious when he began to tell them of his life with Gloria Swanson. The first 1933 preview of <u>King Kong</u> was very helpful for its producers because one scene so terrified the audience that many of them ran screaming from the theater and would not return. In this particular scene, four men who had first been attacked by Kong were being eaten by giant spiders.

3.___

4. I.   It is common for supervisors to view employees as "things" to be manipulated.   4.____
    II. This approach does not motivate employees, nor does the carrot-and-stick
         approach because employees often recognize these behaviors and resent them.
    III. Supervisors can change these behaviors by using self-inquiry and persistence.
    IV. The best managers genuinely respect those they work with, are supportive and
         helpful, and are interested in working as a team with those they supervise.
    V.   They disagree with the Golden Rule that says "he or she who has the gold
         makes the rules."

    A.   Some managers act as if they think the Golden Rule means "he or she who has
         the gold makes the rules." They show disrespect to employees by seeing them as
         "things" to be manipulated. Obviously, this approach does not motivate employees
         any more than the carrot-and-stick approach motivates them. The employees are
         smart enough to spot these behaviors and resent them. On the other hand, the
         managers genuinely respect those they work with, are supportive and helpful, and
         are interested in working as a team. Self-inquiry and persistence can change even
         the former type of supervisor into the latter.
    B.   Many supervisors fall into the trap of viewing employees as "things" to be manipu-
         lated, or try to motivate them by using a earrot-and-stick approach. These methods
         do not motivate employees, who often recognize the behaviors and resent them.
         Supervisors can change these behaviors, however, by using self-inquiry and per-
         sistence. The best managers are supportive and helpful, and have genuine respect
         for those with whom they work. They are interested in working as a team with those
         they supervise. To them, the Golden Rule is not "he or she who has the gold makes
         the rules."
    C.   Some supervisors see employees as "things" to be used or manipulated using a
         carrot-and-stick technique. These methods don't work. Employees often see
         through them and resent them. A supervisor who wants to change may do so. The
         techniques of self-inquiry and persistence can be used to turn him or her into the
         type of supervisor who doesn't think the Golden Rule is "he or she who has the
         gold makes the rules." They may become like the best managers who treat those
         with whom they work with respect and give them help and support. These are the
         managers who know how to build a team.
    D.   Unfortunately, many supervisors act as if their employees are objects whose move-
         ments they can position at will. This mistaken belief has the same result as another
         popular motivational technique—the carrot-and-stick approach. Both attitudes can
         lead to the same result — resentment from those employees who recognize the
         behaviors for what they are. Supervisors who recognize these behaviors can
         change through the use of persistence and the use of self-inquiry. It's important to
         remember that the best managers respect their employees. They readily give nec-
         essary help and support and are interested in working as a team with those they
         supervise. To these managers, the Golden Rule is not "he or she who has the gold
         makes the rules."

5. I. The first half of the nineteenth century produced a group of pessimistic poets — Byron, De Musset, Heine, Pushkin, and Leopardi.

    II. It also produced a group of pessimistic composers—Schubert, Chopin, Schumann, and even the later Beethoven.

    III. Above all, in philosophy, there was the profoundly pessimistic philosopher, Schopenhauer.

    IV. The Revolution was dead, the Bourbons were restored, the feudal barons were reclaiming their land, and progress everywhere was being suppressed, as the great age was over.

    V. "I thank God," said Goethe, "that I am not young in so thoroughly finished a world."

    A. "I thank God," said Goethe, "that I am not young in so thoroughly finished a world." The Revolution was dead, the Bourbons were restored, the feudal barons were reclaiming their land, and progress everywhere was being suppressed. The first half of the nineteenth century produced a group of pessimistic poets: Byron, De Musset, Heine, Pushkin, and Leopardi. It also produced pessimistic composers: Schubert, Chopin, Schumann. Although Beethoven came later, he fits into this group, too. Finally and above all, it also produced a profoundly pessimistic philosopher, Schopenhauer. The great age was over.

    B. The first half of the nineteenth century produced a group of pessimistic poets: Byron, De Musset, Heine, Pushkin, and Leopardi. It produced a group of pessimistic composers: Schubert, Chopin, Schumann, and even the later Beethoven. Above all, it produced a profoundly pessimistic philosopher, Schopenhauer. For each of these men, the great age was over. The Revolution was dead, and the Bourbons were restored. The feudal barons were reclaiming their land, and progress everywhere was being suppressed.

    C. The great age was over. The Revolution was dead—the Bourbons were restored, and the feudal barons were reclaiming their land. Progress everywhere was being suppressed. Out of this climate came a profound pessimism. Poets, like Byron, De Musset, Heine, Pushkin, and Leopardi; composers, like Schubert, Chopin, Schumann, and even the later Beethoven; and, above all, a profoundly pessimistic philosopher, Schopenauer. This pessimism which arose in the first half of the nineteenth century is illustrated by these words of Goethe, "I thank God that I am not young in so thoroughly finished a world."

    D. The first half of the nineteenth century produced a group of pessimistic poets, Byron, De Musset, Heine, Pushkin, and Leopardi — and a group of pessimistic composers, Schubert, Chopin, Schumann, and the later Beethoven. Above all, it produced a profoundly pessimistic philosopher, Schopenhauer. The great age was over. The Revolution was dead, the Bourbons were restored, the feudal barons were reclaiming their land, and progress everywhere was being suppressed. "I thank God," said Goethe, "that I am not young in so thoroughly finished a world."

6. I. A new manager sometimes may feel insecure about his or her competence in the new position.

    II. The new manager may then exhibit defensive or arrogant behavior towards those one supervises, or the new manager may direct overly flattering behavior toward one's new supervisor.

A.   Sometimes, a new manager may feel insecure about his or her ability to perform well in this new position. The insecurity may lead him or her to treat others differently. He or she may display arrogant or defensive behavior towards those he or she supervises, or be overly flattering to his or her new supervisor.

B.   A new manager may sometimes feel insecure about his or her ability to perform well in the new position. He or she may then become arrogant, defensive, or overly flattering towards those he or she works with.

C.   There are times when a new manager may be insecure about how well he or she can perform in the new job. The new manager may also behave defensive or act in an arrogant way towards those he or she supervises, or overly flatter his or her boss.

D.   Sometimes, a new manager may feel insecure about his or her ability to perform well in the new position. He or she may then display arrogant or defensive behavior towards those they supervise, or become overly flattering towards their supervisors.

7.   I.   It is possible to eliminate unwanted behavior by bringing it under stimulus control — tying the behavior to a cue, and then never, or rarely, giving the cue.   7.____

   II.   One trainer successfully used this method to keep an energetic young porpoise from coming out of her tank whenever she felt like it, which was potentially dangerous.

   III.   Her trainer taught her to do it for a reward, in response to a hand signal, and then rarely gave the signal.

A.   Unwanted behavior can be eliminated by tying the behavior to a cue, and then never, or rarely, giving the cue. This is called stimulus control. One trainer was able to use this method to keep an energetic young porpoise from coming out of her tank by teaching her to come out for a reward in response to a hand signal, and then rarely giving the signal.

B.   Stimulus control can be used to eliminate unwanted behavior. In this method, behavior is tied to a cue, and then the cue is rarely, if ever, given. One trainer was able to successfully use stimulus control to keep an energetic young porpoise from coming out of her tank whenever she felt like it — a potentially dangerous practice. She taught the porpoise to come out for a reward when she gave a hand signal, and then rarely gave the signal.

C.   It is possible to eliminate behavior that is undesirable by bringing it under stimulus control by tying behavior to a signal, and then rarely giving the signal. One trainer successfully used this method to keep an energetic young porpoise from coming out of her tank, a potentially dangerous situation. Her trainer taught the porpoise to do it for a reward, in response to a hand signal, and then would rarely give the signal.

D.   By using stimulus control, it is possible to eliminate unwanted behavior by tying the behavior to a cue, and then rarely or never give the cue. One trainer was able to use this method to successfully stop a young porpoise from coming out of her tank whenever she felt like it. To curb this potentially dangerous practice, the porpoise was taught by the trainer to come out of the tank for a reward, in response to a hand signal, and then rarely given the signal.

8.   I.   There is a great deal of concern over the safety of commercial trucks, caused by   8.___
           their greatly increased role in serious accidents since federal deregulation in 1981.
     II.   Recently, 60 percent of trucks in New York and Connecticut and 70 percent of
           trucks in Maryland randomly stopped by state troopers failed safety inspections.
     III.   Sixteen states in the United States require no training at all for truck drivers.

     A.   Since federal deregulation in 1981, there has been a great deal of concern over the
           safety of commercial trucks, and their greatly increased role in serious accidents.
           Recently, 60 percent of trucks in New York and Connecticut, and 70 percent of
           trucks in Maryland failed safety inspections. Sixteen states in the United States
           require no training at all for truck drivers.
     B.   There is a great deal of concern over the safety of commercial trucks since federal
           deregulation in 1981. Their role in serious accidents has greatly increased.
           Recently, 60 percent of trucks randomly stopped in Connecticut and New York, and
           70 percent in Maryland failed safety inspections conducted by state troopers. Six-
           teen states in the United States provide no training at all for truck drivers.
     C.   Commercial trucks have a greatly increased role in serious accidents since federal
           deregulation in 1981. This has led to a great deal of concern. Recently, 70 percent
           of trucks in Maryland and 60 percent of trucks in New York and Connecticut failed
           inspection of those that were randomly stopped by state troopers. Sixteen states in
           the United States require no training for all truck drivers.
     D.   Since federal deregulation in 1981, the role that commercial trucks have played in
           serious accidents has greatly increased, and this has led to a great deal of con-
           cern. Recently, 60 percent of trucks in New York and Connecticut, and 70 percent
           of trucks in Maryland randomly stopped by state troopers failed safety inspections.
           Sixteen states in the U.S. don't require any training for truck drivers.

9.   I.   No matter how much some people have, they still feel unsatisfied and want more,   9.___
           or want to keep what they have forever.
     II.   One recent television documentary showed several people flying from New York
           to Paris for a one-day shopping spree to buy platinum earrings, because they
           were bored.
     III.   In Brazil, some people are ordering coffins that cost a minimum of $45,000 and
           are equipping them with deluxe stereos, televisions and other graveyard neces-
           sities.

     A.   Some people, despite having a great deal, still feel unsatisfied and want more, or
           think they can keep what they have forever. One recent documentary on television
           showed several people enroute from Paris to New York for a one day shopping
           spree to buy platinum earrings, because they were bored. Some people in Brazil
           are even ordering coffins equipped with such graveyard necessities as deluxe ste-
           reos and televisions. The price of the coffins start at $45,000.
     B.   No matter how much some people have, they may feel unsatisfied. This leads them
           to want more, or to want to keep what they have forever. Recently, a television doc-
           umentary depicting several people flying from New York to Paris for a one day
           shopping spree to buy platinum earrings. They were bored. Some people in Brazil
           are ordering coffins that cost at least $45,000 and come equipped with deluxe tele-
           visions, stereos and other necessary graveyard items.
     C.   Some people will be dissatisfied no matter how much they have. They may want
           more, or they may want to keep what they have forever. One recent television doc-
           umentary showed several people, motivated by boredom, jetting from New York to

Paris for a one-day shopping spree to buy platinum earrings. In Brazil, some people are ordering coffins equipped with deluxe stereos, televisions and other graveyard necessities. The minimum price for these coffins - $45,000.

D. Some people are never satisfied. No matter how much they have they still want more, or think they can keep what they have forever. One television documentary recently showed several people flying from New York to Paris for the day to buy platinum earrings because they were bored. In Brazil, some people are ordering coffins that cost $45,000 and are equipped with deluxe stereos, televisions and other graveyard necessities.

10. I.   A television signal or Video signal has three parts.   10._____
     II.   Its parts are the black-and-white portion, the color portion, and the synchronizing (sync) pulses, which keep the picture stable.
     III. Each video source, whether it's a camera or a video-cassette recorder, contains its own generator of these synchronizing pulses to accompany the picture that it's sending in order to keep it steady and straight.
     IV.   In order to produce a clean recording, a video-cassette recorder must "lock-up" to the sync pulses that are part of the video it is trying to record, and this effort may be very noticeable if the device does not have genlock.

     A. There are three parts to a television or video signal: the black-and-white part, the color part, and the synchronizing (sync) pulses, which keep the picture stable. Whether it's a video-cassette recorder or a camera, each each video source contains its own pulse that synchronizes and generates the picture it's sending in order to keep it straight and steady. A video-cassette recorder must "lock up" to the sync pulses that are part of the video it's trying to record. If the device doesn't have genlock, this effort must be very noticeable.
     B. A video signal or television is comprised of three parts: the black-and-white portion, the color portion, and the the sync (synchronizing) pulses, which keep the picture stable. Whether it's a camera or a video-cassette recorder, each video source contains its own generator of these synchronizing pulses. These accompany the picture that it's sending in order to keep it straight and steady. A video-cassette recorder must "lock up" to the sync pulses that are part of the video it is trying to record in order to produce a clean recording. This effort may be very noticeable if the device does not have genlock.
     C. There are three parts to a television or video signal: the color portion, the black-and-white portion, and the sync (synchronizing pulses). These keep the picture stable. Each video source, whether it's a video-cassette recorder or a camera, generates these synchronizing pulses accompanying the picture it's sending in order to keep it straight and steady. If a clean recording is to be produced, a video-cassette recorder must store the sync pulses that are part of the video it is trying to record. This effort may not be noticeable if the device does not have genlock.
     D. A television signal or video signal has three parts: the black-and-white portion, the color portion, and the synchronizing (sync) pulses. It's the sync pulses which keep the picture stable, which accompany it and keep it steady and straight. Whether it's a camera or a video-cassette recorder, each video source contains its own generator of these synchronizing pulses. To produce a clean recording, a video-cassette recorder must "lock-up" to the sync pulses that are part of the video it is trying to record. If the device does not have genlock, this effort may be very noticeable.

KEY (CORRECT ANSWERS)

1.	C		6.	A
2.	B		7.	B
3.	A		8.	D
4.	B		9.	C
5.	D		10.	D

———

PREPARING WRITTEN MATERIAL

EXAMINATION SECTION
TEST 1

DIRECTIONS: Each of the sentences in the Tests that follow may be classified under one of the following four categories:

      A. *Faulty* because of incorrect grammar or word usage
      B. *Faulty* because of incorrect punctuation
      C. *Faulty* because of incorrect capitalization or incorrect spelling
      D. *Correct*

Examine each sentence carefully to determine under which of the above four options it is best classified. Then, in the space to the right, print the capital letter preceding the option which is the best of the four suggested above.

(Note that each faulty sentence contains but one type of error. Consider a sentence to be correct if it contains none of the types of errors mentioned, even though there may be other correct ways of expressing the same thought.)

1. He sent the notice to the clerk who you hired yesterday.   1.____

2. It must be admitted, however that you were not informed of this change.   2.____

3. Only the employees who have served in this grade for at least two years are eligible for promotion.   3.____

4. The work was divided equally between she and Mary.   4.____

5. He thought that you were not available at that time.   5.____

6. When the messenger returns; please give him this package.   6.____

7. The new secretary prepared, typed, addressed, and delivered, the notices.   7.____

8. Walking into the room, his desk can be seen at the rear.   8.____

9. Although John has worked here longer than She, he produces a smaller amount of work.   9.____

10. She said she could of typed this report yesterday.   10.____

11. Neither one of these procedures are adequate for the efficient performance of this task.   11.____

12. The typewriter is the tool of the typist; the cashe register, the tool of the cashier.   12.____

13. "The assignment must be completed as soon as possible" said the supervisor.   13.____

14. As you know, office handbooks are issued to all new Employees.   14.____

15. Writing a speech is sometimes easier than to deliver it before an audience.   15.____

16. Mr. Brown our accountant, will audit the accounts next week.   16.____

17. Give the assignment to whomever is able to do it most efficiently. 17.___

18. The supervisor expected either your or I to file these reports. 18.___

KEY (CORRECT ANSWERS)

1.	A	10.	A
2.	B	11.	A
3.	D	12.	C
4.	A	13.	B
5.	D	14.	C
6.	B	15.	A
7.	B	16.	B
8.	A	17.	A
9.	C	18.	A

TEST 2

DIRECTIONS: Each of the sentences in the Tests that follow may be classified under one of the following four categories:
- A. *Faulty* because of incorrect grammar or word usage
- B. *Faulty* because of incorrect punctuation
- C. *Faulty* because of incorrect capitalization or incorrect spelling
- D. *Correct*

Examine each sentence carefully to determine under which of the above four options it is best classified. Then, in the space to the right, print the capital letter preceding the option which is the best of the four suggested above.

Note that each faulty sentence contains but one type of error. Consider a sentence to be correct if it contains none of the types of errors mentioned, even though there may be other correct ways of expressing the same thought.)

1. The fire apparently started in the storeroom, which is usually locked.   1.____

2. On approaching the victim two bruises were noticed by this officer.   2.____

3. The officer, who was there examined the report with great care.   3.____

4. Each employee in the office had a seperate desk.   4.____

5. All employees including members of the clerical staff, were invited to the lecture.   5.____

6. The suggested Procedure is similar to the one now in use.   6.____

7. No one was more pleased with the new procedure than the chauffeur.   7.____

8. He tried to persaude her to change the procedure.   8.____

9. The total of the expenses charged to petty cash were high.   9.____

10. An understanding between him and I was finally reached.   10.____

———

KEY (CORRECT ANSWERS)

1. D	6. C
2. A	7. D
3. B	8. C
4. C	9. A
5. B	10. A

———

TEST 3

DIRECTIONS: Each of the sentences in the Tests that follow may be classified under one of the following four categories:
  A. *Faulty* because of incorrect grammar or word usage
  B. *Faulty* because of incorrect punctuation
  C. *Faulty* because of incorrect capitalization or incorrect spelling
  D. *Correct*

Examine each sentence carefully to determine under which of the above four options it is best classified. Then, in the space to the right, print the capital letter preceding the option which is the best of the four suggested above.

(Note that each faulty sentence contains but one type of error. Consider a sentence to be correct if it contains none of the types of errors mentioned, even though there may be other correct ways of expressing the same thought.)

1. They told both he and *I* that the prisoner had escaped. 1.____

2. Any superior officer, who, disregards the just complaints of his subordinates, is remiss in the performance of his duty. 2.____

3. Only those members of the national organization who resided in the Middle West attended the conference in Chicago. 3.____

4. We told him to give the investigation assignment to whoever was available. 4.____

5. Please do not disappoint and embarass us by not appearing in court. 5.____

6. Although the officer's speech proved to be entertaining, the topic was not relevent to the main theme of the conference. 6.____

7. In February all new officers attended a training course in which they were learned in their principal duties and the fundamental operating procedures of the department. 7.____

8. I personally seen inmate Jones threaten inmates Smith and Green with bodily harm if they refused to participate in the plot. 8.____

9. To the layman, who on a chance visit to the prison observes everything functioning smoothly, the maintenance of prison discipline may seem to be a relatively easily realizable objective. 9.____

10. The prisoners in cell block fourty were forbidden to sit on the cell cots during the recreation hour. 10.____

KEY (CORRECT ANSWERS)

1.	A	6.	C
2.	B	7.	A
3.	C	8.	A
4.	D	9.	D
5.	C	10.	C

———

TEST 4

DIRECTIONS: Each of the sentences in the Tests that follow may be classified under one of
the following four categories:
A.   *Faulty* because of incorrect grammar or word usage
B.   *Faulty* because of incorrect punctuation
C.   *Faulty* because of incorrect capitalization or incorrect spelling
D.   *Correct*

Examine each sentence carefully to determine under which of the above four options it is
best classified. Then, in the space to the right, print the capital letter preceding the option
which is the best of the four suggested above.

(Note that each faulty sentence contains but one type of error. Consider a sentence to be
correct if it contains none of the types of errors mentioned, even though there may be other
correct ways of expressing the same thought.)

1.   I cannot encourage you any.   1._____

2.   You always look well in those sort of clothes.   2._____

3.   Shall we go to the park?   3._____

4.   The man whome he introduced was Mr. Carey.   4._____

5.   She saw the letter laying here this morning.   5._____

6.   It should rain before the Afternoon is over.   6._____

7.   They have already went home.   7._____

8.   That Jackson will be elected is evident.   8._____

9.   He does not hardly approve of us.   9._____

10. It was he, who won the prize.   10._____

———————

KEY (CORRECT ANSWERS)

1.	A		6.	C
2.	A		7.	A
3.	D		8.	D
4.	C		9.	A
5.	A		10.	B

TEST 5

DIRECTIONS: Each of the sentences in the Tests that follow may be classified under one of the following four categories:

DIRECTIONS: Each of the sentences in the Tests that follow may be classified under one of the following four categories:
   A. *Faulty* because of incorrect grammar or word usage
   B. *Faulty* because of incorrect punctuation
   C. *Faulty* because of incorrect capitalization or incorrect spelling
   D. *Correct*

Examine each sentence carefully to determine under which of the above four options it is best classified. Then, in the space to the right, print the capital letter preceding the option which is the best of the four suggested above.

Note that each faulty sentence contains but one type of error. Consider a sentence to be correct if it contains none of the types of errors mentioned, even though there may be other correct ways of expressing the same thought.)

1. Shall we go to the park.   1._____

2. They are, alike, in this particular.   2._____

3. They gave the poor man sume food when he knocked on the door.   3._____

4. I regret the loss caused by the error.   4._____

5. The students' will have a new teacher.   5._____

6. They sweared to bring out all the facts.   6._____

7. He decided to open a branch store on 33rd street.   7._____

8. His speed is equal and more than that of a racehorse.   8._____

9. He felt very warm on that Summer day.   9._____

10. He was assisted by his friend, who lives in the next house.   10._____

KEY (CORRECT ANSWERS)

1.	B	6.	A
2.	B	7.	C
3.	C	8.	A
4.	D	9.	C
5.	B	10.	D

————

TEST 6

DIRECTIONS: Each of the sentences in the Tests that follow may be classified under one of the following four categories:

DIRECTIONS: Each of the sentences in the Tests that follow may be classified under one of the following four categories:

    A. *Faulty* because of incorrect grammar or word usage
    B. *Faulty* because of incorrect punctuation
    C. *Faulty* because of incorrect capitalization or incorrect spelling
    D. *Correct*

Examine each sentence carefully to determine under which of the above four options it is best classified. Then, in the space to the right, print the capital letter preceding the option which is the best of the four suggested above.

Note that each faulty sentence contains but one type of error. Consider a sentence to be correct if it contains none of the types of errors mentioned, even though there may be other correct ways of expressing the same thought.)

1. The climate of New York is colder than California.   1.____

2. I shall wait for you on the corner.   2.____

3. Did we see the boy who, we think, is the leader.   3.____

4. Being a modest person, John seldom talks about his invention .   4.____

5. The gang is called the smith street boys.   5.____

6. He seen the man break into the store.   6.____

7. We expected to lay still there for quite a while.   7.____

8. He is considered to be the Leader of his organization.   8.____

9. Although I recieved an invitation, I won't go.   9.____

10. The letter must be here some place.   10.____

KEY (CORRECT ANSWERS)

1.	A	6.	A
2.	D	7.	A
3.	B	8.	C
4.	D	9.	C
5.	C	10.	A

———————

TEST 7

DIRECTIONS: Each of the sentences in the Tests that follow may be classified under one of the following four categories:

DIRECTIONS: Each of the sentences in the Tests that follow may be classified under one of the following four categories:
   A. *Faulty* because of incorrect grammar or word usage
   B. *Faulty* because of incorrect punctuation
   C. *Faulty* because of incorrect capitalization or incorrect spelling
   D. *Correct*

Examine each sentence carefully to determine under which of the above four options it is best classified. Then, in the space to the right, print the capital letter preceding the option which is the best of the four suggested above.

Note that each faulty sentence contains but one type of error. Consider a sentence to be correct if it contains none of the types of errors mentioned, even though there may be other correct ways of expressing the same thought.)

1. I though it to be he.   1._____

2. We expect to remain here for a long time.   2._____

3. The committee was agreed.   3._____

4. Two-thirds of the building are finished.   4._____

5. The water was froze.   5._____

6. Everyone of the salesmen must supply their own car.   6._____

7. Who is the author of Gone With the Wind?   7._____

8. He marched on and declaring that he would never surrender.   8._____

9. Who shall I say called?   9._____

10. Everyone has left but they.   10._____

———

KEY (CORRECT ANSWERS)

1.	A	6.	A
2.	D	7.	B
3.	D	8.	A
4.	A	9.	D
5.	A	10.	D

———

TEST 8

DIRECTIONS: Each of the sentences in the Tests that follow may be classified under one of the following four categories:

DIRECTIONS: Each of the sentences in the Tests that follow may be classified under one of the following four categories:
    A. *Faulty* because of incorrect grammar or word usage
    B. *Faulty* because of incorrect punctuation
    C. *Faulty* because of incorrect capitalization or incorrect spelling
    D. *Correct*

Examine each sentence carefully to determine under which of the above four options it is best classified. Then, in the space to the right, print the capital letter preceding the option which is the best of the four suggested above.

Note that each faulty sentence contains but one type of error. Consider a sentence to be correct if it contains none of the types of errors mentioned, even though there may be other correct ways of expressing the same thought.)

1. Who did we give the order to?   1.____

2. Send your order in immediately.   2.____

3. I believe I paid the Bill.   3.____

4. I have not met but one person.   4.____

5. Why aren't Tom, and Fred, going to the dance?   5.____

6. What reason is there for him not going?   6.____

7. The seige of Malta was a tremendous event.   7.____

8. I was there yesterday I assure you.   8.____

9. Your ukelele is better than mine.   9.____

10. No one was there only Mary.   10.____

KEY (CORRECT ANSWERS)

1.	A		6.	A
2.	D		7.	C
3.	C		8.	B
4.	A		9.	C
5.	B		10.	A

———

TEST 9

DIRECTIONS: In each of the following groups of sentences, one of the four sentences is faulty in grammar, punctuation, or capitalization. Select the incorrect sentence in each case.

1.   A.   If you had stood at home and done your homework, you would not have failed in arithmetic.
     B.   Her affected manner annoyed every member of the audience.
     C.   How will the new law affect our income taxes?
     D.   The plants were not affected by the long, cold winter, but they succumbed to the drought of summer.

     1._____

2.   A.   He is one of the most able men who have been in the Senate.
     B.   It is he who is to blame for the lamentable mistake.
     C.   Haven't you a helpful suggestion to make at this time?
     D.   The money was robbed from the blind man's cup.

     2._____

3.   A.   The amount of children in this school is steadily increasing.
     B.   After taking an apple from the table, she went out to play.
     C.   He borrowed a dollar from me.
     D.   I had hoped my brother would arrive before me.

     3._____

4.   A.   Whom do you think I hear from every week?
     B.   Who do you think is the right man for the job?
     C.   Who do you think I found in the room?
     D.   He is the man whom we considered a good candidate for the presidency.

     4._____

5.   A.   Quietly the puppy laid down before the fireplace.
     B.   You have made your bed; now lie in it.
     C.   I was badly sunburned because I had lain too long in the sun.
     D.   I laid the doll on the bed and left the room.

     5._____

KEY (CORRECT ANSWERS)

1. A
2. D
3. A
4. C
5. A

EXAMINATION SECTION
TEST 1

DIRECTIONS: In each of the following questions, only one of the four sentences conforms to standards of correct usage. The other three contain errors in grammar, diction, or punctuation. Select the choice in each question which BEST conforms to standards of correct usage. Consider a choice correct if it contains none of the errors mentioned above, even though there may be other ways of expressing the same thought. *PRINT THE LETTER OF THE CORRECT ANSWER IN THE SPACE AT THE RIGHT.*

1. A. Because he was ill was no excuse for his behavior.
    B. I insist that he see a lawyer before he goes to trial.
    C. He said "that he had not intended to go."
    D. He wasn't out of the office only three days.   1.____

2. A. He came to the station and pays a porter to carry his bags into the train.
    B. I should have liked to live in medieval times.
    C. My father was born in Linville. A little country town where everyone knows every-
        one else.
    D. The car, which is parked across the street, is disabled.   2.____

3. A. He asked the desk clerk for a clean, quiet, room.
    B. I expected James to be lonesome and that he would want to go home.
    C. I have stopped worrying because I have heard nothing further on the subject.
    D. If the board of directors controls the company, they may take actions which are dis-
        approved by the stockholders.   3.____

4. A. Each of the players knew their place.
    B. He whom you saw on the stage is the son of an actor.
    C. Susan is the smartest of the twin sisters.
    D. Who ever thought of him winning both prizes?   4.____

5. A. An outstanding trait of early man was their reliance on omens.
    B. Because I had never been there before.
    C. Neither Mr. Jones nor Mr. Smith has completed his work.
    D. While eating my dinner, a dog came to the window.   5.____

6. A. A copy of the lease, in addition to the Rules and Regulations, are to be given to
        each tenant.
    B. The Rules and Regulations and a copy of the lease is being given to each tenant.
    C. A copy of the lease, in addition to the Rules and Regulations, is to be given to each
        tenant.
    D. A copy of the lease, in addition to the Rules and Regulations, are being given to
        each tenant.   6.____

7. A. Although we understood that for him music was a passion, we were disturbed by
        the fact that he was addicted to sing along with the soloists.
    B. Do you believe that Steven is liable to win a scholarship?
    C. Give the picture to whomever is a connoisseur of art.
    D. Whom do you believe to be the most efficient worker in the office?   7.____

8. A. Each adult who is sure they know all the answers will some day realize their mis-   8.___
    take.
    B. Even the most hardhearted villain would have to feel bad about so horrible a trag-
    edy.
    C. Neither being licensed teachers, both aspirants had to pass rigorous tests before
    being appointed.
    D. The principal reason why he wanted to be designated was because he had never
    before been to a convention.

9. A. Being that the weather was so inclement, the party has been postponed for at least   9.___
    a month.
    B. He is in New York City only three weeks and he has already seen all the thrilling
    sights in Manhattan and in the other four boroughs.
    C. If you will look it up in the official directory, which can be consulted in the library
    during specified hours, you will discover that the chairman and director are Mr.
    T. Henry Long.
    D. Working hard at college during the day and at the post office during the night, he
    appeared to his family to be indefatigable.

10. A. I would have been happy to oblige you if you only asked me to do it.   10.___
    B. The cold weather, as well as the unceasing wind and rain, have made us decide to
    spend the winter in Florida.
    C. The politician would have been more successful in winning office if he would have
    been less dogmatic.
    D. These trousers are expensive; however, they will wear well.

11. A. All except him wore formal attire at the reception for the ambassador.   11.___
    B. If that chair were to be blown off of the balcony, it might injure someone below.
    C. Not a passenger, who was in the crash, survived the impact.
    D. To borrow money off friends is the best way to lose them.

12. A. Approaching Manhattan on the ferry boat from Staten Island, an unforgettable   12.___
    sight of the skyscrapers is seen.
    B. Did you see the exhibit of modernistic paintings as yet?
    C. Gesticulating wildly and ranting in stentorian tones, the speaker was the sinecure
    of all eyes.
    D. The airplane with crew and passengers was lost somewhere in the Pacific Ocean.

13. A. If one has consistently had that kind of training, it is certainly too late to change   13.___
    your entire method of swimming long distances.
    B. The captain would have been more impressed if you would have been more con-
    scientious in evacuation drills.
    C. The passengers on the stricken ship were all ready to abandon it at the signal.
    D. The villainous shark lashed at the lifeboat with it's tail, trying to upset the rocking
    boat in order to partake of it's contents.

14.   A. As one whose been certified as a professional engineer, I believe that the decision to build a bridge over that harbor is unsound.   14.____
      B. Between you and me, this project ought to be completed long before winter arrives.
      C. He fervently hoped that the men would be back at camp and to find them busy at their usual chores.
      D. Much to his surprise, he discovered that the climate of Korea was like his home town.

15.   A. An industrious executive is aided, not impeded, by having a hobby which gives him a fresh point of view on life and its problems.   15.____
      B. Frequent absence during the calendar year will surely mitigate against the chances of promotion.
      C. He was unable to go to the committee meeting because he was very ill.
      D. Mr. Brown expressed his disapproval so emphatically that his associates were embarassed.

16.   A. At our next session, the office manager will have told you something about his duties and responsibilities.   16.____
      B. In general, the book is absorbing and original and have no hesitation about recommending it.
      C. The procedures followed by private industry in dealing with lateness and absence are different from ours.
      D. We shall treat confidentially any information about Mr. Doe, to whom we understand you have sent reports to for many years.

17.   A. I talked to one official, whom I knew was fully impartial.   17.____
      B. Everyone signed the petition but him.
      C. He proved not only to be a good student but also a good athlete.
      D. All are incorrect.

18.   A. Every year a large amount of tenants are admitted to housing projects.   18.____
      B. Henry Ford owned around a billion dollars in industrial equipment.
      C. He was aggravated by the child's poor behavior.
      D. All are incorrect.

19.   A. Before he was committed to the asylum he suffered from the illusion that he was Napoleon.   19.____
      B. Besides stocks, there were also bonds in the safe.
      C. We bet the other team easily.
      D. All are incorrect.

20.   A. Bring this report to your supervisor immediately.   20.____
      B. He set the chair down near the table.
      C. The capitol of New York is Albany.
      D. All are incorrect.

21.   A. He was chosen to arbitrate the dispute because everyone knew he would be disinterested.   21.____
      B. It is advisable to obtain the best council before making an important decision.
      C. Less college students are interested in teaching than ever before.
      D. All are incorrect.

22. A. She, hearing a signal, the source lamp flashed.
     B. While hearing a signal, the source lamp flashed.
     C. In hearing a signal, the source lamp flashed.
     D. As she heard a signal, the source lamp flashed.   22.___

23. A. Every one of the time records have been initialed in the designated spaces.
     B. All of the time records has been initialed in the designated spaces.
     C. Each one of the time records was initialed in the designated spaces.
     D. The time records all been initialed in the designated spaces.   23.___

24. A. If there is no one else to answer the phone, you will have to answer it.
     B. You will have to answer it yourself if no one else answers the phone.
     C. If no one else is not around to pick up the phone, you will have to do it.
     D. You will have to answer the phone when nobodys here to do it.   24.___

25. A. Dr. Barnes not in his office. What could I do for you?
     B. Dr. Barnes is not in his office. Is there something I can do for you?
     C. Since Dr. Barnes is not in his office, might there be something I may do for you?
     D. Is there any ways I can assist you since Dr. Barnes is not in his office?   25.___

26. A. She do not understand how the new console works.
     B. The way the new console works, she doesn't understand.
     C. She doesn't understand how the new console works.
     D. The new console works, so that she doesn't understand.   26.___

27. A. Certain changes in family income must be reported as they occur.
     B. When certain changes in family income occur, it must be reported.
     C. Certain family income changes must be reported as they occur.
     D. Certain changes in family income must be reported as they have been occuring. 27.___

28. A. Each tenant has to complete the application themselves.
     B. Each of the tenants have to complete the application by himself.
     C. Each of the tenants has to complete the application himself.
     D. Each of the tenants has to complete the application by themselves.   28.___

29. A. Yours is the only building that the construction will effect.
     B. Your's is the only building affected by the construction.
     C. The construction will only effect your building.
     D. Yours is the only building that will be affected by the construction.   29.___

30. A. There is four tests left.
     B. The number of tests left are four.
     C. There are four tests left.
     D. Four of the tests remains.   30.___

31. A. Each of the applicants takes a test.
     B. Each of the applicants take a test.
     C. Each of the applicants take tests.
     D. Each of the applicants have taken tests.   31.___

32. A. The applicant, not the examiners, are ready.   32.____
     B. The applicants, not the examiner, is ready.
     C. The applicants, not the examiner, are ready.
     D. The applicant, not the examiner, are ready.

33. A. You will not progress except you practice.   33.____
     B. You will not progress without you practicing.
     C. You will not progress unless you practice.
     D. You will not progress provided you do not practice.

34. A. Neither the director or the employees will be at the office tomorrow.   34.____
     B. Neither the director nor the employees will be at the office tomorrow.
     C. Neither the director, or the secretary nor the other employees will be at the office
         tomorrow.
     D. Neither the director, the secretary or the other employees will be at the office
         tomorrow.

35. A. In my absence he and her will have to finish the assignment.   35.____
     B. In my absence he and she will have to finish the assignment.
     C. In my absence she and him, they will have to finish the assignment.
     D. In my absence he and her both will have to finish the assignment.

───────

KEY (CORRECT ANSWERS)

1.	B	16.	C
2.	B	17.	B
3.	C	18.	D
4.	B	19.	B
5.	C	20.	B
6.	C	21.	A
7.	D	22.	D
8.	B	23.	C
9.	D	24.	A
10.	D	25.	B
11.	A	26.	C
12.	D	27.	A
13.	C	28.	C
14.	B	29.	D
15.	A	30.	C

31.	A
32.	C
33.	C
34.	B
35.	B

TEST 2

Questions 1-4.

DIRECTIONS: Questions 1 through 4 consist of three sentences each. For each question, select the sentence which contains NO error in grammar or usage.

1. A. Be sure that everybody brings his notes to the conference.   1._____
    B. He looked like he meant to hit the boy.
    C. Mr. Jones is one of the clients who was chosen to represent the district
    B. All are incorrect.

2. A. He is taller than I.   2._____
    B. I'll have nothing to do with these kind of people.
    C. The reason why he will not buy the house is because it is too expensive.
    D. All are incorrect.

3. A. Aren't I eligible for this apartment.   3._____
    B. Have you seen him anywheres?
    C. He should of come earlier.
    D. All are incorrect.

4. A. He graduated college in 1982.   4._____
    B. He hadn't but one more line to write.
    C. Who do you think is the author of this report?
    D. All are incorrect.

Questions 5-35.

DIRECTIONS: In each of the following questions, only one of the four sentences conforms to standards of correct usage. The other three contain errors in grammar, diction, or punctuation. Select the choice in each question which BEST conforms to standards of correct usage. Consider a choice correct if it contains none of the errors mentioned above, even though there may be other ways of expressing the same thought.

5. A. It is obvious that no one wants to be a kill-joy if they can help it.   5._____
    B. It is not always possible, and perhaps it never ispossible, to judge a person's character by just looking at him.
    C. When Yogi Berra of the New York Yankees hit an immortal grandslam home run, everybody in the huge stadium including Pittsburgh fans, rose to his feet.
    D. Every one of us students must pay tuition today.

6.   A.   The physician told the young mother that if the baby is not able to digest its milk, it should be boiled.   6.___

       B.   There is no doubt whatsoever that he felt deeply hurt because John Smith had betrayed the trust.

       C.   Having partaken of a most delicious repast prepared by Tessie Breen, the hostess, the horses were driven home immediately thereafter.

       D.   The attorney asked my wife and myself several questions.

7.   A.   Despite all denials, there is no doubt in my mind that   7.___

       B.   At this time everyone must deprecate the demogogic attack made by one of our Senators on one of our most revered statesmen.

       C.   In the first game of a crucial two-game series, Ted Williams, got two singles, both of them driving in a run.

       D.   Our visitor brought good news to John and I.

8.   A.   If he would have told me, I should have been glad to help him in his dire financial emergency.   8.___

       B.   Newspaper men have often asserted that diplomats or so-called official spokes-men sometimes employ equivocation in attempts to deceive.

       C.   I think someones coming to collect money for the Red Cross.

       D.   In a masterly summation, the young attorney expressed his belief that the facts clearly militate against this opinion.

9.   A.   We have seen most all the exhibits.   9.___

       B.   Without in the least underestimating your advice, in my opinion the situation has grown immeasurably worse in the past few days.

       C.   I wrote to the box office treasurer of the hit show that a pair of orchestra seats would be preferable.

       D.   As the grim story of Pearl Harbor was broadcast on that fateful December 7, it was the general opinion that war was inevitable.

10.   A.   Without a moment's hesitation, Casey Stengel said that Larry Berra works harder than any player on the team.   10.___

       B.   There is ample evidence to indicate that many animals can run faster than any human being.

       C.   No one saw the accident but I.

       D.   Example of courage is the heroic defense put up by the paratroopers against over-whelming odds.

11.   A.   If you prefer these kind, Mrs. Grey, we shall be more than willing to let you have them reasonably.   11.___

       B.   If you like these here, Mrs. Grey, we shall be more than willing to let you have them reasonably.

       C.   If you like these, Mrs. Grey, we shall be more than willing to let you have them.

       D.   Who shall we appoint?

12.   A.   The number of errors are greater in speech than in writing.   12.___

       B.   The doctor rather than the nurse was to blame for his being neglected.

       C.   Because the demand for these books have been so great, we reduced the price.

       D.   John Galsworthy, the English novelist, could not have survived a serious illness; had it not been for loving care.

13.　A.　Our activities this year have seldom ever been as interesting as they have been this month.
　　B.　Our activities this month have been more interesting, or at least as interesting as those of any month this year.
　　C.　Our activities this month has been more interesting than those of any other month this year.
　　D.　Neither Jean nor her sister was at home.

13.____

14.　A.　George B. Shaw's view of common morality, as well as his wit sparkling with a dash of perverse humor here and there, have led critics to term him "The Incurable Rebel."
　　B.　The President's program was not always received with the wholehearted endorsement of his own party, which is why the party faces difficulty in drawing up a platform for the coming election.
　　C.　The reason why they wanted to travel was because they had never been away from home.
　　D.　Facing a barrage of cameras, the visiting celebrity found it extremely difficult to express his opinions clearly.

14.____

15.　A.　When we calmed down, we all agreed that our anger had been kind of unnecessary and had not helped the situation.
　　B.　Without him going into all the details, he made us realize the horror of the accident.
　　C.　Like one girl, for example, who applied for two positions.
　　D.　Do not think that you have to be so talented as he is in order to play in the school orchestra.

15.____

16.　A.　He looked very peculiarly to me.
　　B.　He certainly looked at me peculiar.
　　C.　Due to the train's being late, we had to wait an hour.
　　D.　The reason for the poor attendance is that it is raining.

16.____

17.　A.　About one out of four own an automobile.
　　B.　The collapse of the old Mitchell Bridge was caused by defective construction in the central pier.
　　C.　Brooks Atkinson was well acquainted with the best literature, thus helping him to become an able critic.
　　D.　He has to stand still until the relief man comes up, thus giving him no chance to move about and keep warm.

17.____

18.　A.　He is sensitive to confusion and withdraws from people whom he feels are too noisy.
　　B.　Do you know whether the data is statistically correct?
　　C.　Neither the mayor or the aldermen are to blame.
　　D.　Of those who were graduated from high school, a goodly percentage went to college.

18.____

19.　A.　Acting on orders, the offices were searched by a designated committee.
　　B.　The answer probably is nothing.
　　C.　I thought it to be all right to excuse them from class.
　　D.　I think that he is as successful a singer, if not more successful, than Mary.

19.____

20. A. $120,000 is really very little to pay for such a wellbuilt house.   20.___
    B. The creatures looked like they had come from outer space.
    C. It was her, he knew!
    D. Nobody but me knows what to do.

21. A. Mrs. Smith looked good in her new suit.   21.___
    B. New York may be compared with Chicago.
    C. I will not go to the meeting except you go with me.
    D. I agree with this editorial.

22. A. My opinions are different from his.   22.___
    B. There will be less students in class now.
    C. Helen was real glad to find her watch.
    D. It had been pushed off of her dresser.

23. A. Almost everone, who has been to California, returns with glowing reports.   23.___
    B. George Washington, John Adams, and Thomas Jefferson, were our first presidents.
    C. Mr. Walters, whom we met at the bank yesterday, is the man, who gave me my first job.
    D. One should study his lessons as carefully as he can.

24. A. We had such a good time yesterday.   24.___
    B. When the bell rang, the boys and girls went in the schoolhouse.
    C. John had the worst headache when he got up this morning.
    D. Today's assignment is somewhat longer than yesterday's.

25. A. Neither the mayor nor the city clerk are willing to talk.   25.___
    B. Neither the mayor nor the city clerk is willing to talk.
    C. Neither the mayor or the city clerk are willing to talk.
    D. Neither the mayor or the city clerk is willing to talk.

26. A. Being that he is that kind of boy, cooperation cannot be expected.   26.___
    B. He interviewed people who he thought had something to say.
    C. Stop whomever enters the building regardless of rank or office held.
    D. Passing through the countryside, the scenery pleased us.

27. A. The childrens' shoes were in their closet.   27.___
    B. The children's shoes were in their closet.
    C. The childs' shoes were in their closet.
    D. The childs' shoes were in his closet.

28. A. An agreement was reached between the defendant, the plaintiff, the plaintiff's attorney and the insurance company as to the amount of the settlement.   28.___
    B. Everybody was asked to give their versions of the accident.
    C. The consensus of opinion was that the evidence was inconclusive.
    D. The witness stated that if he was rich, he wouldn't have had to loan the money.

29. A. Before beginning the investigation, all the materials relating to the case were carefully assembled.
    B. The reason for his inability to keep the appointment is because of his injury in the accident.
    C. This here evidence tends to support the claim of the defendant.
    D. We interviewed all the witnesses who, according to the driver, were still in town.

29.____

30. A. Each claimant was allowed the full amount of their medical expenses.
    B. Either of the three witnesses is available.
    C. Every one of the witnesses was asked to tell his story.
    D. Neither of the witnesses are right.

30.____

31. A. The commissioner, as well as his deputy and various bureau heads, were present.
    B. A new organization of employers and employees have been formed.
    C. One or the other of these men have been selected.
    D. The number of pages in the book is enough to discourage a reader.

31.____

32. A. Between you and me, I think he is the better man.
    B. He was believed to be me.
    C. Is it us that you wish to see?
    D. The winners are him and her.

32.____

33. A. Beside the statement to the police, the witness spoke to no one.
    B. He made no statement other than to the police and I.
    C. He made no statement to any one else, aside from the police.
    D. The witness spoke to no one but me.

33.____

34. A. The claimant has no one to blame but himself.
    B. The boss sent us, he and I, to deliver the packages.
    C. The lights come from mine and not his car.
    D. There was room on the stairs for him and myself.

34.____

35. A. Admission to this clinic is limited to patients' inability to pay for medical care.
    B. Patients who can pay little or nothing for medical care are treated in this clinic.
    C. The patient's ability to pay for medical care is the determining factor in his admissibility to this clinic.
    D. This clinic is for the patient's that cannot afford to pay or that can pay a little for medical care.

35.____

KEY (CORRECT ANSWERS)

1.	A		16.	D
2.	A		17.	B
3.	D		18.	D
4.	C		19.	B
5.	D		20.	D
6.	D		21.	A
7.	B		22.	A
8.	B		23.	D
9.	D		24.	D
10.	B		25.	B
11.	C		26.	B
12.	B		27.	B
13.	D		28.	C
14.	D		29.	D
15.	D		30.	C

31.	D
32.	A
33.	D
34.	A
35.	B

———

EXAMINATION SECTION
TEST 1

DIRECTIONS: Each question or incomplete statement is followed by several suggested answers or completions. Select the one that BEST answers the question or completes the statement. *PRINT THE LETTER OF THE CORRECT ANSWER IN THE SPACE AT THE RIGHT.*

Questions 1-25.

A student has written an article for the high school newspaper, using the skills learned in a stenography and typewriting class in its preparation. In the article which follows, certain words or groups of words are underlined and numbered. The underlined word or group of words may be incorrect because they present an error in grammar, usage, sentence structure, capitalization, diction, or punctuation. For each numbered word or group of words, there is an identically numbered question consisting of four choices based only on the underlined portion. Indicate the BEST choice. <u>Unnecessary changes will be considered incorrect</u>.

TIGERS VIE FOR CITY CHAMPIONSHIP

In their second year of varsity football, the North Side Tigers have gained a shot at the city championship. Last Saturday in the play-offs, the Tigers defeated the Western High
(1)
School Cowboys, <u>thus eliminated that team</u> from contention. Most of the credit for the
(2)
team's improvement must go to Joe Harris, the coach. <u>To play as well as they do</u> now, the coach
(3)
must have given the team superior instruction. There is no doubt that, <u>if a coach is effective, his</u>
<u>influence is over</u> many young minds.
(4)

With this major victory behind them, the Tigers can now look forward <u>to meet</u> the defending champions, the Revere Minutemen, in the finals.

(5)
The win over the Cowboys was <u>due to</u> North Side's supremacy in the air. The Tigers'
(6)
players have the advantages of strength and of <u>being speedy</u>. Our sterling quarterback, Butch
(7)
Carter, a master of the long pass, used <u>these kind of passes</u> to bedevil the boys from
(8)
Western. As a matter of fact, if the Tigers <u>would have used</u> the passing offense earlier in the game, the score would have been more one-sided. Butch, by the way, our all-around senior stu-dent, has already been tapped for bigger things. Having the highest marks in his class, <u>Barton</u>
(9)
<u>College has offered him a scholarship</u>.

The team's defense is another story. During the last few weeks, neither the linebackers

(10)
nor the safety man <u>have shown</u> sufficient ability to contain their oppo nents' running game.

(11)
In the city final, <u>the defensive unit's failing to complete it's assignments</u> may lead to disaster.

(12)
However, the coach said that this unit <u>not only has been cooperative but also the coach raise</u>

(13)
<u>their eagerness to learn</u>. He also said that this team <u>has</u> not <u>and never will give up</u>.

(14)
This kind of spirit is contagious, <u>therefore</u> I predict that the Tigers will   win because I have

(15)
<u>affection and full confidence in</u> the team.

(16)
One of the happy surprises this season is Peter Yisko, our punter. Peter <u>is</u> in the United
States for only two years. When he was in grammar school in the old country, it was not nec-

(17)
essary for him <u>to have studied</u> hard. Now, he depends on the football team to help him with

(18)
his English. Everybody <u>but the team mascot and I have</u> been pressed into service. Peter was

(19)
ineligible last year when he <u>learned that he would only obtain half</u> of the credits he had completed in Europe. Nevertheless, he attended occasional practice sessions, but he soon found

(20)
out that, if one wants to be a success ful player, <u>you</u> must realize that regular practice is

(21)
required. In fact, if a team is to be successful, it is necessary that everyone <u>be</u> present for all

(22)
practice sessions. "The life of a football player," says Peter, "is better than <u>a scholar</u>."

Facing the Minutemen, the Tigers will meet their most formidable opposition yet. This

(23)
team <u>is not only gaining a bad reputation</u> but also indulging in illegal practices on the field.

(24)
They <u>can't hardly object to us being</u> technical about penalties under these circumstances.

(25)
As far as the Minutemen are concerned, a <u>victory will taste sweet like a victory should</u>.

1.   A.   that eliminated that team
      B.   and they were eliminated
      C.   and eliminated them
      D.   Correct as is

2.   A.   To make them play as well as they do
      B.   Having played so well
      C.   After they played so well
      D.   Correct as is

3.   A.   if coaches are effective; they have influence over
      B.   to be effective, a coach influences
      C.   if a coach is effective, he influences
      D.   Correct as is

1.__

2.__

3.__

4. A. to meet with   B. to meeting   4.____
    C. to a meeting of   D. Correct as is

5. A. because of   B. on account of   5.____
    C. motivated by   D. Correct as is

6. A. operating swiftly   B. speed   6.____
    C. running speedily   D. Correct as is

7. A. these kinds of pass   B. this kind of passes   7.____
    C. this kind of pass   D. Correct as is

8. A. would of used   B. had used   8.____
    C. were using   D. Correct as is

9. A. he was offered a scholarship by Barton College.   9.____
    B. Barton College offered a scholarship to him.
    C. a scholarship was offered him by Barton College.
    D. Correct as is

10. A. had shown   B. were showing   10.____
    C. has shown   D. Correct as is

11. A. the defensive unit failing to complete its assignment   11.____
    B. the defensive unit's failing to complete its assignment
    C. the defensive unit failing to complete it's assignment
    D. Correct as is

12. A. has been not only cooperative, but also eager to learn   12.____
    B. has not only been cooperative, but also shows eagerness to learn
    C. has been not only cooperative, but also they were eager to learn
    D. Correct as is

13. A. has not given up and never will   13.____
    B. has not and never would give up
    C. has not given up and never will give up
    D. Correct as is

14. A. . Therefore   B. : therefore   14.____
    C. -- therefore   D. Correct as is

15. A. full confidence and affection for   15.____
    B. affection for and full confidence in
    C. affection and full confidence concerning
    D. Correct as is

16. A. is living   B. was living   16.____
    C. has been   D. Correct as is

17. A. to study   B. to be studying   17.____
    C. to have been studying D. Correct as is

18. A. but the team mascot and me has   18._
     B. but the team mascot and myself has
     C. but the team mascot and me have
     D. Correct as is

19. A. only learned that he would obtain half   19._
     B. learned that he would obtain only half
     C. learned that he only would obtain half
     D. Correct as is

20. A. a person   B. everyone   20._
     C. one   D. one

21. A. is   B. will be   21._
     C. shall be   D. Correct as is

22. A. to be a scholar   B. being a scholar   22._
     C. that of a scholar   D. Correct as is

23. A. not only is gaining a bad reputation   23._
     B. is gaining not only a bad reputation
     C. is not gaining only a bad reputation
     D. Correct as is

24. A. can hardly object to us being   24._
     B. can hardly object to our being
     C. can't hardly object to our being
     D. Correct as is

25. A. victory will taste sweet like it should   25._
     B. victory will taste sweetly as it should taste
     C. victory will taste sweet as a victory should
     D. Correct as is

Questions 26-30.

DIRECTIONS: Questions 26 through 30 are to be answered on the basis of the instructions
               and paragraph which follow.

               The paragraph which follows is part of a report prepared by a buyer for sub-
               mission to his superior. The paragraph contains 5 underlined groups of words,
               each one bearing a number which identifies the question relating to it. Each of
               these groups of words MAY or MAY NOT represent standard written English,
               suitable for use in a formal report. For each question, decide whether the
               group of words used in the paragraph which is always choice A is standard
               written English and should be retained, or whether choice B, C, or D.

On October 23, 2009 the vendor delivered two microscopes to the using agency. When
     (26)
they inspected, one microscope was found to have a defective part. The vendor was notified,

and offered to replace the defective part; the using agency, however, requested that the
                                                                                   (27)
microscope be replaced. The vendor claimed that complete replacement was unnecessary and

(28)

refused to comply with the agency's demand, <u>having the result that the agency declared</u> that it

(29)

will pay only for the acceptable microscope. At that point <u>I got involved by the agency's</u>

<u>contacting me</u>. The agency requested that I speak to the vendor since I handled the original

(30)

purchase and <u>have dealt with this vendor before.</u>

26.   A.   When they inspected,   26._____
           B.   Upon inspection,
           C.   The inspection report said that
           D.   Having inspected,

27.   A.   that the microscope be replaced.   27._____
           B.   a whole new microscope in replacement.
           C.   to have a replacement for the microscope.
           D.   that they get the microscope replaced.

28.   A.   , having the result that the agency declared   28._____
           B.   ; the agency consequently declared
           C.   , which refusal caused the agency to consequently declare
           D.   , with the result of the agency's declaring

29.   A.   I got involved by the agency's contacting me.   29._____
           B.   I became involved, being contacted by the agency.
           C.   the agency contacting me, I got involved.
           D.   the agency contacted me and I became involved.

30.   A.   have dealt with this vendor before.   30._____
           B.   done business before with this vendor.
           C.   know this vendor by prior dealings.
           D.   have dealt with this vendor before.

KEY (CORRECT ANSWERS)

1.	C	16.	C
2.	A	17.	A
3.	C	18.	A
4.	B	19.	B
5.	A	20.	C
6.	B	21.	D
7.	C	22.	C
8.	B	23.	D
9.	D	24.	A
10.	C	25.	C
11.	B	26.	B
12.	A	27.	A
13.	B	28.	B
14.	A	29.	D
15.	B	30.	D

EXAMINATION SECTION
TEST 1

DIRECTIONS: Each question or incomplete statement is followed by several suggested answers or completions. Select the one that BEST answers the question or completes the statement. *PRINT THE LETTER OF THE CORRECT ANSWER IN THE SPACE AT THE RIGHT.*

1. Which of the following sentences is punctuated INCORRECTLY?　　　　　　　　　1.____

   A. Johnson said, "One tiny virus, Blanche, can multiply so fast that it will become 200 viruses in 25 minutes."
   B. With economic pressures hitting them from all sides, American farmers have become the weak link in the food chain.
   C. The degree to which this is true, of course, depends on the personalities of the people involved, the subject matter, and the atmosphere in general.
   D. "What loneliness, asked George Eliot, is more lonely than distrust?"

2. Which of the following sentences is punctuated INCORRECTLY?　　　　　　　　　2.____

   A. Based on past experiences, do you expect the plumber to show up late, not have the right parts, and overcharge you.
   B. When polled, however, the participants were most concerned that it be convenient.
   C. No one mentioned the flavor of the coffee, and no one seemed to care that china was used instead of plastic.
   D. As we said before, sometimes people view others as things; they don't see them as living, breathing beings like themselves.

3. Convention members travelled here from Kingston New York Pittsfield Massachusetts Bennington Vermont and Hartford Connecticut.　　　　　　　　　3.____
How many commas should there be in the above sentence?

   A. 3　　　　　　　B. 4　　　　　　　C. 5　　　　　　　D. 6

4. Of the two speakers the one who spoke about human rights is more famous and more humble.　　　　　　　　　4.____
How many commas should there be in the above sentence?

   A. 1　　　　　　　B. 2　　　　　　　C. 3　　　　　　　D. 4

5. Which sentence is punctuated INCORRECTLY?　　　　　　　　　5.____

   A. Five people voted no; two voted yes; one person abstained.
   B. Well, consider what has been said here today, but we won't make any promises.
   C. Anthropologists divide history into three major periods: the Stone Age, the Bronze Age, and the Iron Age.
   D. Therefore, we may create a stereotype about people who are unsuccessful; we may see them as lazy, unintelligent, or afraid of success.

6. Which sentence is punctuated INCORRECTLY?　　　　　　　　　6.____

   A. Studies have found that the unpredictability of customer behavior can lead to a great deal of stress, particularly if the behavior is unpleasant or if the employee has little control over it.

B. If this degree of emotion and variation can occur in spectator sports, imagine the role that perceptions can play when there are <u>real</u> stakes involved.

C. At other times, however hidden expectations may sabotage or severely damage an encounter without anyone knowing what happened.

D. There are usually four issues to look for in a conflict: differences in values, goals, methods, and facts.

Questions 7-10.

DIRECTIONS: Questions 7 through 10 test your ability to distinguish between words that sound alike but are spelled differently and have different meanings. In the following groups of sentences, one of the underlined words is used incorrectly.

7. A. By accepting responsibility for their actions, managers promote trust.
    B. Dropping hints or making <u>illusions</u> to things that you would like changed sometimes leads to resentment.
    C. The entire unit <u>loses</u> respect for the manager and resents the reprimand.
    D. Many people are <u>averse</u> to confronting problems directly; they would rather avoid them.
7.___

8. A. What does this say about the <u>effect</u> our expectations have on those we supervise?
    B. In an effort to save time between 9 A.M. and 1 P.M., the staff members devised their own interpretation of what was to be done on these forms.
    C. The task master's <u>principal</u> concern is for getting the work done; he or she is not concerned about the needs or interests of employees.
    D. The advisor's main objective was increasing Angela's ability to invest her <u>capitol</u> wisely.
8.___

9. A. A typical problem is that people have to cope with the internal <u>censer</u> of their feelings.
    B. Sometimes, in their attempt to sound more learned, people speak in ways that are barely <u>comprehensible</u>.
    C. The <u>council</u> will meet next Friday to decide whether Abrams should continue as representative.
    D. His <u>descent</u> from grace was assured by that final word.
9.___

10. A. The doctor said that John's leg had to remain <u>stationary</u> or it would not heal properly.
    B. There is a city <u>ordinance</u> against parking too close to fire hydrants.
    C. Meyer's problem is that he is never <u>discrete</u> when talking about office politics.
    D. Mrs. Thatcher probably worked harder <u>than</u> any other British Prime Minister had ever worked.
10.___

Questions 11-20.

DIRECTIONS: For each of the following groups of sentences in Questions 11 through 20, select the sentence which is the BEST example of English usage and grammar.

11. A. She is a woman who, at age sixty, is distinctly attractive and cares about how they look.
    B. It was a seemingly impossible search, and no one knew the problems better than she.
    C. On the surface, they are all sweetness and light, but his morbid character is under it.
    D. The minicopier, designed to appeal to those who do business on the run like architects in the field or business travelers, weigh about four pounds.

11._____

12. A. Neither the administrators nor the union representa- tive regret the decision to settle the disagreement.
    B. The plans which are made earlier this year were no longer being considered.
    C. I would have rode with him if I had known he was leaving at five.
    D. I don't know who she said had it.

12._____

13. A. Writing at a desk, the memo was handed to her for immediate attention.
    B. Carla didn't water Carl's plants this week, which she never does.
    C. Not only are they good workers, with excellent writing and speaking skills, and they get to the crux of any problem we hand them.
    D. We've noticed that this enthusiasm for undertaking new projects sometimes interferes with his attention to detail.

13._____

14. A. It's obvious that Nick offends people by being unruly, inattentive, and having no patience.
    B. Marcia told Genie that she would have to leave soon.
    C. Here are the papers you need to complete your investigation.
    D. Julio was startled by you're comment.

14._____

15. A. The new manager has done good since receiving her promotion, but her secretary has helped her a great deal.
    B. One of the personnel managers approached John and tells him that the client arrived unexpectedly.
    C. If somebody can supply us with the correct figures, they should do so immediately.
    D. Like zealots, advocates seek power because they want to influence the policies and actions of an organization .

15._____

16. A. Between you and me, Chris probably won't finish this assignment in time.
    B. Rounding the corner, the snack bar appeared before us.
    C. Parker's radical reputation made to the Supreme Court his appointment impossible.
    D. By the time we arrived, Marion finishes briefing James and returns to Hank's office.

16._____

17.   A. As we pointed out earlier, the critical determinant of the success of middle manag-   17.___
         ers is their ability to communicate well with others.
     B. The lecturer stated there wasn't no reason for bad supervision.
     C. We are well aware whose at fault in this instance.
     D. When planning important changes, it's often wise to seek the partic-
         ipation of others because employees often have much valuable
         ideas to offer.

18.   A. Joan had ought to throw out those old things that were damaged when the roof   18.___
         leaked.
     B. I spose he'll let us know what he's decided when he finally comes to
         a decision.
     C. Carmen was walking to work when she suddenly realized that she
         had left her lunch on the table as she passed the market.
     D. Are these enough plants for your new office?

19.   A. First move the lever forward, and then they should lift the ribbon casing before try-   19.___
         ing to take it out.
     B. Michael finished quickest than any other person in the office.
     C. There is a special meeting for we committee members today at 4
         p.m.
     D. My husband is worried about our having to work overtime next
         week.

20.   A. Another source of conflicts are individuals who possess very poor interpersonal   20.___
         skills.
     B. It is difficult for us to work with him on projects because these kinds
         of people are not interested in team building.
     C. Each of the departments was represented at the meeting.
     D. Poor boy, he never should of past that truck on the right.

Questions 21-28.

DIRECTIONS: In Questions 21 through 28, there may be a problem with English grammar or
                usage. If a problem does exist, select the letter that indicates the most effec-
                tive change. If no problem exists, select choice A.

21. He rushed her to the hospital and stayed with her, even though this took quite a bit of his   21.___
    time, he didn't charge her anything.

    A. No changes are necessary
    B. Change <u>even though</u> to <u>although</u>
    C. Change the first comma to a period and capitalize <u>even</u>
    D. Change <u>rushed</u> to <u>had rushed</u>

22. Waiting that appears unfairly feels longer than waiting that seems justified.   22.___

    A. No changes are necessary
    B. Change <u>unfairly</u> to <u>unfair</u>
    C. Change <u>appears</u> to <u>seems</u>
    D. Change <u>longer</u> to <u>longest</u>

23. May be you and the person who argued with you will be able to reach an agreement.   23._____

    A. No changes are necessary
    B. Change will be to <u>were</u>
    C. Change <u>argued with</u> to <u>had an argument with</u>
    D. Change <u>may be</u> to <u>maybe</u>

24. Any one of them could of taken the file while you were having coffee.   24._____

    A. No changes are necessary
    B. Change <u>any one</u> to <u>anyone</u>
    C. Change <u>of</u> to <u>have</u>
    D. Change <u>were having</u> to <u>were out having</u>

25. While people get jobs or move from poverty level to better paying employment, they stop receiving benefits and start paying taxes.   25._____

    A. No changes are necessary
    B. Change <u>While</u> to <u>As</u>
    C. Change <u>stop</u> to <u>will stop</u>
    D. Change <u>get</u> to <u>obtain</u>

26. Maribeth's phone rang while talking to George about the possibility of their meeting Tom at three this afternoon.   26._____

    A. No changes are necessary
    B. Change <u>their</u> to <u>her</u>
    C. Move <u>to George</u> so that it follows <u>Tom</u>
    D. Change <u>talking</u> to <u>she was talking</u>

27. According to their father, Lisa is smarter than Chris, but Emily is the smartest of the three sisters.   27._____

    A. No changes are necessary
    B. Change <u>their</u> to <u>her</u>
    C. Change <u>is</u> to <u>was</u>
    D. Make two sentences, changing the second comma to a period and omitting <u>but</u>

28. Yesterday, Mark and he claim that Carl took Carol's ideas and used them inappropriately.   28._____

    A. No changes are necessary
    B. Change <u>claim</u> to <u>claimed</u>
    C. Change <u>inappropriately</u> to <u>inappropriate</u>
    D. Change <u>Carol's</u> to <u>Carols'</u>

Questions 29-34.

DIRECTIONS: For each group of sentences in Questions 29 through 34, select the choice that represents the BEST editing of the problem sentence.

29. The managers expected employees to be at their desks at all times, but they would always be late or leave unannounced.   29._____

A. The managers wanted employees to always be at their desks, but they would always be late or leave unannounced.

B. Although the managers expected employees to be at their desks no matter what came up, they would always be late and leave without telling anyone.

C. Although the managers expected employees to be at their desks at all times, the managers would always be late or leave without telling anyone.

D. The managers expected the employee to never leave their desks, but they would always be late or leave without telling anyone.

30. The one who is department manager he will call you to discuss the problem tomorrow morning at 10 A.M.   30.___

A. The one who is department manager will call you tomorrow morning at ten to discuss the problem.

B. The department manager will call you to discuss the problem tomorrow at 10 A.M.

C. Tomorrow morning at 10 A.M., the department manager will call you to discuss the problem.

D. Tomorrow morning the department manager will call you to discuss the problem.

31. A conference on child care in the workplace the $200 cost of which to attend may be prohibitive to childcare workers who earn less than that weekly.   31.___

A. A conference on child care in the workplace that costs $200 may be too expensive for childcare workers who earn less than that each week.

B. A conference on child care in the workplace, the cost of which to attend is $200, may be prohibitive to childcare workers who earn less than that weekly.

C. A conference on child care in the workplace who costs $200 may be too expensive for childcare workers who earn less than that a week.

D. A conference on child care in the workplace which costs $200 may be too expensive to childcare workers who earn less than that on a weekly basis.

32. In accordance with estimates recently made, there are 40,000 to 50,000 nuclear weapons in our world today.   32.___

A. Because of estimates recently, there are 40,000 to 50,000 nuclear weapons in the world today.

B. In accordance with estimates made recently, there are 40,000 to 50,000 nuclear weapons in the world today.

C. According to estimates made recently, there are 40,000 to 50,000 weapons in the world today.

D. According to recent estimates, there are 40,000 to 50,000 nuclear weapons in the world today.

33. Motivation is important in problem solving, but they say that excessive motivation can inhibit the creative process.   33.___

A. Motivation is important in problem solving, but, as they say, too much of it can inhibit the creative process.

B. Motivation is important in problem solving and excessive motivation will inhibit the creative process.

C. Motivation is important in problem solving, but excessive motivation can inhibit the creative process.

    D.   Motivation is important in problem solving because excessive motivation can inhibit the creative process.

34. In selecting the best option calls for consulting with all the people that are involved in it.   34._____

    A.   In selecting the best option consulting with all the people concerned with it.
    B.   Calling for the best option, we consulted all the affected people.
    C.   We called all the people involved to select the best option.
    D.   To be sure of selecting the best option, one should consult all the people involved.

35. There are a number of problems with the following letter. From the options below, select the version that is MOST in accordance with standard business style, tone, and form.   35._____

Dear Sir:

We are so sorry that we have had to backorder your order for 15,000 widgets and 2,300 whatzits for such a long time. We have been having incredibly bad luck lately. When your order first came in no one could get to it because my secretary was out with the flu and her replacement didn't know what she was doing, then there was the dock strike in Cucamonga which held things up for awhile, and then it just somehow got lost. We think it may have fallen behind the radiator.

We are happy to say that all these problems have been taken care of, we are caught up on supplies, and we should have the stuff to you soon, in the near future --about two weeks. You may not believe us after everything you've been through with us, but it's true.

We'll let you know as soon as we have a secure date for delivery. Thank you so much for continuing to do business with us after all the problems this probably has caused you.

Yours very sincerely,

Rob Barker

    A.   Dear Sir:

    We are so sorry that we have had to backorder your order for 15,000 widgets and 2,300 whatzits. We have been having problems with staff lately and the dock strike hasn't helped anything.

    We are happy to say that all these problems have been taken care of. I've told my secretary to get right on it, and we should have the stuff to you soon. Thank you so much for continuing to do business with us after all the problems this must have caused you.

    We'll let you know as soon as we have a secure date for delivery.

    Sincerely,

    Rob Barker

B.   Dear Sir:

We regret that we haven't been able to fill your order for 15,000 widgets and 2,300 whatzits in a timely fashion.

We'll let you know as soon as we have a secure date for delivery.

Sincerely,

Rob Barker

C.   Dear Sir:

We are so very sorry that we haven't been able to fill your order for 15,000 widgets and 2,300 whatzits. We have been having incredibly bad luck lately, but things are much better now.

Thank you so much for bearing with us through all of this. We'll let you know as soon as we have a secure date for delivery.

Sincerely,

Rob Barker

D.   Dear Sir:

We are very sorry that we haven't been able to fill your order for 15,000 widgets and 2,300 whatzits. Due to unforeseen difficulties, we have had to back-order your request. At this time, supplies have caught up to demand, and we foresee a delivery date within the next two weeks.

We'll let you know as soon as we have a secure date for delivery. Thank you for your patience.

Sincerely,

Rob Barker

———

KEY (CORRECT ANSWERS)

1.	D		16.	A
2.	A		17.	A
3.	B		18.	D
4.	A		19.	D
5.	B		20.	C
6.	C		21.	C
7.	B		22.	B
8.	D		23.	D
9.	A		24.	C
10.	C		25.	B
11.	B		26.	D
12.	D		27.	A
13.	D		28.	B
14.	C		29.	C
15.	D		30.	B

31. A
32. D
33. C
34. D
35. D

EXAMINATION SECTION
TEST 1

DIRECTIONS: Each question or incomplete statement is followed by several suggested answers or completions. Select the one that BEST answers the question or completes the statement.

Questions 1-17.

DIRECTIONS: In each of the following groups of sentences, there are three sentences which are correct and one which is incorrect because it contains an error in grammar, usage, diction, or punctuation. Indicate the letter of the INCORRECT sentence.

1. A. The business was organized under the name of Allen & Co.
    B. The price of admission was two dollars.
    C. The news was brought to Mr. Walters.
    D. There are less slips to be checked today than there were yesterday.

1.____

2. A. He only wants you to go with him; consequently I would be in the way.
    B. Whom do you think I saw on my way to lunch today?
    C. I am very much pleased with the work you are doing in my office.
    D. I think he is better than anyone else in his class.

2.____

3. A. I do not believe in his going so far away from home.
    B. She dresses exactly like her sister does.
    C. Neither Flora nor I are going to the movies tonight.
    D. The reason for my lateness is that the train was derailed.

3.____

4. A. I cannot understand its being on the bottom shelf because I remember putting it on the top shelf.
    B. If you do not agree with the statement above, please put a check next to it.
    C. We were both chosen to represent the association.
    D. The doctor assured us that she would not have to be operated.

4.____

5. A. Near the desk stand three chairs.
    B. How many crates of oranges were delivered?
    C. Where's your coat and hat?
    D. Either you or your mother is wrong.

5.____

6. A. She attacked the proposal with bitter words.
    B. Last year our team beat your team.
    C. The careless child spilled some milk on the table cloth.
    D. For three weeks last summer, Molly stood with her aunt.

6.____

7. A. Don't blame me for it.
    B. I have met but four.
    C. Loan me five dollars.
    D. May I leave early tonight?

7.____

8. A. It's time you knew how to divide by two numbers.   8.___
    B. Are you sure the bell has rung?
    C. Whose going to prepare the luncheon?
    D. Will it be all right if you are called at ten o'clock?

9. A. He had a wide knowledge of birds.   9.___
    B. New Orleans is further from Seattle than from Camden.
    C. Keats's poetry is characterized by rich imagery.
    D. He objected to several things—the cost, the gaudiness, and the congestion.

10. A. There was, in the first place, no indication that a crime had been committed.   10.___
    B. She is taller than any other member of the class.
    C. She decided to leave the book lay on the table.
    D. Haven't you any film in stock at this time?

11. A. Why do you still object to him coming with us to the party?   11.___
    B. If I were you, I should wait for them.
    C. If I were ten years older, I should like this kind of job.
    D. I shall go if you desire it.

12. A. Swimming in the pool, the water looked green.   12.___
    B. His speech is so precise as to seem affected.
    C. I would like to go overseas.
    D. We read each other's letters.

13. A. It must be here somewhere.   13.___
    B. The reason is that there is no bread.
    C. Of all other cities, New York is the largest.
    D. The sand was very warm at the beach.

14. A. If he were wealthy, he would build a hospital for the poor.   14.___
    B. I shall insist that he obey you.
    C. They saw that it was him.
    D. What kind of cactus is this one?

15. A. Because they had been trained for emergencies, the assault did not catch them by   15.___
        surprise.
    B. They divided the loot between the four of them in proportion to their efforts.
    C. The number of strikes is gradually diminishing.
    D. Between acts we went out to the lobby for a brief chat.

16. A. Through a ruse, the prisoners affected their escape from the concentration camp.   16.___
    B. Constant esposure to danger has affected his mind.
    C. Her affected airs served to alienate her from her friends.
    D. Her vivacity was an affectation.

17. A. It is difficult to recollect what life was like before the war.   17.___
    B. Will each of the pupils please hand their home work in?
    C. There are fewer serious mistakes in this pamphlet than I had thought.
    D. "Leave Her to Heaven" is the title of a novel by Ben Ames Williams.

Questions 18-25.

DIRECTIONS: Each of Questions 18 through 25 consists of three sentences lettered A, B, and C. In each of these questions, one of the sentences may contain an error in grammar, sentence structure, or punctuation, or all three sentences may be correct. If one of the sentences in a question contains an error in grammar, sentence structure, or punctuation, write in the space at the right the letter preceding the sentence which contains the error. If all three sentences are correct, write the letter D.

18. A. Mr. Smith appears to be less competent than I in performing these duties.　18.____
    B. The supervisor spoke to the employee, who had made the error, but did not reprimand him.
    C. When he found the book lying on the table, he immediately notified the owner.

19. A. Being locked in the desk, we were certain that the papers would not be taken.　19.____
    B. It wasn't I who dictated the telegram; I believe it was Eleanor.
    C. You should interview whoever comes to the office today.

20. A. The clerk was instructed to set the machine on the table before summoning the manager.　20.____
    B. He said that he was not familiar with those kind of activities.
    C. A box of pencils, in addition to erasers and blotters, was included in the shipment of supplies.

21. A. The supervisor remarked, "Assigning an employee to the proper type of work is not always easy."　21.____
    B. The employer found that each of the applicants were qualified to perform the duties of the position.
    C. Any competent student is permitted to take this course if he obtains the consent of the instructor.

22. A. The prize was awarded to the employee whom the judges believed to be most deserving.　22.____
    B. Since the instructor believes this book is the better of the two, he is recommending it for use in the school.
    C. It was obvious to the employees that the completion of the task by the scheduled date would require their working overtime.

23. A. These reports have been typed by employees who are trained by a capable supervisor.　23.____
    B. This employee is as old, if not older, than any other employee in the department.
    C. Running rapidly down the street, the messenger soon reached the office.

24. A. It is believed, that if these terms are accepted, the building can be constructed at a reasonable cost.　24.____
    B. The typists are seated in the large office; the stenographers, in the small office.
    C. Either the operators or the machines are at fault.

25. A. Mr. Jones, who is the head of the agency, will come today to discuss the plans for   25.____
       the new training program.
    B. The reason the report is not finished is that the supply of paper is exhausted.
    C. It is now obvious that neither of the two employees is able to handle this type of
       assignment.

KEY (CORRECT ANSWERS)

1.	D	11.	A
2.	A	12.	A
3.	B	13.	C
4.	D	14.	C
5.	C	15.	B
6.	D	16.	A
7.	C	17.	B
8.	C	18.	B
9.	B	19.	A
10.	C	20.	B

21.	B
22.	D
23.	B
24.	A
25.	D

TEST 2

DIRECTIONS: In each of the following groups of sentences, one sentence is incorrect because it includes an error in grammar, usage, sentence structure, diction, capitalization, or punctuation. Indicate the INCORRECT sentence in each group.

1. A. We shall have to leave it to the jury to make a determination of the facts.
   B. His precision resulted in a nice discrimination between their relative merits.
   C. Green vegetables are healthy foods.
   D. We shall attempt to ascertain whether there has been any tampering with the lock.

   1.____

2. A. Have you made any definitive plans which may be applied to budget preparation?
   B. We planned on taking a walking trip through the mountains.
   C. I would much rather he had called me after we had taken the trip.
   D. Do you believe that he has a predisposition toward that kind of response?

   2.____

3. A. He carried out the orders with great dispatch but with little effect.
   B. The cook's overbearing manner overawed his employer.
   C. All of us shall partake of the benefits of exercise.
   D. Miss Smith made less errors than the other typists.

   3.____

4. A. I believe that we are liable to have good weather tomorrow.
   B. From what I could see, I thought he acted like the others.
   C. Perpetual motion is an idea which is not unthinkable.
   D. Many of us taxpayers are displeased with the service.

   4.____

5. A. She was incredulous when I told her the incredible tale.
   B. She was told that the symptoms would disappear within a week.
   C. If possible, I should like to sit in front of the very tall couple.
   D. Punish whomever disobeys our commands.

   5.____

6. A. The men were trapped inside the cave for four days.
   B. The man seated in back of me was talking throughout the play.
   C. He told me that he doesn't know whether he will be able to visit us.
   D. Please bring me the pair of scissors from the table.

   6.____

7. A. He was charged with having committed many larcenous acts.
   B. Material wealth is certainly not something to be dismissed cavalierly.
   C. He is one of those people who do everything promptly.
   D. I hope to be able to retaliate for the assistance you have given me.

   7.____

8. A. Have you noted the unusual phenomena to be seen in that portion of the heavens?
   B. The data is as accurate as it is possible to make it.
   C. The enormity of the crime was such that we could not comprehend it.
   D. The collection of monies from some clients was long overdue.

   8.____

9. A. What you are doing is not really different than what I had suggested.
   B. The enormousness of the animal was enough to make her gasp.
   C. The judge brought in a decision which aroused antagonism in the community.
   D. I asked the monitor to take the papers to the principal.

   9.____

10.   A.   He talks as if he were tired.   10.____
         B.   He amended his declaration to include additional income.
         C.   I know that he would have succeeded if he had tried.
         D.   Whom does Mrs. Jones think wrote the play?

11.   A.   The stone made a very angry bruise on his forearm.   11.____
         B.   He said to me: "I'm very mad at you."
         C.   In all likelihood, we shall be unable to go to the fair.
         D.   He would have liked to go to the theatre with us.

12.   A.   The lawyers tried to settle the case out of court.   12.____
         B.   "Get out of my life!" she cried.
         C.   Walking down the road, the lake comes into view.
         D.   The loan which I received from the bank helped me to keep the business going.

13.   A.   I shall go with you providing that we return home early.   13.____
         B.   He has been providing us with excellent baked goods for many years.
         C.   It has been proved, to my satisfaction, to be correct.
         D.   Whether we go or not is for you to decide.

14.   A.   He does not seem able to present a logical and convincing argument.   14.____
         B.   Each of the goaltenders was trying to protect his respective cage.
         C.   He said, "I shall go there directly."
         D.   The reason he was late was on account of the delay in transportation.

15.   A.   Her mien revealed her abhorrence of his actions.   15.____
         B.   She used a great deal of rope so it would not come apart.
         C.   After he had lived among them, he found much to admire in their way of life.
         D.   He waited patiently for the fish to snatch at the bait.

16.   A.   As a result of constant exposure to the elements, he took sick and required medical attention.   16.____
         B.   Although the automobile is very old, we think it can still be used for a long trip.
         C.   He purchased all the supplies she requested with one exception.
         D.   He has repeated the story so frequently that I think he has begun to believe it.

17.   A.   It is the noise made by the crickets that you hear.   17.____
         B.   She told us that she would be at home on Sunday.
         C.   She said, "If I'm not there on time, don't wait on me."
         D.   Please try to maintain a cheerful disposition under any and all provocations.

18.   A.   Who is the tallest boy in the class?   18.____
         B.   Where shall I look to find a similar kind of stone?
         C.   The horse took the jumps with a great deal of ease.
         D.   He is as good, if not better than, any other jumper in the country.

19.   A.   Which of the two machines would be the most practical?   19.____
         B.   All of us are entitled to a reply if we are to determine whether you should remain as a member of the club.
         C.   Everyone who was listening got to his feet and applauded.
         D.   There was no indication from his actions that he knew he was wrong.

20.   A. I beg leave to call upon you in case of emergency.   20._____
        B. Do not deter me from carrying out the demands of my office.
        C. Please see me irregardless of the time of day.
        D. The intrepid captain shouted: "Into the fray!"

21.   A. The teacher asked me whether she could lend the book from me.   21._____
        B. You are not permitted to enter the public address system control room while an announcement is being made.
        C. The mother announced loudly that she was going to the district office to find out whether we could refuse to accept her daughter.
        D. It was my opinion that the salesman arrived at a most inopportune time to demonstrate his machine.

22.   A. Perhaps we can eliminate any possibility of a misunderstanding by placing a special notice on the bulletin board.   22._____
        B. The heavy snow storm caused a noticeable drop in student attendance.
        C. We received two different relays, due to the fact that both the district office and the division office sent out separate notices.
        D. Nevertheless, I urge you to prepare for the regular examination by taking the required courses.

23.   A. By rotating the secretaries' tasks, we should be able to train the entire office staff in all duties.   23._____
        B. The boy who had fallen told me that he felt alright, so that I didn't make out an accident report.
        C. The flowers that the secretary had brought added a delightful touch of color to the office.
        D. We shall have to work fast to complete the task before the deadline.

24.   A. The telephone caller said that he was the boy's father, but his voice sounded immature.   24._____
        B. There are very few situations which would require that we close the office and send the staff home early.
        C. Although a packing slip accompanied the package, we had not received an invoice.
        D. The parent claimed that the child had been in school, but the roll book indicated that the boy had been absent from school.

25.   A. Needless to say, I could not grant the parent her request to see the teacher immediately since the teacher was teaching a class.   25._____
        B. The small boy entered the office crying bitterly, and he refused to tell me the cause of his tears.
        C. In describing her son, the mother told me that he was smaller than any boy in his class.
        D. By holding teachers' checks until after lunch, you prevent many teachers from getting to the bank.

KEY (CORRECT ANSWERS)

1.	C		11.	B
2.	B		12.	C
3.	D		13.	A
4.	A		14.	D
5.	D		15.	B
6.	B		16.	A
7.	D		17.	C
8.	B		18.	D
9.	A		19.	A
10.	D		20.	C

21.	A
22.	C
23.	B
24.	D
25.	C

TEST 3

DIRECTIONS: In each of the following groups of sentences, one of the four sentences contains one or more errors in grammar, sentence structure, English usage, or diction. Select the INCORRECT sentence in each case.

1. A. Protest as much as you like, I shall stick to my plan to the bitter end.   1.____
   B. It took two men to lift the refrigerator off of the truck.
   C. The dancer, with her company, her orchestra, and her manager, occupies the sixth floor.
   D. When one has worked with his hands he has really earned his keep.

2. A. The large number of crises among African governments indicate the difficulty of   2.____
      transition to independence.
   B. No sooner had the final bell rung than there was a mad scramble toward the door.
   C. Being as helpful as he could, the traffic policeman offered to send for a mechanic.
   D. They climbed higher that they might reach the little souvenir shop.

3. A. That angry retort of Father's came after long provocation.   3.____
   B. The frankness of the book presented a difficult problem as far as advertising it.
   C. It is the glory of Yale that she has many famous men to select from.
   D. The stars of the team were the following: Jones, center Smith, end; and Harris, quarterback.

4. A. Next year we shall nominate whomever we please.   4.____
   B. The story is so well told that anything but the author's desired effect is impossible.
   C. My Oldsmobile has a Mercury motor, which makes it hard to shift gears.
   D. He is one of those people who believe in existentialist ideas.

5. A. After my previous experiences, I never expect to come this far again.   5.____
   B. I like my present work as preparing the way to my future occupation.
   C. To sit and smoke and think and dream was his idea of gratification.
   D. The snowball of knowledge sweeps relentlessly on, stamping additional rivets into the body of science.

6. A. The student racked his brains back and forth over the algebra problem.   6.____
   B. It must be conceded that all the young men adapted themselves to the new regulations.
   C. Formal talks were held between the three great powers in an effort to achieve disarmament.
   D. The librarian felt bad about the damaged encyclopedia.

7. A. The policeman wanted to know if the driver of the car had a license.   7.____
   B. Not many of these churches are less than thirty years old.
   C. The athlete failed to break his unofficial world decathlon record by a narrow margin.
   D. How different things appear in Washington than in London.

8. A. The agenda for the next meeting contains several highly important topics.   8.____
    B. Stemming from the prelate's remarks was the inference that all was not well at the council.
    C. Because the weight of majority opinion is so great is no reason why a dissenter should remain silent.
    D. The general dominating the conference, there was no danger of chaos erupting.

9. A. Our company, which has thousands of employees, rates Jones one of its best men.   9.____
    B. That wars go on may be considered somewhat of an inherited curse for posterity to bear.
    C. Either Italian dressing or mayonnaise goes well with lettuce hearts.
    D. Granted that he had the best intentions, his conduct was not above reproach.

10. A. There are two "i's" and two "e's" in privilege.   10.____
    B. There is no use in Harry's brother saying anything about the situation.
    C. I, not you, am to blame for the condition of this desk.
    D. By relentless logic the group was lead to accept the statements of the eloquent stranger.

11. A. "It is one of those cars that go faster than 90 miles an hour," said the salesman.   11.____
    B. Elementary school children are not the only ones who are tardy; it is also true of high school and college students.
    C. My handsome brother who is in college writes that he is "having a wonderful time"; he is, however, not doing too well scholastically.
    D. A number of clerks were drinking coffee during the coffee break; the number of cups they drank was unbelievable.

12. A. He asked what had caused the accident. She replied that she did not know since she had not been present when it had occurred.   12.____
    B. The new party headed by Prime Minister Wilson advocated government for the people, not by the people.
    C. Five hundred yards of cloth are sufficient to do the work satisfactorily, and I plan to work continually until I finish.
    D. She thought it would be all right for her to do the work in advance of the due date owing to the fact that none of the machines was being used by others.

13. A. "Oh! please stop that," he said; but when he looked up, they were nowhere to be seen.   13.____
    B. The president of the company often told us workers of his experiences as a penniless, untrained beginner forty years ago.
    C. The family showed its approval of the plan and decided to leave for Detroit, Michigan, on May 18th, or, if delay was unavoidable, on May 25th.
    D. "I'm not buying," he said, "it's too expensive.

14. A. We expect in the next decade to more than hold our own in our race to the moon.   14.____
    B. The teachers who have been considering the annual promotion plan today gave their report to the principal.
    C. You are likely to find him sitting beside the brook in the park.
    D. I shall have eaten by the time we go if my plans proceed according to schedule.

15. A. If you must know — of course, however, this is a secret — Billy just asked to borrow   15.____
         my car.
     B. The job is over with, and neither my wife nor my children will ever persuade me
         to do it again.
     C. You ought not to have said what you said, and I suggest that you apologize at
         once.
     D. His friends had begun to understand how much he had done for the organiza-
         tion, but then they seemed to forget everything.

16. A. Unlike Bill and me, Ted looks really good in a stylish suit.   16.____
     B. They have good teachers in our high schools; therefore, I plan to become a high
         school teacher.
     C. Do you remember the name of the book? the author? the copyright date? the
         name of the publisher? of the editor?
     D. The secretary and treasurer of the firm intends to hold a meeting with his presi-
         dent within a week or two.

17. A. Foreign films may be interesting, but I do not see them often. I usually prefer listen-   17.____
         ing to music.
     B. Court reporting has always fascinated me, but last spring I went to a lecture by a
         famous reporter. Then I made up my mind to be a reporter.
     C. Haven't I asked you a hundred times to take the damaged typewriter to the repair
         shop which is in the store next to Jones's Candy Store?
     D. Your typewriter should be kept absolutely clean and should be dusted as soon as
         you have completed your day's work.

18. A. The salesmen felt very pleased when they heard the manager say that their sales   18.____
         for the month of July, August, and September were much higher than that for the
         same months the previous year.
     B. Four hundred dollars is too much to pay for these typewriters; I therefore suggest
         that you do some additional shopping before you make a final decision.
     C. John said that he had swum around the lake three times and that he was now eli-
         gible for his swimming certificate.
     D. I recently read "Trade Winds" in <u>The Saturday Review</u>.

19. A. Neither being sufficiently prepared for it, both brothers had to apply for additional   19.____
         training at the technical school.
     B. The question was laid before them, and after weeks of argument it was still
         unsettled.
     C. If all goes satisfactorily — and why shouldn't it? — we shall be in Europe before
         the middle of May
     D. In his first year he was only an office boy, and in his fifth year he was president of
         the company.

20. A. Of all my friends he is the one on whom I can most surely depend.   20.____
     B. We value the Constitution because of it's guarantees to freedom.
     C. The audience was deeply stirred by the actor's performance.
     D. Give the book to whoever comes into the room first.

21. A. Everything was in order: the paper rules, the pencils sharpened, the chairs placed.   21.____
    B. Neither John nor Peter were able to attend the reception .
    C. In April the streets which had been damaged by cold weather were repaired by the workmen.
    D. You may lend my book to the pupil who you think will enjoy it most.

22. A. He fidgeted, like most children do, while the grown-ups were discussing the prob-   22.____
        lem.
    B. I won't go unless you go with me.
    C. Sitting beside the charred ruins of his cabin, the frontiersman told us the story of the attack.
    D. Certainly there can be no objection to the boys' working on a volunteer basis.

23. A. The congregation was dismissed.   23.____
    B. The congregation were deeply moved by the sermon.
    C. What kind of an automobile is that?
    D. His explanation and mine agree.

24. A. There is no danger of him being elected.   24.____
    B. There is no doubt of his election.
    C. John and he are to be the speakers.
    D. John and she are to be the speakers.

25. A. Them that honor me I will honor.   25.____
    B. They that believe in me shall be rewarded.
    C. Who did you see at the meeting?
    D. Whom are you writing to?

KEY (CORRECT ANSWERS)

1.	B		11.	B
2.	A		12.	B
3.	B		13.	D
4.	C		14.	D
5.	D		15.	B
6.	A		16.	B
7.	C		17.	B
8.	C		18.	A
9.	B		19.	A
10.	D		20.	B

21.	B
22.	A
23.	C
24.	A
25.	C

VERBAL & CLERICAL ABILITIES
EXAMINATION SECTION

TEST 1

DIRECTIONS: Read each question carefully. Select the best answer and write the letter in the answer space at the right.

1. PREVIOUS means most nearly
   A. abandoned
   B. timely
   C. former
   D. successive
   E. younger

1._____

2. CONSENSUS means most nearly
   A. accord
   B. abridgment
   C. presumption
   D. quota
   E. exception

2._____

3. LACONIC means most nearly
   A. slothful
   B. concise
   C. punctual
   D. melancholy
   E. indifferent

3._____

4. TRENCHANT means most nearly
   A. urgent
   B. witty
   C. decisive
   D. sharp
   E. merciless

4._____

5. MANDATORY means most nearly
   A. basic
   B. obligatory
   C. discretionary
   D. discriminatory
   E. advisory

5._____

6. OPTION means most nearly
   A. use
   B. choice
   C. value
   D. blame
   E. rule

6._____

7. INNATE means most nearly
    A. eternal
    B. well-developed
    C. native
    D. prospective
    E. understandable

7._____

8. To CONFINE means most nearly to
    A. restrict
    B. hide
    C. eliminate
    D. punish
    E. ruin

8._____

9. A small crane was used to *raise* the heavy parts.
   Raise means most nearly
    A. drag
    B. unload
    C. deliver
    D. lift
    E. guide

9._____

10. The reports were *consolidated* by the secretary.
   Consolidated means most nearly
    A. combined
    B. concluded
    C. distributed
    D. protected
    E. weighed

10._____

11. CROWD is related to PERSONS as FLEET is related to
    A. guns
    B. officers
    C. navy
    D. expedition
    E. ships

11._____

12. SPEEDOMETER is related to POINTER as WATCH is related to
    A. case
    B. hands
    C. dial
    D. numerals
    E. band

12._____

13. PLUMBER is related to WRENCH as PAINTER is related to
    A. brush
    B. pipe
    C. shop
    D. hammer
    E. painting

13._____

14. BODY is related to FOOD as ENGINE is related to   14._____
    A. wheels
    B. smoke
    C. motion
    D. fuel
    E. conductor

15. ABUNDANT is related to CHEAP as SCARCE is related to   15._____
    A. ample
    B. inexpensive
    C. costly
    D. unobtainable
    E. frugal

Reading

16. "One type of advertising on which it is difficult to calculate the return is the radio   16._____
program, offered by so many industries today. The chief return of radio
advertising is goodwill, which industries consider so valuable that they spend
vast sums of money to obtain it."

The quotation BEST supports the statement that radio advertising by industries
    A. is more expensive than other advertising
    B. has its chief value in creating goodwill
    C. is used by all large industries
    D. is of little value
    E. is the most valuable form of advertising

17. "Just as the procedure of a collection department must be clear-cut and definite,   17._____
the steps being taken with the sureness of a skilled chess player, so the various
paragraphs of a collection letter must show clear organization, giving evidence of
a mind that, from the beginning, has had a specific end in view."

The quotation BEST supports the statement that a collection letter should always
    A. show a spirit of sportsmanship
    B. be divided into several paragraphs
    C. express confidence in the debtor
    D. be brief, but courteous
    E. be carefully planned

18. "One of the primary steps in the development of management in any enterprise is   18._____
proper organization. After the business has been conceived and the broad
policies that are to be pursued have been established, before any operating
methods may be devised, at least a skeleton organization must be developed."

The quotation BEST supports the statement that, in industry, some kind of
organization is necessary in order that
    A. the type of enterprise may be decided upon
    B. policies may be established
    C. routine work may be planned
    D. capital may be invested
    E. a manager may be selected

19. "The division of labor into the categories of physical and mental labor is not   19._____
strictly accurate. The labor of even the most unskilled workman calls for the
exercise of certain mental qualities, like attention, memory, and prudence; and
on the other hand, the intellectual effort of the great captains of industry is
associated with a certain amount of waste of tissue."

The quotation BEST supports the statement that
    A. There is no real distinction between physical and mental labor.
    B. Manual labor does not call for so great a waste of tissue as intellectual
        effort does.
    C. The exercise of mental qualities remains the most important feature of
        labor.
    D. Physical and mental labor require use of the same mental qualities.
    E. The difference between various forms of labor is one of degree.

20. "Proper supervision of play involves a recognition of the fact that a happy   20._____
childhood through play is essential to a child's normal growth and personal
development. Self-discipline and right conduct are natural results of a situation in
which a child engages in activities of absorbing interest under wise guidance."

The quotation BEST supports the statement that the proper supervision of play
    A. is of greater benefit to some children than to others
    B. has as its chief purpose training for self-discipline
    C. helps a child to obtain satisfactory results from his recreation
    D. is less essential as a child becomes more absorbed in his play
    E. provides for the natural development of differences in personalities

21. "Alertness and attentiveness are qualities essential for success as a receptionist.   21._____
The work the receptionist performs often takes careful attention under conditions
of stress."

The quotation BEST supports the statement that a receptionist
    A. always works under great strain
    B. cannot be successful unless she memorizes many extensions
    C. must be trained before she can render good service
    D. must be able to work under difficulties
    E. performs more difficult work than do clerical office workers

22. "Probably few people realize, as they drive on a concrete road, that steel is used to keep the surface flat and even, in spite of the weight of busses and trucks. Steel bars, deeply imbedded in the concrete, provide sinews to take the stresses so that they cannot crack the slab or make it wavy."

22._____

The quotation BEST supports the statement that a concrete road
   A. is expensive to build
   B. usually cracks under heavy weights
   C. is used exclusively for heavy traffic
   D. is reinforced with other material

23. "Whenever two groups of people whose interests at the moment conflict meet to discuss a solution of that conflict, there is laid the basis for an interchange of facts and ideas which increases the total range of knowledge of both parties and tends to break down the barrier which their restricted field of information has helped to create."

23._____

The quotation BEST supports the statement that conflicts between two parties may be brought closer to a settlement through
   A. frank acknowledgment of error
   B. the exchange of accusations
   C. gaining a wider knowledge of facts
   D. submitting the dispute to an impartial judge
   E. limiting discussion to plans acceptable to both groups

24. "What constitutes skill in any line of work is not always easy to determine; economy of time must be carefully distinguished from economy of energy, as the quickest method may require the greatest expenditure of muscular effort, and may not be essential or at all desirable."

24._____

The quotation BEST supports the statement that
   A. energy and time cannot both be conserved in the performing of a single task
   B. the most efficiently executed task is not always the one done in the shortest time
   C. if a task requires muscular energy, it is not being performed economically
   D. skill in performing a task should not be acquired at the expense of time
   E. a task is well done when it is performed in the shortest time

25. "The secretarial profession is a very old one and has increased in importance with the passage of time. In modern times, the vast expansion of business and industry has greatly increased the need and opportunities for secretaries, and for the first time in history their number has become large."

25._____

The quotation BEST supports the statement that the secretarial profession
   A. is older than business and industry
   B. did not exist in ancient times
   C. has greatly increased in size
   D. demands higher training than it did formerly
   E. is not in high enough demand

26. "It is difficult to distinguish between bookkeeping and accounting. In attempts to do so, bookkeeping is called the art, and accounting the science, of recording business transactions. Bookkeeping gives the history of the business in a systematic manner; and accounting classifies, analyzes, and interprets the facts thus recorded."

    The quotation BEST supports the statement that
    A. accounting is less systematic than bookkeeping
    B. accounting and bookkeeping are closely related
    C. bookkeeping and accounting cannot be distinguished from one another
    D. bookkeeping has been superseded by accounting
    E. bookkeeping is more practical than accounting

26._____

Spelling. Find which choice is spelled correctly and mark the letter in the space at the right.

27. A. athalete
    B. athlete
    C. athelete
    D. none of the above

27._____

28. A. predesessor
    B. predecesar
    C. predecesser
    D. none of the above

28._____

29. A. occasion
    B. occasion
    C. ocassion
    D. none of the above

29._____

30. A. Mobile, Ala.
    B. Brocton, Mass.
    C. Yeork, Pa.
    D. Sou Falls, S. Dak.
    E. none of the above

30._____

31. A. Brookelin, N.Y.
    B. Alambra, Calif.
    C. Attlanta, Ga.
    D. Joplinn, Mo.
    E. none of the above

31._____

Grammar. Decide which sentence is preferable with respect to grammar and usage suitable for a formal letter or report and mark the letter in the space at the right.

32. A. They do not ordinarily present these kind of reports in detail like this.
    B. Reports like this is not generally given in such great detail.
    C. A report of this kind is not hardly ever given in such detail as this one.
    D. This report is more detailed than what such reports ordinarily are.
    E. A report of this kind is not ordinarily presented in such detail as this one.

32._____

33. A. No other city anywheres in the State has grown so fast as this city.
    B. This city has grown more rapidly than any other city in the State.
    C. No other city in the State has grown as fast or faster than this city.
    D. The growth of this city has been more rapid than any other city in the State.
    E. This city has grown the fastest of all the others in the State.

33._____

34. A. The manager told Mr. Jones and I that we were expected to attend the meeting.
    B. Mr. Jones and I were told by the manager that is was necessary for both of us to have attended the meeting.
    C. In his talk with Mr. Jones and I, the manager explained that our attendance at the meeting was expected.
    D. The manager said that he expected Mr. Jones and me to attend the meeting.
    E. The manager explained to Mr. Jones and myself that it was necessary for us to be present at the meeting.

34._____

35. A. Neither the editor nor his assistant will approve that type of report.
    B. That kind of a report is not acceptable to either the editor or his assistant.
    C. A report of that kind is acceptable to neither the editor or his assistant.
    D. Both the editor and his assistant are sort of unwilling to approve a report like that.
    E. Neither the editor nor his assistant are willing to approve that type of report.

35._____

36. A. I haven't no report on your call yet.
    B. I had ought to receive a report on your call soon.
    C. Can I ring you when I have a report on your call?
    D. Do you want for me to ring as soon as I receive a report on your call?
    E. I do not have any report on your call yet.

36._____

37. A. Our activities this month have been as interesting, if not more interesting than those of any other month this year.
    B. Our activities this year have seldom ever been as interesting as they have been this month.
    C. Our activities this month have been more interesting than those of any other month this year.
    D. Our activities this month have been more interesting, or at least as interesting as those of any month this year.
    E. This month's activities have been more interesting than any previous month during the year.

37._____

38. A. If properly addressed, the letter will reach my mother and I.
    B. The letter had been addressed to myself and my mother.
    C. I believe the letter was addressed to either my mother or I.
    D. My mother's name, as well as mine, was on the letter.
    E. The letter will get to my mother and myself if properly addressed.

    38._____

39. A. Most all these statements have been supported by persons who are reliable and can be depended upon.
    B. The persons which have guaranteed these statements are reliable.
    C. Reliable persons guarantee the facts with regards to the truth of these statements.
    D. These statements can be depended on, for their truth has been guaranteed by reliable persons.
    E. The persons who guarantee these statements are very much reliable.

    39._____

40. A. Brown's & Company employees have recently received increases in salary.
    B. Brown & Company recently increased the salaries of all its employees.
    C. Recently Brown & Company has increased their employees' salaries.
    D. Brown & Company have recently increased the salaries of all its employees.
    E. Brown & Company employees have all been increased in salary.

    40._____

KEY (CORRECT ANSWERS)

1.	C	16.	B	31.	E
2.	A	17.	E	32.	E
3.	B	18.	C	33.	B
4.	D	19.	E	34.	D
5.	B	20.	C	35.	A
6.	B	21.	D	36.	E
7.	C	22.	D	37.	C
8.	A	23.	C	38.	D
9.	D	24.	B	39.	D
10.	A	25.	C	40.	B
11.	E	26.	B		
12.	B	27.	B		
13.	A	28.	D		
14.	D	29.	B		
15.	C	30.	A		

TEST 2

DIRECTIONS: Below are underlined names, followed by alphabetical names. The spaces between names are lettered A, B, C, D, and E. Decide in which space the underlined name belongs and write the letter in the answer space at right.

1. <u>Kessler, Neilson</u>   1._____

    A)_____

      Kessel, Oscar

    B)_____

      Kessinger, D.J.

    C)_____

      Kessler, Karl

    D)_____

      Kessner, Lewis

    E)_____

2. <u>Jones, Jane</u>   2._____

    A)_____

      Goodyear, G.L.

    B)_____

      Haddon, Harry

    C)_____

      Jackson, Mary

    D)_____

      Jenkins, William

    E)_____

3. <u>Olsen, C.C.</u>   3._____

    A)_____

       Olsen, C.A.

    B)_____

       Olsen, C.D.

    C)_____

       Olsen, Charles

    D)_____

       Olsen, Christopher

    E)_____

4. <u>DeMattia, Jessica</u>   4._____

    A)_____

       DeLong, Jesse

    B)_____

       DeMatteo, Jessie

    C)_____

       Derby, Jessie S.

    D)_____

       DeShazo, L.M.

    E)_____

Question 5.

DIRECTIONS: Following are a group of four related sentences, which may or may not be in logical order. Following the sentences are five suggested sequences, lettered A, B, C, D, and E, from which you are to select the one that indicates the best arrangement of sentences. Indicate your choice of letters in the space at right.

5. (1) It must be comparatively scarce, and it should have a stable value. 5._____
   (2) In order to serve satisfactorily as money, a substance must have certain qualities.
   (3) It should also be durable, and its value should be high in proportion to its bulk.
   (4) Gold and silver have been widely used for money because they possess these qualities to a greater extent than do other commodities.

    A. 2-4-1-3
    B. 2-3-1-4
    C. 2-1-4-3
    D. 2-1-3-4
    E. 2-4-3-1

Question 6.

DIRECTIONS: Following is a sentence with an underlined word that is spelled as it is pronounced. Write the correct spelling of the word in the blank. Then decide which one of the suggested answers, A, B, C, or D, is the correct answer to the question, and write the letter in the space at right.

6. The new treasurer uses the same system that his pred-eh-sess´-urr did. 6._____
   In the correct spelling, _____, what is the tenth letter?
    A. s
    B. e
    C. o
    D. none of the above

Questions 7-11.

DIRECTIONS: In each line there are three names or numbers that are much alike. Compare the three names or numbers and decide which ones are exactly alike. Fill in the letter
- A. if ALL THREE names or number are exactly ALIKE
- B. if only the FIRST and SECOND names or numbers are exactly ALIKE
- C. if only the FIRST and THIRD names or numbers are exactly ALIKE
- D. if only the SECOND and THIRD names or numbers are exactly ALIKE
- E. if ALL THREE names or numbers are DIFFERENT

7. Davis Hazen	David Hozen	David Hazen	7._____
8. Lois Appel	Lois Appel	Lois Apfel	8._____
9. June Allan	Jane Allan	Jane Allan	9._____
10. 10235	10235	10235	10._____
11. 32614	32164	32614	11._____

Questions 12-22.

DIRECTIONS: Compute the answer and compare it with suggested answers. Mark the letter in the space at right.

12. Add: 12._____

```
 963
 257
+416
```

- A. 1,516
- B. 1,526
- C. 1,636
- D. 1,726
- E. none of the above

13. Add: 13._____

    22
  +33

    A. 44
    B. 45
    C. 54
    D. 55
    E. none of the above

14. Add: 14._____

  5.2 + .96 + 47.0 =

    A. 19.5
    B. 48.48
    C. 53.16
    D. 42.98
    E. none of the above

15. Subtract: 15._____

    24
  - 3

    A. 20
    B. 21
    C. 27
    D. 29
    E. none of the above

16. Subtract: 16._____

    33
  -8

    A. 25
    B. 26
    C. 35
    D. 36
    E. none of the above

17. Subtract: 17._____

    219
  -110

    A. 99
    B. 109
    C. 199
    D. 189
    E. none of the above

18. Multiply: 18._____

    25
   X5

    A. 100
    B. 115
    C. 125
    D. 135
    E. none of the above

19. Multiply: 19._____

    45
   X5

    A. 200
    B. 215
    C. 225
    D. 235
    E. none of the above

20. 47% of 538 =   20._____

    A. 11.45
    B. 252.86
    C. 285.14
    D. 265.66
    E. none of the above

21. Divide: 21._____

$6\overline{)126}$

    A. 20
    B. 22
    C. 24
    D. 26
    E. none of the above

22. Divide: 22._____

40 ⟌ 1,208

    A. 3
    B. 30
    C. 33
    D. 40
    E. none of the above

Questions 23-32.

DIRECTIONS: For each question, find which one of the suggested answers
               contains numbers and letters all of which appear in that question.
               These numbers and letters may be in any order in the question, but
               all four must appear. If neither A, B, C, nor D fits, mark E for that
               question. Mark your answer in the space at right.

23. 8 N K 9 G T 4 6   23._____

24. T 9 7 Z 6 L 3 K   24._____

25. Z 7 G K 3 9 8 N   25._____

26. 3 K 9 4 6 G Z L   26._____

27. Z N 7 3 8 K T 9   27._____

Suggested Answers for Questions 23-27:
A = 7, 9, G, K
B = 8, 9, T, Z
C = 6, 7, K, Z
D = 6, 8, G, T
E = none of the above

28. 2 3 P 6 V Z 4 L   28._____

29. T 7 4 3 P Z 9 G   29._____

30. 6 N G Z 3 9 P 7   30._____

31. 9 6 P 4 N G Z 2   31._____

32. 4 9 7 T L P 3 V   32._____

Suggested Answers for Questions 28-32:
A = 3, 6, G, P
B = 3, 7, P, V
C = 4, 6, V, Z
D = 4, 7, G, Z
E = none of the above

Questions 33-34.

DIRECTIONS: Consider the figures below to be correct figures.

The figures below are incorrect because the slope of one of the lines differs from the slope in one of the similar correct figures.

The following questions show four correct figures and one incorrect figure. Select the letter of the incorrect figure and mark the letter in the space at right.

33.      33._____

     A   B   C   D   E

34.

_____ _____ _____ _____ _____
_____ _____ _____ _____ _____

  A   B   C   D   E

34._____

Questions 35-48

DIRECTIONS: On the left is a series of numbers or letters which follow some
definite order. Pick the answer that follows the order and write the
letter of your choice in the space at right.

35. x c x d x e x

35._____

    A. f x
    B. f g
    C. x f
    D. e f
    E. x g

36. a b d c e f h

36._____

    A. c h
    B. i g
    C. g i
    D. k l
    E. i h

37. 15 14 13 12 11 10 9

37._____

    A. 2 1
    B. 17 16
    C. 8 9
    D. 8 7
    E. 9 8

38. 20 20 21 21 22 22 23

38._____

    A. 23 23
    B. 23 24
    C. 19 19
    D. 22 23
    E. 21 22

39. 17 3 17 4 17 5 17

    A. 6 17
    B. 6 7
    C. 17 6
    D. 5 6
    E. 17 7

40. 1 2 4 5 7 8 10

    A. 11 12
    B. 12 14
    C. 10 13
    D. 12 13
    E. 11 13

41. 21 21 20 20 19 19 18

    A. 18 18
    B. 18 17
    C. 17 18
    D. 17 17
    E. 18 19

42. 1 20 3 19 5 18 7

    A. 8 9
    B. 8 17
    C. 17 10
    D. 17 9
    E. 9 18

43. 30 2 28 4 26 6 24

    A. 23 9
    B. 26 8
    C. 8 9
    D. 26 22
    E. 8 22

44. 5 6 20 7 8 19 9

    A. 10 18
    B. 18 17
    C. 10 17
    D. 18 19
    E. 10 11

39._____

40._____

41._____

42._____

43._____

44._____

45. 9 10 1 11 12 2 13

45._____

    A. 2 14
    B. 3 14
    C. 14 3
    D. 14 15
    E. 14 1

46. 4 6 9 11 14 16 19

46._____

    A. 21 24
    B. 22 25
    C. 20 22
    D. 21 23
    E. 22 24

47. 8 8 1 10 10 3 12

47._____

    A. 13 13
    B. 12 5
    C. 12 4
    D. 13 5
    E. 4 12

48. 20 21 23 24 27 28 32 33 38 39

48._____

    A. 45 46
    B. 45 54
    C. 44 45
    D. 44 49
    E. 40 46

Questions 49-53.

DIRECTIONS: Each of the following questions consists of two sets of symbols. Find the one rule that (a) explains the similarity of the symbols within each set, and (b) also explains the difference between the sets. Among the five suggested answers, find the symbol that can best be substituted for the question mark in the second set. In all these questions you will find details that have nothing to do with the principle of the question: to find the similarity between the symbols within a set and the difference between the sets. Mark the letter of your answer choice in the space at right.

49.   SET 1   SET 2

49._____

50.

SET 1   SET 2

50._____

51.

SET 1   SET 2

51._____

52.

SET 1   SET 2

52._____

53.

SET 1   SET 2

53._____

Questions 54-56.

DIRECTIONS: Following are word problems. Mark the letter of the answer you choose in the space at right.

54. The safety rules of Factory X require that the operator of a certain machine take a rest period of 15 minutes after working 2 consecutive hours. If the workday consists of 3 3/4 hours in the morning, 30 minutes for lunch, and 4 1/4 hours in the afternoon, a job that requires 29 machine hours to complete will take the operator of this machine

54._____

    A. less than 3 days
    B. between 3 and 3 1/2 days
    C. 3 1/2 days
    D. between 3 1/2 and 4 days
    E. 4 days or longer

55. The weight of water is 62.4 pounds per cubic foot. What is the weight of the water that fills a rectangular container 6 inches by 6 inches by 1 foot?

55._____

    A. 1.7 pounds
    B. 10.4 pounds
    C. 31.2 pounds
    D. 249.6 pounds
    E. none of the above

56. The inventor of a machine which operates by solar heat claims that it accumulates heat in the daytime at the rate of 10 units an hour on sunny days and 3 units an hour on cloudy days. During rain there is no accumulation of heat. In July there were 22 hours of daylight rain and 42 hours of cloudy daylight. Assuming on the average 13 hours of daylight per day in July, how many units should the machine have accumulated that month?

    A. 339
    B. 403
    C. 3,516
    D. 3,810
    E. none of the above

56._____

Questions 57-60

DIRECTIONS: Refer to the tables and charts to answer the following questions, and mark the letter of the correct answer in the space at right.

CONSUMPTION OF FUELS FOR PRODUCTION OF ELECTRIC ENERGY
1998-2003

	1998	1999	2000	2001	2002	2003
Bituminous and lignite coal (thousands short tons)	165,794	173,882	179,612	190,941	200,193	223,162
Anthracite coal (thousands short tons)	2,629	2,751	2,509	2,297	2,139	2,289
Fuel oil (thousands of barrels)	88,263	85,340	85,736	85,768	93,314	101,162
Gas (millions of cubic feet)	1,628,509	1,724,762	1,825,117	1,955,974	2,144,473	2,321,889

57. In which year did the greatest number of kinds of fuel show an increase in consumption over that of the preceding year?

    A. 1999
    B. 2000
    C. 2001
    D. 2002
    E. 2003

57._____

58. The total amount of coal consumed in the production of electric energy in 2003   58._____
    was approximately what percent of that consumed in 1998?

    A. 57%
    B. 75%
    C. 134%
    D. 150%
    E. 168%

POPULATION MOVEMENT TO AND FROM COUNTY X
1982 TO 2003

MOVING TO COUNTY -----------
MOVING FROM COUNTY ————

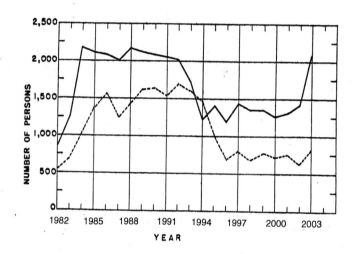

59. The graph above indicates that, with respect to County X, migratory activities   59._____
    during the period from 1982 to 2003 tended mostly to result in

    A. population gains
    B. population losses
    C. gradual stabilization of population
    D. irregular fluctuations in population without consistent direction
    E. cycles of alternating losses and gains in population which tended to
       balance each other

60. The ratio of the number of persons who left to the number who entered County X   60._____
    in 2003 is approximately

    A. 12 to 7
    B. 7 to 12
    C. 2 to 5
    D. 5 to 2
    E. 5 to 3

KEY (CORRECT ANSWERS)

1.	D	16.	A	31.	E	46.	A
2.	E	17.	B	32.	B	47.	B
3.	B	18.	C	33.	A	48.	A
4.	C	19.	C	34.	B	49.	E
5.	D	20.	B	35.	A	50.	D
6.	C	21.	E	36.	C	51.	B
7.	E	22.	E	37.	D	52.	E
8.	B	23.	D	38.	B	53.	B
9.	D	24.	C	39.	A	54.	D
10.	A	25.	A	40.	E	55.	E
11.	C	26.	E	41.	B	56.	C
12.	C	27.	B	42.	D	57.	E
13.	D	28.	C	43.	E	58.	C
14.	C	29.	D	44.	A	59.	B
15.	B	30.	A	45.	C	60.	D

CLERICAL ABILITIES

EXAMINATION SECTION
TEST 1

DIRECTIONS: Each question or incomplete statement is followed by several suggested answers or completions. Select the one that BEST answers the question or completes the statement. *PRINT THE LETTER OF THE CORRECT ANSWER IN THE SPACE AT THE RIGHT.*

Questions 1-4.

DIRECTIONS: Questions 1 through 4 are to be answered on the basis of the information given below.

The most commonly used filing system and the one that is easiest to learn is alphabetical filing. This involves putting records in an A to Z order, according to the letters of the alphabet. The name of a person is filed by using the following order: first, the surname or last name; second, the first name; third, the middle name or middle initial. For example, *Henry C. Young* is filed under *Y* and thereafter under *Young, Henry C.* The name of a company is filed in the same way. For example, *Long Cabinet Co.* is filed under *L,* while *John T. Long Cabinet Co.* is filed under *L* and thereafter under *Long., John T. Cabinet Co.*

1. The one of the following which lists the names of persons in the CORRECT alphabetical order is:

    A. Mary Carrie, Helen Carrol, James Carson, John Carter
    B. James Carson, Mary Carrie, John Carter, Helen Carrol
    C. Helen Carrol, James Carson, John Carter, Mary Carrie
    D. John Carter, Helen Carrol, Mary Carrie, James Carson

1._____

2. The one of the following which lists the names of persons in the CORRECT alphabetical order is:

    A. Jones, John C.; Jones, John A.; Jones, John P.; Jones, John K.
    B. Jones, John P.; Jones, John K.; Jones, John C.; Jones, John A.
    C. Jones, John A.; Jones, John C.; Jones, John K.; Jones, John P.
    D. Jones, John K.; Jones, John C.; Jones, John A.; Jones, John P.

2._____

3. The one of the following which lists the names of the companies in the CORRECT alphabetical order is:

    A. Blane Co., Blake Co., Block Co., Blear Co.
    B. Blake Co., Blane Co., Blear Co., Block Co.
    C. Block Co., Blear Co., Blane Co., Blake Co.
    D. Blear Co., Blake Co., Blane Co., Block Co.

3._____

4. You are to return to the file an index card on *Barry C. Wayne Materials and Supplies Co.* Of the following, the CORRECT alphabetical group that you should return the index card to is

    A. A to G   B. H to M   C. N to S   D. T to Z

4._____

Questions 5-10.

DIRECTIONS: In each of Questions 5 through 10, the names of four people are given. For each question, choose as your answer the one of the four names given which should be filed FIRST according to the usual system of alphabetical filing of names, as described in the following paragraph.

In filing names, you must start with the last name. Names are filed in order of the first letter of the last name, then the second letter, etc. Therefore, BAILY would be filed before BROWN, which would be filed before COLT. A name with fewer letters of the same type comes first; i.e., Smith before Smithe. If the last names are the same, the names are filed alphabetically by the first name. If the first name is an initial, a name with an initial would come before a first name that starts with the same letter as the initial. Therefore, I. BROWN would come before IRA BROWN. Finally, if both last name and first name are the same, the name would be filed alphabetically by the middle name, once again an initial coming before a middle name which starts with the same letter as the initial. If there is no middle name at all, the name would come before those with middle initials or names.

Sample Question;   A.   Lester Daniels
B.   William Dancer
C.   Nathan Danzig
D.   Dan Lester

The last names beginning with D are filed before the last name beginning with L. Since DANIELS, DANCER, and DANZIG all begin with the same three letters, you must look at the fourth letter of the last name to determine which name should be filed first. C comes before I or Z in the alphabet, so DANCER is filed before DANIELS or DANZIG. Therefore, the answer to the above sample question is B.

5.   A.   Scott Biala
   B.   Mary Byala
   C.   Martin Baylor
   D.   Francis Bauer

     5.___

6.   A.   Howard J. Black
   B.   Howard Black
   C.   J. Howard Black
   D.   John H. Black

     6.___

7.   A.   Theodora Garth Kingston
   B.   Theadore Barth Kingston
   C.   Thomas Kingston
   D.   Thomas T. Kingston

     7.___

8.   A.   Paulette Mary Huerta
   B.   Paul M. Huerta
   C.   Paulette L. Huerta
   D.   Peter A. Huerta

     8.___

9. A. Martha Hunt Morgan
    B. Martin Hunt Morgan
    C. Mary H. Morgan
    D. Martine H. Morgan

9.____

10. A. James T. Meerschaum
    B. James M. Mershum
    C. James F. Mearshaum
    D. James N. Meshum

10.____

Questions 11-14.

DIRECTIONS: Questions 11 through 14 are to be answered SOLELY on the basis of the following information.

You are required to file various documents in file drawers which are labeled according to the following pattern:

DOCUMENTS

MEMOS		LETTERS	
File	Subject	File	Subject
84PM1 - (A-L)		84PC1 - (A-L)	
84PM2 - (M-Z)		84PC2 - (M-Z)	

REPORTS		INQUIRIES	
File	Subject	File	Subject
84PR1 - (A-L)		84PQ1 - (A-L)	
84PR2 - (M-Z)		84PQ2 - (M-Z)	

11. A letter dealing with a burglary should be filed in the drawer labeled

    A. 84PM1   B. 84PC1   C. 84PR1   D. 84PQ2

11.____

12. A report on Statistics should be found in the drawer labeled

    A. 84PM1   B. 84PC2   C. 84PR2   D. 84PQ2

12.____

13. An inquiry is received about parade permit procedures. It should be filed in the drawer labeled

    A. 84PM2   B. 84PC1   C. 84PR1   D. 84PQ2

13.____

14. A police officer has a question about a robbery report you filed. You should pull this file from the drawer labeled

    A. 84PM1   B. 84PM2   C. 84PR1   D. 84PR2

14.____

Questions 15-22.

DIRECTIONS: Each of Questions 15 through 22 consists of four or six numbered names. For each question, choose the option (A, B, C, or D) which indicates the order in which the names should be filed in accordance with the following filing instructions:
   - File alphabetically according to last name, then first name, then middle initial.
   - File according to each successive letter within a name.

- When comparing two names in which, the letters in the longer name are identical to the corresponding letters in the shorter name, the shorter name is filed first.
- When the last names are the same, initials are always filed before names beginning with the same letter.

15.   I.   Ralph Robinson   15.__
    II. Alfred Ross
   III. Luis Robles
   IV. James Roberts

The CORRECT filing sequence for the above names should be

  A. IV, II, I, III   B. I, IV, III, II
  C. III, IV, I, II   D. IV, I, III, II

16.   I.   Irwin Goodwin   16.__
    II. Inez Gonzalez
   III. Irene Goodman
   IV. Ira S. Goodwin
   V.   Ruth I. Goldstein
   VI. M.B. Goodman

The CORRECT filing sequence for the above names should be

  A. V, II, I, IV, III, VI   B. V, II, VI, III, IV, I
  C. V, II, III, VI, IV, I   D. V, II, III, VI, I, IV

17.   I.   George Allan   17.__
    II. Gregory Allen
   III. Gary Allen
   IV. George Allen

The CORRECT filing sequence for the above names should be

  A. IV, III, I, II   B. I, IV, II, III
  C. III, IV, I, II   D. I, III, IV, II

18.   I.   Simon Kauffman   18.__
    II. Leo Kaufman
   III. Robert Kaufmann
   IV. Paul Kauffmann

The CORRECT filing sequence for the above names should be

  A. I, IV, II, III   B. II, IV, III, I
  C. III, II, IV, I   D. I, II, III, IV

19.   I.   Roberta Williams   19.__
    II. Robin Wilson
   III. Roberta Wilson
   IV. Robin Williams

The CORRECT filing sequence for the above names should be

  A. III, II, IV, I   B. I, IV, III, II
  C. I, II, III, IV   D. III, I, II, IV

20.
    I.   Lawrence Shultz
    II.   Albert Schultz
    III. Theodore Schwartz
    IV. Thomas Schwarz
    V.   Alvin Schultz
    VI. Leonard Shultz

20.____

The CORRECT filing sequence for the above names should be

A. II, V, III, IV, I, VI
C. II, V, I, VI, III, IV
B. IV, III, V, I, II, VI
D. I, VI, II, V, III, IV

21.
    I.   McArdle
    II.   Mayer
    III. Maletz
    IV. McNiff
    V.   Meyer
    VI. MacMahon

21.____

The CORRECT filing sequence for the above names should be

A. I, IV, VI, III, II, V
C. VI, III, II, I, IV, V
B. II, I, IV, VI, III, V
D. VI, III, II, V, I, IV

22.
    I.   Jack E. Johnson
    II.   R.H. Jackson
    III. Bertha Jackson
    IV. J.T. Johnson
    V.   Ann Johns
    VI. John Jacobs

22.____

The CORRECT filing sequence for the above names should be

A. II, III, VI, V, IV, I
C. VI, II, III, I, V, IV
B. III, II, VI, V, IV, I
D. III, II, VI, IV, V, I

Questions 23-30.

DIRECTIONS: The code table below shows 10 letters with matching numbers. For each question, there are three sets of letters. Each set of letters is followed by a set of numbers which may or may not match their correct letter according to the code table. For each question, check all three sets of letters and numbers and mark your answer:

    A. if no pairs are correctly matched
    B. if only one pair is correctly matched
    C. if only two pairs are correctly matched
    D. if all three pairs are correctly matched

CODE TABLE

T	M	V	D	S	P	R	G	B	H
1	2	3	4	5	6	7	8	9	0

Sample Question: TMVDSP - 123456
                     RGBHTM - 789011
                     DSPRGB - 256789

In the sample question above, the first set of numbers correctly matches its set of letters. But the second and third pairs contain mistakes. In the second pair, M is incorrectly matched with number 1. According to the code table, letter M should be correctly matched with number 2. In the third pair, the letter D is incorrectly matched with number 2. According to the code table, letter D should be correctly matched with number 4. Since only one of the pairs is correctly matched, the answer to this sample question is B.

23. RSBMRM 759262
    GDSRVH 845730
    VDBRTM 349713

23.___

24. TGVSDR 183247
    SMHRDP 520647
    TRMHSR 172057

24.___

25. DSPRGM 456782
    MVDBHT 234902
    HPMDBT 062491

25.___

26. BVPTRD 936184
    GDPHMB 807029
    GMRHMV 827032

26.___

27. MGVRSH 283750
    TRDMBS 174295
    SPRMGV 567283

27.___

28. SGBSDM 489542
    MGHPTM 290612
    MPBMHT 269301

28.___

29. TDPBHM 146902
    VPBMRS 369275
    GDMBHM 842902

29.___

30. MVPTBV 236194
    PDRTMB 647128
    BGTMSM 981232

30.___

KEY (CORRECT ANSWERS)

1.	A	11.	B	21.	C
2.	C	12.	C	22.	B
3.	B	13.	D	23.	B
4.	D	14.	D	24.	B
5.	D	15.	D	25.	C
6.	B	16.	C	26.	A
7.	B	17.	D	27.	D
8.	B	18.	A	28.	A
9.	A	19.	B	29.	D
10.	C	20.	A	30.	A

TEST 2

DIRECTIONS: Each question or incomplete statement is followed by several suggested answers or completions. Select the one that BEST answers the question or completes the statement. *PRINT THE LETTER OF THE CORRECT ANSWER IN THE SPACE AT THE RIGHT.*

Questions 1-10.

DIRECTIONS: Questions 1 through 10 each consists of two columns, each containing four lines of names, numbers and/or addresses. For each question, compare the lines in Column I with the lines in Column II to see if they match exactly, and mark your answer A, B, C, or D, according to the following instructions:
- A. all four lines match exactly
- B. only three lines match exactly
- C. only two lines match exactly
- D. only one line matches exactly

	COLUMN I	COLUMN II	
1.	I. Earl Hodgson II. 1409870 III. Shore Ave. IV. Macon Rd.	Earl Hodgson 1408970 Schore Ave. Macon Rd.	1.____
2.	I. 9671485 II. 470 Astor Court III. Halprin, Phillip IV. Frank D. Poliseo	9671485 470 Astor Court Halperin, Phillip Frank D. Poliseo	2.____
3.	I. Tandem Associates II. 144-17 Northern Blvd. III. Alberta Forchi IV. Kings Park, NY 10751	Tandom Associates 144 17 Northern Blvd. Albert Forchi Kings Point, NY 10751	3.____
4.	I. Bertha C. McCormack II. Clayton, MO. III. 976-4242 IV. New City, NY 10951	Bertha C. McCormack Clayton, MO. 976-4242 New City, NY 10951	4.____
5.	I. George C. Morill II. Columbia, SC 29201 III. Louis Ingham IV. 3406 Forest Ave.	George C. Morrill Columbia, SD 29201 Louis Ingham 3406 Forest Ave.	5.____
6.	I. 506 S. Elliott P1. II. Herbert Hall III. 4712 Rockaway Pkway IV. 169 E. 7 St.	506 S. Elliott P1. Hurbert Hall 4712 Rockaway Pkway 169 E. 7 St.	6.____

	COLUMN I	COLUMN II	

7.
    I.   345 Park Ave.   345 Park P1.   7._____
    II.   Colman Oven Corp.   Coleman Oven Corp.
    III.   Robert Conte   Robert Conti
    IV.   6179846   6179846

8.
    I.   Grigori Schierber   Grigori Schierber   8._____
    II.   Des Moines, Iowa   Des Moines, Iowa
    III.   Gouverneur Hospital   Gouverneur Hospital
    IV.   91-35 Cresskill P1.   91-35 Cresskill P1.

9.
    I.   Jeffery Janssen   Jeffrey Janssen   9._____
    II.   8041071   8041071
    III.   40 Rockefeller Plaza   40 Rockafeller Plaza
    IV.   407 6 St.   406 7 St.

10.
    I.   5971996   5871996   10._____
    II.   3113 Knickerbocker Ave.   3113 Knickerbocker Ave.
    III.   8434 Boston Post Rd.   8424 Boston Post Rd.
    IV.   Penn Station   Penn Station

Questions 11-14.

DIRECTIONS: Questions 11 through 14 are to be answered by looking at the four groups of names and addresses listed below (I, II, III, and IV) and then finding out the number of groups that have their corresponding numbered lines exactly the same.

GROUP I	GROUP II
Line 1. Richmond General Hospital	Richman General Hospital
Line 2. Geriatric Clinic	Geriatric Clinic
Line 3. 3975 Paerdegat St.	3975 Peardegat St.
Line 4 Loudonville, New York 11538	Londonville, New York 11538

GROUP III	GROUP IV
Line 1. Richmond General Hospital	Richmend General Hospital
Line 2. Geriatric Clinic	Geriatric Clinic
Line 3. 3795 Paerdegat St.	3975 Paerdegat St.
Line 4. Loudonville, New York 11358	Loudonville, New York 11538

11.   In how many groups is line one exactly the same?   11._____

    A. Two   B. Three   C. Four   D. None

12.   In how many groups is line two exactly the same?   12._____

    A. Two   B. Three   C. Four   D. None

13.   In how many groups is line three exactly the same?   13._____

    A. Two   B. Three   C. Four   D. None

14. In how many groups is line four exactly the same?   14.___

   A. Two   B. Three   C. Four   D. None

Questions 15-18.

DIRECTIONS: Each of Questions 15 through 18 has two lists of names and addresses. Each list contains three sets of names and addresses. Check each of the three sets in the list on the right to see if they are the same as the corresponding set in the list on the left. Mark your answers:
    A. if none of the sets in the right list are the same as those in the left list
    B. if only one of the sets in the right list is the same as those in the left list
    C. if only two of the sets in the right list are the same as those in the left list
    D. if all three sets in the right list are the same as those in the left list

15.   Mary T. Berlinger   Mary T. Berlinger   15.___
            2351 Hampton St.   2351 Hampton St.
            Monsey, N.Y. 20117   Monsey, N.Y. 20117

            Eduardo Benes   Eduardo Benes
            473 Kingston Avenue   473 Kingston Avenue
            Central Islip, N.Y. 11734   Central Islip, N.Y. 11734

            Alan Carrington Fuchs 17 Gnarled   Alan Carrington Fuchs 17 Gnarled
            Hollow Road Los Angeles, CA   Hollow Road Los Angeles, CA
            91635   91685

16.   David John Jacobson   David John Jacobson   16.___
            178 35 St. Apt. 4C   178 53 St. Apt. 4C
            New York, N.Y. 00927   New York, N.Y. 00927

            Ann-Marie Calonella   Ann-Marie Calonella
            7243 South Ridge Blvd.   7243 South Ridge Blvd.
            Bakersfield, CA 96714   Bakersfield, CA 96714

            Pauline M. Thompson   Pauline M. Thomson 872 Linden
            872 Linden Ave. Houston,   Ave. Houston, Texas 70321
            Texas 70321

17.   Chester LeRoy Masterton   Chester LeRoy Masterson   17.___
            152 Lacy Rd.   152 Lacy Rd.
            Kankakee, 111. 54532   Kankakee, 111. 54532

            William Maloney   William Maloney
            S. LaCrosse Pla.   S. LaCross Pla.
            Wausau, Wisconsin 52146   Wausau, Wisconsin 52146

            Cynthia V. Barnes   Cynthia V. Barnes
            16 Pines Rd.   16 Pines Rd.
            Greenpoint, Miss. 20376   Greenpoint, Miss. 20376

18.
Marcel Jean Frontenac
8 Burton On The Water
Calender, Me. 01471

J. Scott Marsden
174 S. Tipton St.
Cleveland, Ohio

Lawrence T. Haney
171 McDonough St.
Decatur, Ga. 31304

Marcel Jean Frontenac
6 Burton On The Water
Calender, Me. 01471

J. Scott Marsden
174 Tipton St.
Cleveland, Ohio

Lawrence T. Haney
171 McDonough St.
Decatur, Ga. 31304

18.____

Questions 19-26.

DIRECTIONS: Each of Questions 19 through 26 has two lists of numbers. Each list contains three sets of numbers. Check each of the three sets in the list on the right to see if they are the same as the corresponding set in the list on the left. Mark your answers:
   A. if none of the sets in the right list are the same as those in the left list
   B. if only one of the sets in the right list is the same as those in the left list
   C. if only two of the sets in the right list are the same as those in the left list
   D. if all three sets in the right list are the same as those in the left list

19. 7354183476
4474747744
57914302311

7354983476
4474747774
57914302311

19.____

20. 7143592185
8344517699
9178531263

7143892185
8344518699
9178531263

20.____

21. 2572114731
8806835476
8255831246

257214731
8806835476
8255831246

21.____

22. 331476853821
6976658532996
3766042113715

331476858621
6976655832996
3766042113745

22.____

23. 8806663315
74477138449
211756663666

8806663315
74477138449
211756663666

23.____

24. 990006966996
53022219743
4171171117717

99000696996
53022219843
4171171177717

24.____

25. 24400222433004
5300030055000355
20000075532002022

24400222433004
5300030055500355
20000075532002022

25.____

26. 611166640660001116   61116664066001116   26.__
     711130011700110 0733   7111300117001100733
     26666446664476518   26666446664476518

Questions 27-30.

DIRECTIONS: Questions 27 through 30 are to be answered by picking the answer which is in the correct numerical order, from the lowest number to the highest number, in each question.z

27. A. 44533, 44518, 44516, 44547   27.__
     B. 44516, 44518, 44533, 44547
     C. 44547, 44533, 44518, 44516
     D. 44518, 44516, 44547, 44533

28. A. 95587, 95593, 95601, 95620   28.__
     B. 95601, 95620, 95587, 95593
     C. 95593, 95587, 95601, 95620
     D. 95620, 95601, 95593, 95587

29. A. 232212, 232208, 232232, 232223   29.__
     B. 232208, 232223, 232212, 232232
     C. 232208, 232212, 232223, 232232
     D. 232223, 232232, 232208, 232212

30. A. 113419, 113521, 113462, 113588   30.__
     B. 113588, 113462, 113521, 113419
     C. 113521, 113588, 113419, 113462
     D. 113419, 113462, 113521, 113588

KEY (CORRECT ANSWERS)

1.	C	11.	A	21.	C
2.	B	12.	C	22.	A
3.	D	13.	A	23.	D
4.	A	14.	A	24.	A
5.	C	15.	C	25.	C
6.	B	16.	B	26.	C
7.	D	17.	B	27.	B
8.	A	18.	B	28.	A
9.	D	19.	B	29.	C
10.	C	20.	B	30.	D

RECORD KEEPING
EXAMINATION SECTION
TEST 1

DIRECTIONS: Each question or incomplete statement is followed by several suggested answers or completions. Select the one that BEST answers the question or completes the statement. *PRINT THE LETTER OF THE CORRECT ANSWER IN THE SPACE AT THE RIGHT.*

Questions 1-7.

DIRECTIONS: In answering Questions 1 through 7, use the following master list. For each question, determine where the name would fit on the master list. Each answer choice indicates right before or after the name in the answer choice.

Aaron, Jane
Armstead, Brendan
Bailey, Charles
Dent, Ricardo
Grant, Mark
Mars, Justin
Methieu, Justine
Parker, Cathy
Sampson, Suzy
Thomas, Heather

1. Schmidt, William
   A. Right before Cathy Parker
   B. Right after Heather Thomas
   C. Right after Suzy Sampson
   D. Right before Ricardo Dent

1.____

2. Asanti, Kendall
   A. Right before Jane Aaron
   B. Right after Charles Bailey
   C. Right before Justine Methieu
   D. Right after Brendan Armstead

2.____

3. O'Brien, Daniel
   A. Right after Justine Methieu
   B. Right before Jane Aaron
   C. Right after Mark Grant
   D. Right before Suzy Sampson

3.____

4. Marrow, Alison
   A. Right before Cathy Parker
   B. Right before Justin Mars
   C. Right after Mark Grant
   D. Right after Heather Thomas

4.____

5. Grantt, Marissa
   A. Right before Mark Grant
   B. Right after Mark Grant
   C. Right after Justin Mars
   D. Right before Suzy Sampson

5.____

6. Thompson, Heath   6.____
   A. Right after Justin Mars   B. Right before Suzy Sampson
   C. Right after Heather Thomas   D. Right before Cathy Parker

DIRECTIONS: Before answering Question 7, add in all of the names from Questions 1 through
            6. Then fit the name in alphabetical order based on the new list.

7. Francisco, Mildred   7.____
   A. Right before Mark Grant   B. Right after Marissa Grantt
   C. Right before Alison Marrow   D. Right after Kendall Asanti

Questions 8-10.

DIRECTIONS: In answering Questions 8 through 10, compare each pair of names and
            addresses. Indicate whether they are the same or different in any way.

8. William H. Pratt, J.D.   William H. Pratt, J.D.   8.____
   Attourney at Law   Attorney at Law
   A. No differences   B. 1 difference
   C. 2 differences   D. 3 differences

9. 1303 Theater Drive,; Apt. 3-B   1330 Theatre Drive,; Apt. 3-B   9.____
   A. No differences   B. 1 difference
   C. 2 differences   D. 3 differences

10. Petersdorff, Briana and Mary   Petersdorff, Briana and Mary   10.____
    A. No differences   B. 1 difference
    C. 2 differences   D. 3 differences

11. Which of the following words, if any, are misspelled?   11.____
    A. Affordable   B. Circumstansial
    C. Legalese   D. None of the above

Questions 12-13.

DIRECTIONS: Questions 12 and 13 are to be answered on the basis of the following table.

Standardized Test Results for High School Students in District #1230

	English	Math	Science	Reading
High School 1	21	22	15	18
High School 2	12	16	13	15
High School 3	16	181	21	17
High School 4	19	14	15	16

The scores for each high school in the district were averaged out and listed for each
subject tested. Scores of 0-10 are significantly below College Readiness Standards. 11-15 are
below College Readiness, 16-20 meet College Readiness, and 21-25 are above College
Readiness.

12. If the high schools need to meet or exceed in at least half the categories
    in order to NOT be considered "at risk," which schools are considered "at risk"?   12.____
    A. High School 2   B. High School 3
    C. High School 4   D. Both A and C

13. What percentage of subjects did the district as a whole meet or exceed   13.____
    College Readiness standards?
    A. 25%   B. 50%   C. 75%   D. 100%

Questions 14-15.

DIRECTIONS: Questions 14 and 15 are to be answered on the basis of the following
              information.

You have seven employees working as a part of your team: Austin, Emily, Jeremy,
Christina, Martin, Harriet, and Steve. You have just sent an e-mail informing them that
there will be a mandatory training session next week. To ensure that work still gets done,
you are offering the training twice during the week: once on Tuesday and also on
Thursday. This way half the employees will still be working while the other half attend the
training. The only other issue is that Jeremy doesn't work on Tuesdays and Harriet
doesn't work on Thursdays due to compressed work schedules.

14. Which of the following is a possible attendance roster for the first training   14.____
    session?
    A. Emily, Jeremy, Steve   B. Steve, Christina, Harriet
    C. Harriet, Jeremy, Austin   D. Steve, Martin, Jeremy

15. If Harriet, Christina, and Steve attend the training session on Tuesday, which   15.____
    of the following is a possible roster for Thursday's training session?
    A. Jeremy, Emily, and Austin   B. Emily, Martin, and Harriet
    C. Austin, Christina, and Emily   D. Jeremy, Emily, and Steve

Questions 16-20.

DIRECTIONS: In answering Questions 16 through 20, you will be given a word and will need
              to choose the answer choice that is MOST similar or different to the word.

16. Which word means the SAME as *annual*?   16.____
    A. Monthly   B. Usually   C. Yearly   D. Constantly

17. Which word means the SAME as *effort*?   17.____
    A. Energy   B. Equate   C. Cherish   D. Commence

18. Which word means the OPPOSITE of *forlorn*?   18.____
    A. Neglected   B. Lethargy   C. Optimistic   D. Astonished

19. Which word means the SAME as *risk*?   19.____
    A. Admire   B. Hazard   C. Limit   D. Hesitant

20. Which word means the OPPOSITE of *translucent*?
    A. Opaque   B. Transparent   C. Luminous   D. Introverted

20._____

21. Last year, Jamie's annual salary was $50,000. Her boss called her today to inform her that she would receive a 20% raise for the upcoming year. How much more money will Jamie receive next year?
    A. $60,000   B. $10,000   C. $1,000   D. $51,000

21._____

22. You and a co-worker work for a temp hiring agency as part of their office staff. You both are given 6 days off per month. How many days off are you and your co-worker given in a year?
    A. 24   B. 72   C. 144   D. 48

22._____

23. If Margot makes $34,000 per year and she works 40 hours per week for all 52 weeks, what is her hourly rate?
    A. $16.34/hour   B. $17.00/hour   C. $15.54/hour   D. $13.23/hour

23._____

24. How many dimes are there in $175.00?
    A. 175   B. 1,750   C. 3,500   D. 17,500

24._____

25. If Janey is three times as old as Emily, and Emily is 3, how old is Janey?
    A. 6   B. 9   C. 12   D. 15

25._____

KEY (CORRECT ANSWERS)

1.	C		11.	B
2.	D		12.	A
3.	A		13.	D
4.	B		14.	B
5.	B		15.	A
6.	C		16.	C
7.	A		17.	A
8.	B		18.	C
9.	C		19.	B
10.	A		20.	A

21.	B
22.	C
23.	A
24.	B
25.	B

TEST 2

DIRECTIONS: Each question or incomplete statement is followed by several suggested answers or completions. Select the one that BEST answers the question or completes the statement. *PRINT THE LETTER OF THE CORRECT ANSWER IN THE SPACE AT THE RIGHT.*

Questions 1-6.

DIRECTIONS: Questions 1 through 6 are to be answered on the basis of the following information.

item	name of item to be ordered
quantity	minimum number that can be ordered
beginning amount	amount in stock at start of month
amount received	amount receiving during month
ending amount	amount in stock at end of month
amount used	amount used during month
amount to order	will need at least as much of each item as used in the previous month
unit price	cost of each unit of an item
total price	total price for the order

Item	Quantity	Beginning	Received	Ending	Amount Used	Amount to Order	Unit Price	Total Price
Pens	10	22	10	8	24	20	$0.11	$2.20
Spiral notebooks	8	30	13	12			$0.25	
Binder clips	2 boxes	3 boxes	1 box	1 box			$1.79	
Sticky notes	3 packs	12 packs	4 packs	2 packs			$14.29	
Dry erase markers	1 pack (dozen)	34 markers	8 markers	40 markers			$16.49	
Ink cartridges (printer)	1 cartridge	3 cartridges	1 cartridge	2 cartridges			$79.99	
Folders	10 folders	25 folders	15 folders	10 folders			$1.08	

1. How many packs of sticky notes were used during the month?   1.____
   A. 16   B. 10   C. 12   D. 14

2. How many folders need to be ordered for next month?   2.____
   A. 15   B. 20   C. 30   D. 40

3. What is the total price of notebooks that you will need to order?   3.____
   A. $6.00   B. $0.25   C. $4.50   D. $2.75

4. Which of the following will you spend the second most money on?   4.____
   A. Ink cartridges   B. Dry erase markers
   C. Sticky notes   D. Binder clips

5. How many packs of dry erase markers should you order?   5.____
   A. 1   B. 8   C. 12   D. 0

6. What will be the total price of the file folders you order? 6.____
    A. $20.16   B. $2.16   C. $1.08   D. $4.32

Questions 7-11.

DIRECTIONS: Questions 7 through 11 are to be answered on the basis of the following table.

Number of Car Accidents, By Location and Cause, for 2014						
	Location 1		Location 2		Location 3	
Cause	Number	Percent	Number	Percent	Number	Percent
Severe Weather	10		25		30	
Excessive Speeding	20	40	5		10	
Impaired Driving	15		15	25	8	
Miscellaneous	5		15		2	4
TOTALS	50	100	60	100	50	100

7. Which of the following is the third highest cause of accidents for all three 7.____
locations?
    A. Severe Weather   B. Impaired Driving
    C. Miscellaneous   D. Excessive Speeding

8. The average number of Severe Weather accidents per week at Location 3 8.____
for the year (52 weeks) was MOST NEARLY
    A. 0.57   B. 30   C. 1   D. 1.25

9. Which location had the LARGEST percentage of accidents caused by 9.____
Impaired Driving?
    A. 1   B. 2   C. 3   D. Both A and B

10. If one-third of the accidents at all three locations resulted in at least one 10.____
fatality, what is the LEAST amount of deaths caused by accidents last year?
    A. 60   B. 106   C. 66   D. 53

11. What is the percentage of accidents caused by miscellaneous means from 11.____
all three locations in 2014?
    A. 5%   B. 10%   C. 13%   D. 25%

12. How many pairs of the following groups of letters are exactly alike? 12.____
        ACDOBJ   ACDBOJ
        HEWBWR   HEWRWB
        DEERVS   DEERVS
        BRFQSX   BRFQSX
        WEYRVB   WEYRVB
        SPQRZA   SQRPZA

    A. 2   B. 3   C. 4   D. 5

Questions 13-19.

DIRECTIONS: Questions 13 through 19 are to be answered on the basis of the following
information.

In 2012, the most current information on the American population was finished. The
population was compiled by 200 people from each of the 50 states. The territory of Puerto Rico,
a sovereign of the United States, had 25 people assigned to compile data. In February of 2010,
each state began collecting information. In Puerto Rico, data collection finished by January 31st,
2011, while the United States finished on June 30, 2012. Each volunteer gathered data on the
population of each state or sovereign. When the information was compiled, each volunteer had
to send their information to the nation's capital, Washington, D.C. Each worker worked 20
hours per month and put together 10 reports per month. After the data was compiled in total, 50
people reviewed the data and worked from January 2012 to December 2012.

13.   How many reports were generated from February 2010 to April 2010 in Illinois   13._____
      and Ohio?
      A. 3,000   B. 6,000   C. 12,000   D. 15,000

14.   How many workers in total were collecting data in January 2012?   14._____
      A. 200   B. 25   C. 225   D. 0

15.   How many reports were put together in May 2012?   15._____
      A. 2,000   B. 50,000   C. 100,000   D. 100,250

16.   How many hours did the Puerto Rican volunteers work in the fall   16._____
      (September-November)?
      A. 60   B. 500   C. 1,500   D. 0

17.   How many workers were there in February 2011?   17._____
      A. 25   B. 200   C. 225   D. 250

18.   What was the total amount of hours worked in July 2010?   18._____
      A. 500   B. 4,000   C. 4,500   D. 5,000

19.   How many reviewers worked in January 2013?   19._____
      A. 75   B. 50   C. 0   D. 25

20.   John has to file 10 documents per shelf. How many documents would it   20._____
      take for John to fill 40 shelves?
      A. 40   B. 400   C. 4,500   D. 5,000

21.   Jill wants to travel from New York City to Los Angeles by bike, which   21._____
      is approximately 2,772 miles. How many miles per day would Jill need to
      average if she wanted to complete the trip in 4 weeks?
      A. 100   B. 89   C. 99   D. 94

22. If there are 24 CPU's and only 7 monitors, how many more monitors do you need to have the same amount of monitors as CPU's?
    A. Not enough information   B. 17
    C. 31   D. 0

22.____

23. If Gerry works 5 days a week and 8 hours each day, and John works 3 days a week and 10 hours each day, how many more hours per year will Gerry work than John?
    A. They work the same amount of hours.
    B. 450
    C. 520
    D. 832

23.____

24. Jimmy gets transferred to a new office. The new office has 25 employees, but only 16 are there due to a blizzard. How many coworkers was Jimmy able to meet on his first day?
    A. 16   B. 25   C. 9   D. 7

24.____

25. If you do a fundraiser for charities in your area and raise $500 total, how much would you give to each charity if you were donating equal amounts to 3 of them?
    A. $250.00   B. $167.77   C. $50.00   D. $111.11

25.____

KEY (CORRECT ANSWERS)

1.	D		11.	C
2.	B		12.	B
3.	A		13.	C
4.	C		14.	A
5.	D		15.	A
6.	B		16.	C
7.	D		17.	B
8.	A		18.	C
9.	A		19.	C
10.	D		20.	B

21.	C
22.	B
23.	C
24.	A
25.	B

TEST 3

DIRECTIONS: Each question or incomplete statement is followed by several suggested answers or completions. Select the one that BEST answers the question or completes the statement. *PRINT THE LETTER OF THE CORRECT ANSWER IN THE SPACE AT THE RIGHT.*

Questions 1-3.

DIRECTIONS: In answering Questions 1 through 3, choose the correctly spelled word.

1.   A.   allusion   B.   alusion   C.   allusien   D.   allution   1._____

2.   A.   altitude   B.   alltitude   C.   atlitude   D.   altlitude   2._____

3.   A.   althogh   B.   allthough   C.   althrough   D.   although   3._____

Questions 4-9.

DIRECTIONS: In answering Questions 4 through 9, choose the answer that BEST completes the analogy.

4.   Odometer is to mileage as compass is to   4._____
     A. speed   B. needle   C. hiking   D. direction

5.   Marathon is to race as hibernation is to   5._____
     A. winter   B. dream   C. sleep   D. bear

6.   Cup is to coffee as bowl is to   6._____
     A. dish   B. spoon   C. food   D. soup

7.   Flow is to river as stagnant is to   7._____
     A. pool   B. rain   C. stream   D. canal

8.   paw is to cat as hoof is to   8._____
     A. lamb   B. horse   C. lion   D. elephant

9.   Architect is to building as sculptor is to   9._____
     A. museum   B. chisel   C. stone   D. statue

Questions 10-14.

DIRECTIONS: Questions 10 through 14 are to be answered on the basis of the following graph.

Population of Carroll City Broken Down by Age and Gender			
(In Thousands) Age	Female	Male	Total
Under 15	60	60	80
15-23		22	
24-33		20	44
34-43	13	18	31
44-53	20		67
64 and Over	65	65	130
TOTAL	225	237	422

10. How many people in the city are between the ages of 15-23?
    A. 70
    B. 46,000
    C. 70,000
    D. 225,000

11. Approximately what percentage of the total population of the city was female aged 24-33?
    A. 10%
    B. 5%
    C. 15%
    D. 25%

12. If 33% of the males have a job and 55% of females don't have a job, which of the following statements is TRUE?
    A. Males have 2,251 more jobs than females.
    B. Females have 44,760 more jobs than males.
    C. Females have 22,251 more jobs than males.
    D. None of the above statements are true.

13. How many females between the ages of 15-23 live in Carroll City?
    A. 67,000
    B. 24,000
    C. 48,000
    D. 91,000

14. Assume all males 44-53 living in Carroll city are employed. If two-thirds of males age 44-53 work jobs outside of Carroll City, how many work within city limits?
    A. 31,333
    B. 15,667
    C. 47,000
    D. Cannot answer the question with the information provided

10.____

11.____

12.____

13.____

14.____

Questions 15-16.

DIRECTIONS: Questions 15 and 16 are labeled as shown. Alphabetize them for filing.
Choose the answer that correctly shows the order.

15. (1) AED   15.____
     (2) OOS
     (3) FOA
     (4) DOM
     (5) COB

     A. 2-5-4-3-2   B. 1-4-5-2-3   C. 1-5-4-2-3   D. 1-5-4-3-2

16. Alphabetize the names of the people. Last names are given last.   16.____
     (1) Lindsey Jamestown
     (2) Jane Alberta
     (3) Ally Jamestown
     (4) Allison Johnston
     (5) Lyle Moreno

     A. 2-1-3-4-5   B. 3-4-2-1-5   C. 2-3-1-4-5   D. 4-3-2-1-5

17. Which of the following words is misspelled?   17.____
     A. disgust   B. whisper
     C. vocale   D. none of the above

Questions 18-21.

DIRECTIONS: Questions 18 through 21 are to be answered on the basis of the following list of
employees.

          Robertson, Aaron
          Bacon, Gina
          Jerimiah, Trace
          Gillette, Stanley
          Jacks, Sharon

18. Which employee name would come in third in alphabetized list?   18.____
     A. Robertson, Aaron   B. Jerimiah, Trace
     C. Gillette, Stanley   D. Jacks, Sharon

19. Which employee's first name starts with the letter in the alphabet that is   19.____
     five letters after the first letter of their last name?
     A. Jerimiah, Trace   B. Bacon, Gina
     C. Jacks, Sharon   D. Gillette, Stanley

20. How many employees have last names that are exactly five letters long?   20.____
     A. 1   B. 2   C. 3   D. 4

21. How many of the employees have either a first or last name that starts with the letter "G"?

    A. 1   B. 2   C. 4   D. 5

21.____

Questions 22-25.

DIRECTIONS: Questions 22 through 25 are to be answered on the basis of the following chart.

Bicycle Sales (Model #34JA32)							
Country	May	June	July	August	September	October	Total
Germany	34	47	45	54	56	60	296
Britain	40	44	36	47	47	46	260
Ireland	37	32	32	32	34	33	200
Portugal	14	14	14	16	17	14	89
Italy	29	29	28	31	29	31	177
Belgium	22	24	24	26	25	23	144
Total	176	198	179	206	208	207	1166

22. What percentage of the overall total was sold to the German importer?

    A. 25.3%   B. 22%   C. 24.1%   D. 23%

22.____

23. What percentage of the overall total was sold in September?

    A. 24.1%   B. 25.6%   C. 17.9%   D. 24.6%

23.____

24. What is the average number of units per month imported into Belgium over the first four months shown?

    A. 26   B. 20   C. 24   D. 31

24.____

25. If you look at the three smallest importers, what is their total import percentage?

    A. 35.1%   B. 37.1%   C. 40%   D. 28%

25.____

KEY (CORRECT ANSWERS)

1.	A		11.	B
2.	A		12.	C
3.	D		13.	C
4.	D		14.	B
5.	C		15.	D
6.	D		16.	C
7.	A		17.	D
8.	B		18.	D
9.	D		19.	B
10.	C		20.	B

21.	B
22.	A
23.	C
24.	C
25.	A

TEST 4

DIRECTIONS: Each question or incomplete statement is followed by several suggested answers or completions. Select the one that BEST answers the question or completes the statement. *PRINT THE LETTER OF THE CORRECT ANSWER IN THE SPACE AT THE RIGHT.*

Questions 1-6.

DIRECTIONS: In answering Questions 1 through 6, choose the sentence that represents the BEST example of English grammar.

1. A. Joey and me want to go on a vacation next week.   1.____
    B. Gary told Jim he would need to take some time off.
    C. If turning six years old, Jim's uncle would teach Spanish to him.
    D. Fax a copy of your resume to Ms. Perez and me.

2. A. Jerry stood in line for almost two hours.   2.____
    B. The reaction to my engagement was less exciting than I thought it would
        be.
    C. Carlos and me have done great work on this project.
    D. Two parts of the speech needs to be revised before tomorrow.

3. A. Arriving home, the alarm was tripped.   3.____
    B. Jonny is regarded as a stand up guy, a responsible parent, and he
        doesn't give up until a task is finished.
    C. Each employee must submit a drug test each month.
    D. One of the documents was incinerated in the explosion.

4. A. As soon as my parents get home, I told them I finished all of my chores. 4.____
    B. I asked my teacher to send me my missing work, check my absences,
        and how did I do on my test.
    C. Matt attempted to keep it concealed from Jenny and me.
    D. If Mary or him cannot get work done on time, I will have to split them up.

5. A. Driving to work, the traffic report warned him of an accident on   5.____
        Highway 47.
    B. Jimmy has performed well this season.
    C. Since finishing her degree, several job offers have been given to Cam.
    D. Our boss is creating unstable conditions for we employees.

6. A. The thief was described as a tall man with a wiry mustache weighing   6.____
        approximately 150 pounds.
    B. She gave Patrick and I some more time to finish our work.
    C. One of the books that he ordered was damaged in shipping.
    D. While talking on the rotary phone, the car Jim was driving skidded off the
        road.

Questions 7-9.

DIRECTIONS: Questions 7 through 9 are to be answered on the basis of the following graph.

Ice Lake Frozen Flight (2002-2013)		
Year	Number of Participants	Temperature (Fahrenheit)
2002	22	4°
2003	50	33°
2004	69	18°
2005	104	22°
2006	108	24°
2007	288	33°
2008	173	9°
2009	598	39°
2010	698	26°
2011	696	30°
2012	777	28°
2013	578	32°

7.   Which two year span had the LARGEST difference between temperatures?   7.____
     A. 2002 and 2003   B. 2011 and 2012
     C. 2008 and 2009   D. 2003 and 2004

8.   How many total people participated in the years after the temperature   8.____
     reached at least 29°?
     A. 2,295   B. 1,717   C. 2,210   D. 4,543

9.   In 2007, the event saw 288 participants, while in 2008 that number   9.____
     dropped to 173. Which of the following reasons BEST explains the drop in
     participants?
     A. The event had not been going on that long and people didn't know about
         it.
     B. The lake water wasn't cold enough to have people jump in.
     C. The temperature was too cold for many people who would have normally
         participated.
     D. None of the above reasons explain the drop in participants.

10. In the following list of numbers, how many times does 4 come just after 2   10.____
     when 2 comes just after an odd number?
     2365247653898632488572486392424
     A. 2   B. 3   C. 4   D. 5

11. Which choice below lists the letter that is as far after B as S is after N in   11.____
     the alphabet?
     A. G   B. H   C. I   D. J

Questions 12-15.

DIRECTIONS: Questions 12 through 15 are to be answered on the basis of the following directory and list of changes.

Directory		
Name	Emp. Type	Position
Julie Taylor	Warehouse	Packer
James King	Office	Administrative Assistant
John Williams	Office	Salesperson
Ray Moore	Warehouse	Maintenance
Kathleen Byrne	Warehouse	Supervisor
Amy Jones	Office	Salesperson
Paul Jonas	Office	Salesperson
Lisa Wong	Warehouse	Loader
Eugene Lee	Office	Accountant
Bruce Lavine	Office	Manager
Adam Gates	Warehouse	Packer
Will Suter	Warehouse	Packer
Gary Lorper	Office	Accountant
Jon Adams	Office	Salesperson
Susannah Harper	Office	Salesperson

Directory Updates:
- Employee e-mail address will adhere to the following guidelines: lastnamefirstname@apexindustries.com (ex. Susannah Harper is harpersusannah@apexindustries.com). Currently, employees in the warehouse share one e-mail, distribution@apexindustries.com.
- The "Loader" position was now be referred to as "Specialist I"
- Adam Gates has accepted a Supervisor position within the Warehouse and is no longer a Packer. All warehouses employees report to the two Supervisors and all office employees report to the Manager.

12. Amy Jones tried to send an e-mail to Adam Gates, but it wouldn't send. Which of the following offers the BEST explanation?
    A. Amy put Adam's first name first and then his last name.
    B. Adam doesn't check his e-mail, so he wouldn't know if he received the e-mail or not.
    C. Adam does not have his own e-mail.
    D. Office employees are not allowed to send e-mails to each other.

12.____

13. How many Packers currently work for Apex Industries?
    A. 2   B. 3   C. 4   D. 5

13.____

14. What position does Lisa Wong currently hold?
    A. Specialist I   B. Secretary
    C. Administrative Assistant   D. Loader

14.____

15. If an employee wanted to contact the office manager, which of the following e-mails should the e-mail be sent to?
    A. officemanager@apexindustries.com
    B. brucelavine@apexindustries.com
    C. lavinebruce@apexindustries.com
    D. distribution@apexindustries.com

15.____

Questions 16-19.

DIRECTIONS: In answering Questions 16 through 19, compare the three names, numbers or addresses.

16. Smiley Yarnell   Smiley Yarnel   Smily Yarnell   16.____
    A. All three are exactly alike.
    B. The first and second are exactly alike.
    C. The second and third are exactly alike.
    D. All three are different.

17. 1583 Theater Drive   1583 Theater Drive   1583 Theatre Drive   17.____
    A. All three are exactly alike.
    B. The first and second are exactly alike.
    C. The second and third are exactly alike.
    D. All three are different.

18. 3341893212   3341893212   3341893212   18.____
    A. All three are exactly alike.
    B. The first and second are exactly alike.
    C. The second and third are exactly alike.
    D. All three are different.

19. Douglass Watkins   Douglas Watkins   Douglass Watkins   19.____
    A. All three are exactly alike.
    B. The first and second are exactly alike.
    C. The second and third are exactly alike.
    D. All three are different.

Questions 20-24.

DIRECTIONS: In answering Questions 20 through 24, you will be presented with a word. Choose the synonym that BEST represents the word in question.

20. Flexible   20.____
    A. delicate   B. inflammable   C. strong   D. pliable

21. Alternative   21.____
    A. choice   B. moderate   C. lazy   D. value

22. Corroborate
    A. examine   B. explain   C. verify   D. explain

22.____

23. Respiration
    A. recovery   B. breathing   C. sweating   D. selfish

23.____

24. Negligent
    A. lazy   B. moderate   C. hopeless   D. lax

24.____

25. Plumber is to Wrench as Painter is to
    A. pipe   B. shop   C. hammer   D. brush

25.____

KEY (CORRECT ANSWERS)

1.	D		11.	A
2.	A		12.	C
3.	D		13.	A
4.	C		14.	A
5.	B		15.	C
6.	C		16.	D
7.	C		17.	B
8.	B		18.	A
9.	C		19.	B
10.	C		20.	D

21.	A
22.	C
23.	B
24.	D
25.	D

SPELLING

COMMENTARY

Spelling forms an integral part of tests of academic aptitude and achievement and of general and mental ability. Moreover, the spelling question is a staple of verbal and clerical tests in civil service entrance and promotional examinations.

Perhaps, the most rewarding way to learn to spell successfully is the direct, functional approach of learning to spell correctly, both orally and in writing, all words as they appear, both singly and in context.

In accordance with this positive method, the spelling question is presented here in "test" form, as it might appear on an actual examination.

The spelling question may appear on examinations in the following format:

Four words are listed in each question. These are lettered A, B, C, and D. A fifth option, E, is also given, which always reads "none misspelled." The examinee is to select one of the five (lettered) choices: either A, B, C, or D if one of the words is misspelled, or item E, none misspelled, if all four words have been correctly spelled in the question.

SAMPLE QUESTIONS

The directions for this part are approximately as follows:

DIRECTIONS: Mark the space corresponding to the one MISSPELLED word in each of the following groups of words. If NO word is misspelled, mark the last space on the answer sheet.

SAMPLE O

A. walk
B. talk
C. play
D. dance
E. *none misspelled*

Since none of the words is misspelled, E would be marked on the answer sheet.

SAMPLE OO

A. seize
B. yield
C. define
D. reckless
E. *none misspelled*

Since "reckless" (correct spelling, reckless) has been misspelled, D would be marked on the answer. sheet

SPELLING

SAMPLE QUESTION

DIRECTIONS: The spelling test is designed to resemble a proofreading task. You are presented with a passage. Each line of the passage is considered one test question. You are to read the passage and indicate how many spelling errors are contained in each line. In some cases, a spelling error will consist of the use of the wrong form of a word that has several correct spellings. The different correct spellings of such words have different meanings, for example "to," "two," and "too." Be sure that you look for these kinds of errors. *PRINT THE LETTER OF THE CORRECT ANSWER IN THE SPACE AT THE RIGHT.*

KEY

A = The line contains no spelling errors.
B = There is one (1) spelling error in the line.
C = There are two (2) spelling errors in the line.
D = There are three (3) or more spelling errors in the line.

1. The main reasons for in-service training are to inprove the work being done by

2. employees in there present jobs and to meet the system and program goals of the

3. agency. It is the responsability of managers to suport and encourage teh use of

4. skills learned in training classes. In-service training will be done during normal work

5. hours and will be paied for by the employer.

_____

KEY (CORRECT ANSWERS)

1. The correct answer is B. There is one spelling error. The word "improve" is misspelled as "inprove".

2. The correct answer is B. The word "there" is not spelled correctly for the use of the word in this sentence. In this case, we need the plural, possessive pronoun "their", so one spelling error is found in this line.

3. The correct answer is D. There are three misspelled words in this line: "responsibility," "support," and "the".

4. The correct answer is A. This line contains no spelling errors.

5. The correct answer is B. This line contains one spelling error. The word "paied" is misspelled and should be "paid" or "payed". Both are acceptable forms though "paid" is probably more commonly used.

_____

SPELLING
EXAMINATION SECTION
TEST 1

DIRECTIONS: Each question or incomplete statement is followed by several suggested answers or completions. Select the one that BEST answers the question or completes the statement. *PRINT THE LETTER OF THE CORRECT ANSWER IN THE SPACE AT THE RIGHT.*

Questions 1-5.

DIRECTIONS: Questions 1 through 5 consist of four words. Indicate the letter of the word that is CORRECTLY spelled.

1. A. harassment   B. harrasment   1._____
    C. harasment   D. harrassment

2. A. maintainance   B. maintenence   2._____
    C. maintainence   D. maintenance

3. A. comparable   B. comprable   3._____
    C. comparible   D. commparable

4. A. suficient   B. sufficiant   4._____
    C. sufficient   D. suficiant

5. A. fairly   B. fairley   C. farely   D. fairlie   5._____

Questions 6-10.

DIRECTIONS: Questions 6 through 10 consist of four words. Indicate the letter of the word that is INCORRECTLY spelled.

6. A. pallor   B. ballid   C. ballet   D. pallid   6._____

7. A. urbane   B. surburbane
    C. interurban   D. urban

8. A. facial   B. physical   C. fiscle   D. muscle   8._____

9. A. interceed   B. benefited
    C. analogous   D. altogether

10. A. seizure   B. irrelevant
    C. inordinate   D. dissapproved

KEY (CORRECT ANSWERS)

1.	A	6.	B
2.	D	7.	B
3.	A	8.	C
4.	C	9.	A
5.	A	10.	D

TEST 2

DIRECTIONS: Each of Questions 1 through 15 consists of two words preceded by the letters A and B. In each question, one of the words may be spelled INCORRECTLY or both words may be spelled CORRECTLY. If one of the words in a question is spelled INCORRECTLY, print in the space at the right the capital letter preceding the INCORRECTLY spelled word. If both words are spelled CORRECTLY, print the letter C.

1.	A. easely	B. readily	1._
2.	A. pursue	B. decend	2._
3.	A. measure	B. laboratory	3._
4.	A. exausted	B. traffic	4._
5.	A. discussion	B. unpleasant	5._
6.	A. campaign	B. murmer	6._
7.	A. guarantee	B. sanatary	7._
8.	A. communication	B. safty	8._
9.	A. numerus	B. celebration	9._
10.	A. nourish	B. begining	10._
11.	A. courious	B. witness	11._
12.	A. undoubtedly	B. thoroughly	12._
13.	A. accessible	B. artifical	13._
14.	A. feild	B. arranged	14._
15.	A. admittence	B. hastily	15._

KEY (CORRECT ANSWERS)

1.	A	6.	B	11.	A
2.	B	7.	B	12.	C
3.	C	8.	B	13.	B
4.	A	9.	A	14.	A
5.	C	10.	B	15.	A

TEST 3

DIRECTIONS: In each of the following sentences, one word is misspelled. Following each sentence is a list of four words taken from the sentence. Indicate the letter of the word which is MISSPELLED in the sentence. *PRINT THE LETTER OF THE CORRECT ANSWER IN THE SPACE AT THE RIGHT.*

1. The placing of any inflammable substance in any building, or the placing of any device or contrivence capable of producing fire, for the purpose of causing a fire is an attempt to burn.

   A. inflammable   B. substance
   C. device   D. contrivence

1.____

2. The word *break* also means obtaining an entrance into a building by any artifice used for that purpose, or by colussion with any person therein.

   A. obtaining   B. entrance
   C. artifice   D. colussion

2.____

3. Any person who with intent to provoke a breech of the peace causes a disturbance or is offensive to others may be deemed to have committed disorderly conduct.

   A. breech   B. disturbance
   C. offensive   D. committed

3.____

4. When the offender inflicts a grevious harm upon the person from whose possession, or in whose presence, property is taken, he is guilty of robbery.

   A. offender   B. grevious
   C. possession   D. presence

4.____

5. A person who wilfuly encourages or advises another person in attempting to take the latter's life is guilty of a felony.

   A. wilfuly   B. encourages
   C. advises   D. attempting

5.____

6. He maliciously demurred to an ajournment of the proceedings.

   A. maliciously   B. demurred
   C. ajournment   D. proceedings

6.____

7. His innocence at that time is irrelevant in view of his more recent villianous demeanor.

   A. innocence   B. irrelevant
   C. villianous   D. demeanor

7.____

8. The mischievous boys aggrevated the annoyance of their neighbor.

   A. mischievous   B. aggrevated
   C. annoyance   D. neighbor

8.____

9. While his perseverence was commendable, his judgment was debatable.

   A. perseverence   B. commendable
   C. judgment   D. debatable

9.____

10. He was hoping the appeal would facilitate his aquittal. 10.___

   A. hoping   B. appeal
   C. facilitate   D. aquittal

11. It would be preferable for them to persue separate courses. 11.___

   A. preferable   B. persue
   C. separate   D. courses

12. The litigant was complimented on his persistance and achievement. 12.___

   A. litigant   B. complimented
   C. persistance   D. achievement

13. Ocassionally there are discrepancies in the descriptions of miscellaneous items. 13.___

   A. ocassionally   B. discrepancies
   C. descriptions   D. miscellaneous

14. The councilmanic seargent-at-arms enforced the prohibition. 14.___

   A. councilmanic   B. seargent-at-arms
   C. enforced   D. prohibition

15. The teacher had an ingenious device for maintaning attendance. 15.___

   A. ingenious   B. device
   C. maintaning   D. attendance

16. A worrysome situation has developed as a result of the assessment that absenteeism is increasing despite our conscientious efforts. 16.___

   A. worrysome   B. assessment
   C. absenteeism   D. conscientious

17. I concurred with the credit manager that it was practicable to charge purchases on a biennial basis, and the company agreed to adhear to this policy. 17.___

   A. concurred   B. practicable
   C. biennial   D. adhear

18. The pastor was chagrined and embarassed by the irreverent conduct of one of his parishioners. 18.___

   A. chagrined   B. embarassed
   C. irreverent   D. parishioners

19. His inate seriousness was belied by his flippant demeanor. 19.___

   A. inate   B. belied
   C. flippant   D. demeanor

20. It was exceedingly regrettable that the excessive number of challanges in the court delayed the start of the trial. 20.___

   A. exceedingly   B. regrettable
   C. excessive   D. challanges

KEY (CORRECT ANSWERS)

1.	D	11.	B
2.	D	12.	C
3.	A	13.	A
4.	B	14.	B
5.	A	15.	C
6.	C	16.	A
7.	C	17.	D
8.	B	18.	B
9.	A	19.	A
10.	D	20.	D

TEST 4

Questions 1-11.

DIRECTIONS: Each question consists of three words. In each question, one of the words may be spelled incorrectly or all three may be spelled correctly. For each question, if one of the words is spelled INCORRECTLY, write the letter of the incorrect word in the space at the right. If all three words are spelled CORRECTLY, write the letter D in the space at the right.

SAMPLE I: (A) guide (B) department (C) stranger
SAMPLE II: (A) comply (B) valuable (C) window
In Sample I, departmint is incorrect. It should be spelled department. Therefore, B is the answer.
In Sample II, all three words are spelled correctly. Therefore, D is the answer.

1.	A.	argument	B.	reciept	C.	complain	1._
2.	A.	sufficient	B.	postpone	C.	visible	2._
3.	A.	expirience	B.	dissatisfy	C.	alternate	3._
4.	A.	occurred	B.	noticable	C.	appendix	4._
5.	A.	anxious	B.	guarantee	C.	calender	5._
6.	A.	sincerely	B.	affectionately	C.	truly	6._
7.	A.	excellant	B.	verify	C.	important	7._
8.	A.	error	B.	quality	C.	enviroment	8._
9.	A.	exercise	B.	advance	C.	pressure	9._
10.	A.	citizen	B.	expence	C.	memory	10._
11.	A.	flexable	B.	focus	C.	forward	11._

Questions 12-15.

DIRECTIONS: Each of Questions 12 through 15 consists of a group of four words. Examine each group carefully; then in the space at the right, indicate
A - if only one word in the group is spelled correctly
B - if two words in the group are spelled correctly
C - if three words in the group are spelled correctly
D - if all four words in the group are spelled correctly

12. Wendsday, particular, similar, hunderd   12._

13. realize, judgment, opportunities, consistent   13._

14. equel, principle, assistense, commitee   14._

15. simultaneous, privilege, advise, ocassionaly   15._

KEY (CORRECT ANSWERS)

1.	B	6.	D	11.	A
2.	D	7.	A	12.	B
3.	A	8.	C	13.	D
4.	B	9.	D	14.	A
5.	C	10.	B	15.	C

———

TEST 5

1.	A.	justified	B.	offering	1.__
2.	A.	predjudice	B.	license	2.__
3.	A.	label	B.	pamphlet	3.__
4.	A.	bulletin	B.	physical	4.__
5.	A.	assure	B.	exceed	5.__
6.	A.	advantagous	B.	evident	6.__
7.	A.	benefit	B.	occured	7.__
8.	A.	acquire	B.	graditude	8.__
9.	A.	amenable	B.	boundry	9.__
10.	A.	deceive	B.	voluntary	10.__
11.	A.	imunity	B.	conciliate	11.__
12.	A.	acknoledge	B.	presume	12.__
13.	A.	substitute	B.	prespiration	13.__
14.	A.	reputible	B.	announce	14.__
15.	A.	luncheon	B.	wretched	15.__

KEY (CORRECT ANSWERS)

1.	C	6.	A	11.	A
2.	A	7.	B	12.	A
3.	C	8.	B	13.	B
4.	C	9.	B	14.	A
5.	C	10.	C	15.	C

TEST 6

DIRECTIONS: Questions 1 through 15 contain lists of words, one of which is misspelled. Indicate the MISSPELLED word in each group. *PRINT THE LETTER OF THE CORRECT ANSWER IN THE SPACE AT THE RIGHT.*

1. A. felony   B. lacerate
    C. cancellation   D. seperate

2. A. batallion   B. beneficial
    C. miscellaneous   D. secretary

3. A. camouflage   B. changeable   C. embarass   D. inoculate   3._____

4. A. beneficial   B. disasterous
    C. incredible   D. miniature

5. A. auxilliary   B. hypocrisy   C. phlegm   D. vengeance   5._____

6. A. aisle   B. cemetary
    C. courtesy   D. extraordinary

7. A. crystallize   B. innoculate
    C. eminent   D. symmetrical

8. A. judgment   B. maintainance
    C. bouillon   D. eery

9. A. isosceles   B. ukulele   C. mayonaise   D. iridescent   9._____

10. A. remembrance   B. occurence
    C. correspondence   D. countenance

11. A. corpuscles   B. mischievous
    C. batchelor   D. bulletin

12. A. terrace   B. banister   C. concrete   D. masonery   12._____

13. A. balluster   B. gutter   C. latch   D. bridging   13._____

14. A. personnell   B. navel   C. therefor   D. emigrant   14._____

15. A. committee   B. submiting   15._____
    C. amendment   D. electorate

KEY (CORRECT ANSWERS)

1. D	6. B	11. C
2. A	7. B	12. D
3. C	8. B	13. A
4. B	9. C	14. A
5. A	10. B	15. B

TEST 7

Questions 1-5.

DIRECTIONS: Questions 1 through 5 consist of groups of four words. Select answer:
A if only ONE word is spelled correctly in a group
B if TWO words are spelled correctly in a group
C if THREE words are spelled correctly in a group
D if all FOUR words are spelled correctly in a group

1. counterfeit, embarass, panicky, supercede   1.___

2. benefited, personnel, questionnaire, unparalelled   2.___

3. bankruptcy describable, proceed, vacuum   3.___

4. handicapped, mispell, offerred, pilgrimmage   4.___

5. corduroy, interfere, privilege, separator   5.___

Questions 6-10.

DIRECTIONS: Questions 6 through 10 consist of four pairs of words each. Some of the words
are spelled correctly; others are spelled incorrectly. For each question, indicate in the space at the right the letter preceding that pair of words in which
BOTH words are spelled CORRECTLY.

6. A. hygienic, inviegle   B. omniscience, pittance   6.___
    C. plagarize, nullify   D. seargent, perilous

7. A. auxilary, existence   B. pronounciation, accordance   7.___
    C. ignominy, indegence   D. suable, baccalaureate

8. A. discreet, inaudible   B. hypocrisy, currupt   8.___
    C. liquidate, maintainance   D. transparancy, onerous

9. A. facility, stimulent   B. frugel, sanitary   9.___
    C. monetary, prefatory   D. punctileous, credentials

10. A. bankruptsy, perceptible   B. disuade, resilient   10.___
    C. exhilerate, expectancy   D. panegyric, disparate

Questions 11-15

DIRECTIONS: Each question or incomplete statement is followed by several suggested
answers or completions. Select the one that BEST answers the question or
completes the statement. PRINT THE LETTER OF THE CORRECT ANSWER
IN THE SPACE AT THE RIGHT.

11. The silent e must be retained when the suffix -able is added to the word   11.___

    A. argue   B. love   C. move   D. notice

12. The CORRECTLY spelled word in the choices below is   12.___

    A. kindergarden   B. zylophone
    C. hemorrhage   D. mayonaise

13. Of the following words, the one spelled CORRECTLY is   13.____

    A. begger   B. cemetary
    C. embarassed   D. coyote

14. Of the following words, the one spelled CORRECTLY is   14.____

    A. dandilion   B. wiry   C. sieze   D. rythmic

15. Of the following words, the one spelled CORRECTLY is   15.____

    A. beligerent   B. anihilation
    C. facetious   D. adversery

KEY (CORRECT ANSWERS)

1.	B	6.	B	11.	D
2.	C	7.	D	12.	C
3.	D	8.	A	13.	D
4.	A	9.	C	14.	B
5.	D	10.	D	15.	C

TEST 8

DIRECTIONS: In each of the following sentences, one word is misspelled. Following each sentence is a list of four words taken from the sentence. Indicate the letter of the word which is MISSPELLED. *PRINT THE LETTER OF THE CORRECT ANSWER IN THE SPACE AT THE RIGHT.*

1. If the administrator attempts to withold information, there is a good likelihood that there will be serious repercussions.

   A. administrator
   C. likelihood
   B. withold
   D. repercussions

   1.__

2. He condescended to apologize, but we felt that a beligerent person should not occupy an influential position.

   A. condescended
   C. beligerent
   B. apologize
   D. influential

   2.__

3. Despite the sporadic delinquent payments of his indebtedness, Mr. Johnson has been an exemplery customer.

   A. sporadic
   C. indebtedness
   B. delinquent
   D. exemplery

   3.__

4. He was appreciative of the support he consistantly acquired, but he felt that he had waited an inordinate length of time for it.

   A. appreciative
   C. acquired
   B. consistantly
   D. inordinate

   4.__

5. Undeniably they benefited from the establishment of a receivership, but the question of statutary limitations remained unresolved.

   A. undeniably
   C. receivership
   B. benefited
   D. statutary

   5.__

6. Mr. Smith profered his hand as an indication that he considered it a viable contract, but Mr. Nelson alluded to the fact that his colleagues had not been consulted.

   A. profered
   C. alluded
   B. viable
   D. colleagues

   6.__

7. The treatments were beneficial according to the optometrists, and the consensus was that minimal improvement could be expected.

   A. beneficial
   C. consensus
   B. optomotrists
   D. minimal

   7.__

8. Her frivalous manner was unbecoming because the air of solemnity at the cemetery was pervasive.

   A. frivalous
   C. cemetery
   B. solemnity
   D. pervasive

   8.__

9. The clandestine meetings were designed to make the two adversaries more amicable, but they served only to intensify their emnity.

   A. clandestine
   C. amicable
   B. adversaries
   D. emnity

   9.__

10. Do you think that his innovative ideas and financial acumen will help stabalize the fluctu-   10.____
    ations of the stock market?

    A. innovative   B. acumen
    C. stabalize   D. fluctuations

11. In order to keep a perpetual inventory, you will have to keep an uninterrupted surveil-   11.____
    lance of all the miscellanious stock.

    A. perpetual   B. uninterrupted
    C. surveillance   D. miscellanious

12. She used the art of pursuasion on the children because she found that caustic remarks   12.____
    had no perceptible effect on their behavior.

    A. pursuasion   B. caustic
    C. perceptible   D. effect

13. His sacreligious outbursts offended his constituents, and he was summarily removed   13.____
    from office by the City Council.

    A. sacreligious   B. constituents
    C. summarily   D. Council

14. They exhorted the contestants to greater efforts, but the exhorbitant costs in terms of   14.____
    energy expended resulted in a feeling of lethargy.

    A. exhorted   B. contestants
    C. exhorbitant   D. lethargy

15. Since he was knowledgable about illicit drugs, he was served with a subpoena to appear   15.____
    for the prosecution.

    A. knowledgable   B. illicit
    C. subpoena   D. prosecution

16. In spite of his lucid statements, they denigrated his report and decided it should be suc-   16.____
    cintly paraphrased.

    A. lucid   B. denigrated
    C. succintly   D. paraphrased

17. The discussion was not germane to the contraversy, but the indicted man's insistence on   17.____
    further talk was allowed.

    A. germane   B. contraversy
    C. indicted   D. insistence

18. The legislators were enervated by the distances they had traveled during the election   18.____
    year to fullfil their speaking engagements.

    A. legislators   B. enervated
    C. traveled   D. fullfil

19. The plaintiffs' attornies charged the defendant in the case with felonious assault.   19._

    A. plaintiffs'   B. attornies
    C. defendant   D. felonious

20. It is symptomatic of the times that we try to placate all, but a proposal for new forms of   20._
disciplinery action was promulgated by the staff.

    A. symptomatic   B. placate
    C. disciplinery   D. promulgated

KEY (CORRECT ANSWERS)

1. B	6. A	11. D	16. C
2. C	7. B	12. A	17. B
3. D	8. A	13. A	18. D
4. B	9. D	14. C	19. B
5. D	10. C	15. A	20. C

TEST 9

DIRECTIONS: Each of Questions 1 through 15 consists of a single word which is spelled either correctly or incorrectly. If the word is spelled CORRECTLY, you are to print the letter C (Correct) in the space at the right. If the word is spelled INCORRECTLY, you are to print the letter W (Wrong).

1. pospone

1._____

2. diffrent

2._____

3. height

3._____

4. carefully

4._____

5. ability

5._____

6. temper

6._____

7. deslike

7._____

8. seldem

8._____

9. alcohol

9._____

10. expense

10._____

11. vegatable

11._____

12. dispensary

12._____

13. specemin

13._____

14. allowance

14._____

15. exersise

15._____

KEY (CORRECT ANSWERS)

1.	W	6.	C	11.	W
2.	W	7.	W	12.	C
3.	C	8.	W	13.	W
4.	C	9.	C	14.	C
5.	C	10.	C	15.	W

TEST 10

DIRECTIONS: Each of Questions 1 through 10 consists of four words, one of which may be spelled incorrectly or all four words may be spelled correctly. If one of the words in a question is spelled incorrectly, print in the space at the right the capital letter preceding the word which is spelled INCORRECTLY. If all four words are spelled CORRECTLY, print the letter E.

1.	A.	dismissal	B.	collateral	C.	leisure	D.	proffession	1.
2.	A.	subsidary	B.	outrageous	C.	liaison	D.	assessed	2.
3.	A.	already	B.	changeable	C.	mischevous	D.	cylinder	3.
4.	A.	supersede	B.	deceit	C.	dissension	D.	imminent	4.
5.	A.	arguing	B.	contagious	C.	comparitive	D.	accessible	5.
6.	A.	indelible	B.	existance	C.	presumptuous	D.	mileage	6.
7.	A.	extention	B.	aggregate	C.	sustenance	D.	gratuitous	7.
8.	A.	interrogate	B.	exaggeration	C.	vacillate	D.	moreover	8.
9.	A.	parallel	B.	derogatory	C.	admissable	D.	appellate	9.
10.	A.	safety	B.	cumalative	C.	disappear	D.	usable	10.

KEY (CORRECT ANSWERS)

1.	D	6.	B
2.	A	7.	A
3.	C	8.	E
4.	E	9.	C
5.	C	10.	B

TEST 11

DIRECTIONS: Each of Questions 1 through 10 consists of four words, one of which may be spelled incorrectly or all four words may be spelled correctly. If one of the words in a question is spelled INCORRECTLY, print in the space at the right the capital letter preceding the word which is spelled incorrectly. If all four words are spelled CORRECTLY, print the letter E.

1. A. vehicular   B. gesticulate   1._____
    C. manageable   D. fullfil

2. A. inovation   B. onerous   2._____
    C. chastise   D. irresistible

3. A. familiarize   B. dissolution   3._____
    C. oscillate   D. superflous

4. A. census   B. defender   4._____
    C. adherence   D. inconceivable

5. A. voluminous   B. liberalize   5._____
    C. bankrupcy   D. conversion

6. A. justifiable   B. executor   6._____
    C. perpatrate   D. dispelled

7. A. boycott   B. abeyence   7._____
    C. enterprise   D. circular

8. A. spontaineous   B. dubious   8._____
    C. analyze   D. premonition

9. A. intelligible   B. apparently   9._____
    C. genuine   D. crucial

10. A. plentiful   B. ascertain   10._____
    C. carreer   D. preliminary

KEY (CORRECT ANSWERS)

1.	D		6.	C
2.	A		7.	B
3.	D		8.	A
4.	E		9.	E
5.	C		10.	C

TEST 12

DIRECTIONS: Questions 1 through 25 consist of four words each, of which one of the words may be spelled incorrectly or all four words may be spelled correctly. If one of the words in a question is spelled INCORRECTLY, print in the space at the right the capital letter preceding the word which is spelled incorrectly. If all four words are spelled CORRECTLY, print the letter E.

1. A. temporary   B. existance   1.
    C. complimentary   D. altogether

2. A. privilege   B. changeable   2.
    C. jeopardize   D. commitment

3. A. grievous   B. alloted   3.
    C. outrageous   D. mortgage

4. A. tempermental   B. accommodating   4.
    C. bookkeeping   D. panicky

5. A. auxiliary   B. indispensable   5.
    C. ecstasy   D. fiery

6. A. dissappear   B. buoyant   6.
    C. imminent   D. parallel

7. A. loosly   B. medicine   7.
    C. schedule   D. defendant

8. A. endeavor   B. persuade   8.
    C. retroactive   D. desparate

9. A. usage   B. servicable   9.
    C. disadvantageous   D. remittance

10. A. beneficary   B. receipt   10.
    C. excitable   D. implement

11. A. accompanying   B. intangible   11.
    C. offered   D. movable

12. A. controlling   B. seize   12.
    C. repetitious   D. miscellaneous

13. A. installation   B. accommodation   13.
    C. consistant   D. illuminate

14. A. incidentaly   B. privilege   14.
    C. apparent   D. chargeable

15. A. prevalent   B. serial   15.
    C. briefly   D. disatisfied

16.	A. reciprocal	B. concurrence	16.___
	C. persistence	D. withold	

16. A. reciprocal   B. concurrence   16.___
      C. persistence   D. withold

17. A. deferred   B. suing   17.___
      C. fulfilled   D. pursuant

18. A. questionnable   B. omission   18.___
      C. acknowledgment   D. insistent

19. A. guarantee   B. committment   19.___
      C. mitigate   D. publicly

20. A. prerogative   B. apprise   20.___
      C. extrordinary   D. continual

21. A. arrogant   B. handicapped   21.___
      C. judicious   D. perennial

22. A. permissable   B. deceive   22.___
      C. innumerable   D. retrieve

23. A. notable   B. allegiance   23.___
      C. reimburse   D. illegal

24. A. wholly   B. disbursement   24.___
      C. hindrance   D. conciliatory

25. A. guidance   B. condemn   25.___
      C. publically   D. coercion

KEY (CORRECT ANSWERS)

1.	B	11.	C
2.	E	12.	E
3.	B	13.	C
4.	A	14.	A
5.	E	15.	D
6.	A	16.	D
7.	A	17.	E
8.	D	18.	A
9.	B	19.	B
10.	A	20.	C

21.	E
22.	A
23.	E
24.	E
25.	C

---

400 SPELLING DEMONS

The candidate should overlearn the correct spelling of the words that follow.
TEST YOURSELF.

1. partial
2. therefore
3. usually
4. acknowledgment
5. promptly
6. basis
7. envelope
8. actually
9. parcel post
10. executive
11. credited
12. balance
13. asked
14. material
15. receiving
16. commission
17. academy
18. airplane
19. alley
20. accustom
21. already
22. anxiety
23. audience
24. clothes
25. adviser
26. descend
27. encouraging
28. baseball
29. committee
30. destroy
31. everybody
32. beggar
33. digging
34. exceptional
35. biscuit
36. conscience
37. disappoint
38. disavowal
39. buoyant

40. dissatisfied
41. fascinate
42. course
43. finally
44. cemetery
45. dormitories
46. formally
47. characteristic
48. ecstasy
49. fourth
50. chosen
51. incidentally
52. independence
53. obstacle
54. generally
55. influence
56. manufacturer
57. occurrence
58. grandeur
59. intentionally
60. shown
61. existence
62. arrangement
63. having
64. appreciation
65. almost
66. recommend
67. merely
68. remember
69. suggestions
70. apparently
71. possibly
72. suppose

73. instructions
74. definitely
75. due
76. volume
77. referring
78. basketball
79. considerably
80. writer
81. always
82. assistance
83. absurd
84. aggravate
85. among
86. analogous
87. accumulate
88. ally
89. annual
90. athletic
91. addressed
92. alumnus
93. derived
94. eminent
95. barring
96. desperate
97. competent
98. difference
99. benefited
100. conqueror
101. disappear
102. expense
103. Britannica
104. familiar
105. distribute
106. cylinder
107. forfeit
108. changing
109. deceitful
110. forty

111. chose
112. loose
113. nowadays
114. lying
115. infinite
116. manual
117. occurred
118. grammar
119. intelligence
120. material
121. hoping
122. exceedingly
123. planning
124. secretary
125. affectionately
126. necessarily
127. criticism
128. dearest
129. position
130. handling
131. success
132. merchandise
133. opportunities
134. additional
135. doubt
136. returning
137. affects
138. amateur
139. arising
140. arithmetic
141. all right
142. angle
143. across
144. altogether
145. appropriate

400 SPELLING DEMONS (CONT'D)

146. embarrass
147. baring
148. coming
149. despair
150. especially
151. becoming
152. compelled
153. dictionary
154. excellent
155. believing
156. conquer
157. existence
158. Britain
159. continuous
160. discuss
161. business
162. countries
163. fiery
164. candidate
165. cruelty
166. changeable
167. debater
168. forth
169. choose
170. deferred
171. eliminate
172. noticeable
173. furniture
174. oblige
175. induce
176. maintenance
177. occur
178. governor
179. intellectual
180. cede
181. officers
182. Wednesday
183. pleat

184. acceptable
185. quote
186. society
187. error
188. schedule
189. possible
190. stating
191. always
192. argument
193. accommodate
194. angel
195. ascend
196. acquitted
197. alter
198. appearance
199. awkward
200. barbarous
201. column
202. equipped
203. bearing
204. device
205. beginning
206. conferred
207. dining room
208. exhilarate
209. brilliant
210. considered
211. discipline
212. bureau
213. distinction
214. calendar
215. courtesy
216. doctor
217. foreign
218. dealt
219. eighth
220. fraternity
221. incredulous
222. gallant

223. maintain
224. occasionally
225. government
226. instant
227. marriage
228. o'clock
229. apparently
230. guard
231. although
232. already
233. knowledge
234. library
235. service
236. accepted
237. supply
238. extremely
239. benefit
240. arctic
241. allotted
242. analysis
243. arrival
244. auxiliary
245. balance
246. coarse
247. enemy
248. comparative
249. device
250. exaggerate
251. conceivable
252. begging
253. dilemma
254. exhaust
255. boundaries
256. conscientious
257. dissipate
258. February
259. courteous
260. divine

261. financier
262. drudgery
263. formerly
264. decide
265. effects
266. frantically
267. freshman
268. incidents
269. losing
270. indispensable
271. occasion
272. goddess
273. instance
274. grievous
275. intercede
276. omission
277. hiatus
278. irresistible
279. harass
280. mattress
281. miniature
282. misspelled
283. laboratory
284. murmur
285. parliament
286. hurriedly
287. peaceable
288. Negroes
289. neither
290. immigration
291. literature
292. perseverance
293. supersede
294. shiftless
295. tendency
296. recognize
297. precedents

298. sacrilegious	322. bony	349. based	380. sense
299. principle	323. descendant	350. stopped	381. invoice
300. soliloquy	324. liaison	351. exactly	382. usual
301. ophthalmolo-gist	325. accommodate	352. least	383. awful
302. cinnamon	326. despair	353. community	384. college
303. phlegmatic	327. fallacious	354. necessary	385. different
304. berserk	328. caramel	355. business	386. similar
305. cellophane	329. forego	356. probably	387. freight
306. xylophone	330. receipt	357. course	388. cancel
307. calisthenics	331. received	358. remittance	389. weather
308. inebriate	332. believe	359. their	390. tomorrow
309. chlorophyll	333. convenient	360. truly	391. recent
310. broccoli	334. sufficient	361. enclosed	392. guess
311. ecumenical	335. literature	362. instant	393. prior
312. acupuncture	336. beginning	363. whether	394. mutual
313. deterrent	337. clothes	364. referred	395. perhaps
314. assassin	338. cooperation	365. really	396. accept
315. eligible	339. ought	366. original	397. prices
316. all right	340. paid	367. separate	398. semester
317. infrared	341. arrange	368. further	399. regret
318. antidote	342. approval	369. catalog	400. although
319. impresario	343. beautiful	370. forward	
320. beige	344. connection	371. expect	
321. ellipse	345. certificate	372. canceled	
	346. disposition	373. coming	
	347. grateful	374. inquiry	
	348. finally	375. waste	
		376. definite	
		377. great	
		378. courtesy	
		379. assure	

SPELLING DIFFICULTIES
WORDS PRESENTING DIFFICULTIES BECAUSE OF THEIR ENDINGS

1. ENDING IN ABLE
   - acceptable
   - admirable
   - available
   - charitable
   - desirable
   - excitable
   - formidable
   - imaginable
   - incurable
   - inevitable
   - inextricable
   - intolerable
   - justifiable
   - lovable
   - movable
   - pardonable
   - perishable
   - presumable
   - profitable
   - serviceable
   - suitable
   - transferable
   - unconquerable
   - unconscionable

2. ENDING IN ANCE
   - abundance
   - acquaintance
   - annoyance
   - deliverance
   - maintenance
   - repentance
   - resistance
   - resonance
   - significance
   - sustenance

3. ENDING IN AR
   - beggar
   - burglar
   - calendar
   - circular
   - familiar
   - grammar
   - peculiar
   - popular
   - similar
   - solar
   - tabular
   - vinegar

4. ENDING IN ARY
   - actuary
   - auxiliary
   - dictionary
   - lapidary
   - necessary
   - obituary
   - subsidiary
   - stationary
   - supplementary

5. ENDING IN ENCE
   - circumference
   - coherence
   - competence
   - deference
   - excellence
   - obedience
   - opulence
   - reminiscence
   - violence

6. ENDING IN ER
   - adviser
   - clothier
   - colander
   - debater
   - defender
   - embroider
   - foreigner
   - laborer
   - provider
   - reciter
   - subscriber
   - trotter

7. ENDING IN ERY
   - bribery
   - cemetery
   - delivery
   - flattery
   - monastery
   - stationery
   - thievery

8. ENDING IN IBLE
   - accessible
   - admissible
   - discernible
   - infallible
   - indestructible
   - intelligible
   - invisible
   - irresistible
   - ostensible
   - perceptible
   - plausible
   - responsible

9. ENDING IN OR
   - creator
   - demeanor
   - distributor
   - editor
   - endeavor
   - governor
   - impostor
   - inventor
   - legislator
   - monitor
   - orator
   - persecutor
   - predecessor
   - protector

spectator
suitor
survivor
ventilator

10. PLURAL OF WORDS ENDING IN O
cameo -cameos   solo -solos
folio   -folios   mango -mangoes
piano -pianos   potato -potatoes

11. ADDING TO WORDS ENDING IN C
bivouac -bivouacked, bivouacking
colic   -colicky
frolic   -frolicked, frolicking
mimic   -mimicked, mimicking
panic   -panicky
picnic   -picnicked, picnicking

12. WORDS ENDING IN SILENT E
force   -forcible, forcing
love   -lovable, loving
move   -movable, moving
shape   -shaping
write   -writing
use   -using, usage

13. WORDS ENDING IN CE OR GE
manage -manageable
notice   -noticeable
service -serviceable

———

6

ABBREVIATIONS AND CONTRACTIONS

Abbreviations are shortened forms for words and phrases in common use. For example, U.S.P.S. = United States Postal Service. Abbreviations always require <u>periods</u>.

Contractions are shortened forms of words produced by the omission of letters (Sec'y - Secretary) or by combination (it's = it is) in order to save space or time. Contractions always require an <u>apostrophe</u> to indicate the missing letters.

Jan.	- January	Mon.	- Monday	A.M. (or a.m.) -	morning	
Feb.	- February	Tues.	- Tuesday	P.M. (or p.m.) -	afternoon	
Mar.	- March	Wed.	- Wednesday	Mr.	- Mister	
Apr.	- April	Thurs .	- Thursday	Mrs.	- Mistress	
Jun.	- June	Fri.	- Friday	.St.	- Street	
Jul.	- July	Sat.	- Saturday	Ave	.- Avenue	
Aug.	- August	Sun.	- Sunday	Blvd.	- Boulevard	
Sept.	- September	E.	- East	Rd.	- Road	
Oct.	- October	S.	- South	P.S.	- Public School Post Script	
Nov.	- November	N.	- North			
Dec.	- December	W.	- West	No.	- Number	
Rev.	- Reverend	Co.	- Company	R.N.	- Registered Nurse, or	
Dr.	- Doctor	S.S.	- Steamship		Royal Navy	
f.o.b.	- free on board	Dept.	- Department	Pres.	- President	
Gov.	- Governor	Prin.	- Principal	U. S. A.-	United States of America	
Supt.	- Superintendent	Treas.	- Treasurer			
Jr.	- Junior	Sr.	- Senior	C.O.D. -	Cash on Delivery	
Gen.	- General	Capt	.-Captain	Sgt	.- Serveant	
Cpl.	- Corporal	Pvt.	- Private	A.D	.- Anno Domini (year of our Lord)	
B.C.	- Before Christ	chap.	- chapter			
p.	- page	e.g.	- for example	i.e.	- that is	
pp.	- pages	viz.	- namely	etc	.- and so forth	
Hon	--. Honorable	P.O.	- Post Office	Messrs.-	Gentlemen	
oz.	- ounce	masc.	- masculine	R.F.D. -	Rural Free Delivery	
lb.	- pound	fern.	- feminine	R.I. P. -	Rest in Peace	
yd.	- yard	sing.	- singular	Inc.	- Incorporated	
ft.	- foot or feet	pl.	- plural	Ltd	- Limited	
in.	- inch	Bros.	- Brothers			

CONTRACTIONS

n't

isn't = is not	hasn't = has not	aren't = are not
wasn't = was not	hadn't = had not	won't = will not
haven 't= have not	didn't = did not	wouldn' t =would not
don't = do not	doesn't = does not	couldn't = could not
can't = cannot	shouldn't = should not	

'm

I ' m = I am

' ve

I've = Ihave   we've = we have   you've = you have
they've = they have

,

ne'er = never   o'er = over   e'er = ever

ANSWER SHEET

USE THE SPECIAL PENCIL.   MAKE GLOSSY BLACK MARKS.

	A B C D E		A B C D E		A B C D E		A B C D E		A B C D E
1	:: :: :: :: ::	26	:: :: :: :: ::	51	:: :: :: :: ::	76	:: :: :: :: ::	101	:: :: :: :: ::
2	:: :: :: :: ::	27	:: :: :: :: ::	52	:: :: :: :: ::	77	:: :: :: :: ::	102	:: :: :: :: ::
3	:: :: :: :: ::	28	:: :: :: :: ::	53	:: :: :: :: ::	78	:: :: :: :: ::	103	:: :: :: :: ::
4	:: :: :: :: ::	29	:: :: :: :: ::	54	:: :: :: :: ::	79	:: :: :: :: ::	104	:: :: :: :: ::
5	:: :: :: :: ::	30	:: :: :: :: ::	55	:: :: :: :: ::	80	:: :: :: :: ::	105	:: :: :: :: ::
6	:: :: :: :: ::	31	:: :: :: :: ::	56	:: :: :: :: ::	81	:: :: :: :: ::	106	:: :: :: :: ::
7	:: :: :: :: ::	32	:: :: :: :: ::	57	:: :: :: :: ::	82	:: :: :: :: ::	107	:: :: :: :: ::
8	:: :: :: :: ::	33	:: :: :: :: ::	58	:: :: :: :: ::	83	:: :: :: :: ::	108	:: :: :: :: ::
9	:: :: :: :: ::	34	:: :: :: :: ::	59	:: :: :: :: ::	84	:: :: :: :: ::	109	:: :: :: :: ::
10	:: :: :: :: ::	35	:: :: :: :: ::	60	:: :: :: :: ::	85	:: :: :: :: ::	110	:: :: :: :: ::

Make only ONE mark for each answer.   Additional and stray marks may be
counted as mistakes.   In making corrections, erase errors COMPLETELY.

	A B C D E		A B C D E		A B C D E		A B C D E		A B C D E
11	:: :: :: :: ::	36	:: :: :: :: ::	61	:: :: :: :: ::	86	:: :: :: :: ::	111	:: :: :: :: ::
12	:: :: :: :: ::	37	:: :: :: :: ::	62	:: :: :: :: ::	87	:: :: :: :: ::	112	:: :: :: :: ::
13	:: :: :: :: ::	38	:: :: :: :: ::	63	:: :: :: :: ::	88	:: :: :: :: ::	113	:: :: :: :: ::
14	:: :: :: :: ::	39	:: :: :: :: ::	64	:: :: :: :: ::	89	:: :: :: :: ::	114	:: :: :: :: ::
15	:: :: :: :: ::	40	:: :: :: :: ::	65	:: :: :: :: ::	90	:: :: :: :: ::	115	:: :: :: :: ::
16	:: :: :: :: ::	41	:: :: :: :: ::	66	:: :: :: :: ::	91	:: :: :: :: ::	116	:: :: :: :: ::
17	:: :: :: :: ::	42	:: :: :: :: ::	67	:: :: :: :: ::	92	:: :: :: :: ::	117	:: :: :: :: ::
18	:: :: :: :: ::	43	:: :: :: :: ::	68	:: :: :: :: ::	93	:: :: :: :: ::	118	:: :: :: :: ::
19	:: :: :: :: ::	44	:: :: :: :: ::	69	:: :: :: :: ::	94	:: :: :: :: ::	119	:: :: :: :: ::
20	:: :: :: :: ::	45	:: :: :: :: ::	70	:: :: :: :: ::	95	:: :: :: :: ::	120	:: :: :: :: ::
21	:: :: :: :: ::	46	:: :: :: :: ::	71	:: :: :: :: ::	96	:: :: :: :: ::	121	:: :: :: :: ::
22	:: :: :: :: ::	47	:: :: :: :: ::	72	:: :: :: :: ::	97	:: :: :: :: ::	122	:: :: :: :: ::
23	:: :: :: :: ::	48	:: :: :: :: ::	73	:: :: :: :: ::	98	:: :: :: :: ::	123	:: :: :: :: ::
24	:: :: :: :: ::	49	:: :: :: :: ::	74	:: :: :: :: ::	99	:: :: :: :: ::	124	:: :: :: :: ::
25	:: :: :: :: ::	50	:: :: :: :: ::	75	:: :: :: :: ::	100	:: :: :: :: ::	125	:: :: :: :: ::

ANSWER SHEET

TEST NO. _____ PART _____ TITLE OF POSITION _____

(AS GIVEN IN EXAMINATION ANNOUNCEMENT - INCLUDE OPTION, IF ANY)

PLACE OF EXAMINATION _____ (CITY OR TOWN) WITHDRAWN (STATE) DATE_____

	RATING

USE THE SPECIAL PENCIL.   MAKE GLOSSY BLACK MARKS.

	A B C D E		A B C D E		A B C D E		A B C D E		A B C D E
1	:: :: :: :: ::	26	:: :: :: :: ::	51	:: :: :: :: ::	76	:: :: :: :: ::	101	:: :: :: :: ::
2	:: :: :: :: ::	27	:: :: :: :: ::	52	:: :: :: :: ::	77	:: :: :: :: ::	102	:: :: :: :: ::
3	:: :: :: :: ::	28	:: :: :: :: ::	53	:: :: :: :: ::	78	:: :: :: :: ::	103	:: :: :: :: ::
4	:: :: :: :: ::	29	:: :: :: :: ::	54	:: :: :: :: ::	79	:: :: :: :: ::	104	:: :: :: :: ::
5	:: :: :: :: ::	30	:: :: :: :: ::	55	:: :: :: :: ::	80	:: :: :: :: ::	105	:: :: :: :: ::
6	:: :: :: :: ::	31	:: :: :: :: ::	56	:: :: :: :: ::	81	:: :: :: :: ::	106	:: :: :: :: ::
7	:: :: :: :: ::	32	:: :: :: :: ::	57	:: :: :: :: ::	82	:: :: :: :: ::	107	:: :: :: :: ::
8	:: :: :: :: ::	33	:: :: :: :: ::	58	:: :: :: :: ::	83	:: :: :: :: ::	108	:: :: :: :: ::
9	:: :: :: :: ::	34	:: :: :: :: ::	59	:: :: :: :: ::	84	:: :: :: :: ::	109	:: :: :: :: ::
10	:: :: :: :: ::	35	:: :: :: :: ::	60	:: :: :: :: ::	85	:: :: :: :: ::	110	:: :: :: :: ::

Make only ONE mark for each answer.   Additional and stray marks may be
counted as mistakes.   In making corrections, erase errors COMPLETELY.

	A B C D E		A B C D E		A B C D E		A B C D E		A B C D E
11	:: :: :: :: ::	36	:: :: :: :: ::	61	:: :: :: :: ::	86	:: :: :: :: ::	111	:: :: :: :: ::
12	:: :: :: :: ::	37	:: :: :: :: ::	62	:: :: :: :: ::	87	:: :: :: :: ::	112	:: :: :: :: ::
13	:: :: :: :: ::	38	:: :: :: :: ::	63	:: :: :: :: ::	88	:: :: :: :: ::	113	:: :: :: :: ::
14	:: :: :: :: ::	39	:: :: :: :: ::	64	:: :: :: :: ::	89	:: :: :: :: ::	114	:: :: :: :: ::
15	:: :: :: :: ::	40	:: :: :: :: ::	65	:: :: :: :: ::	90	:: :: :: :: ::	115	:: :: :: :: ::
16	:: :: :: :: ::	41	:: :: :: :: ::	66	:: :: :: :: ::	91	:: :: :: :: ::	116	:: :: :: :: ::
17	:: :: :: :: ::	42	:: :: :: :: ::	67	:: :: :: :: ::	92	:: :: :: :: ::	117	:: :: :: :: ::
18	:: :: :: :: ::	43	:: :: :: :: ::	68	:: :: :: :: ::	93	:: :: :: :: ::	118	:: :: :: :: ::
19	:: :: :: :: ::	44	:: :: :: :: ::	69	:: :: :: :: ::	94	:: :: :: :: ::	119	:: :: :: :: ::
20	:: :: :: :: ::	45	:: :: :: :: ::	70	:: :: :: :: ::	95	:: :: :: :: ::	120	:: :: :: :: ::
21	:: :: :: :: ::	46	:: :: :: :: ::	71	:: :: :: :: ::	96	:: :: :: :: ::	121	:: :: :: :: ::
22	:: :: :: :: ::	47	:: :: :: :: ::	72	:: :: :: :: ::	97	:: :: :: :: ::	122	:: :: :: :: ::
23	:: :: :: :: ::	48	:: :: :: :: ::	73	:: :: :: :: ::	98	:: :: :: :: ::	123	:: :: :: :: ::
24	:: :: :: :: ::	49	:: :: :: :: ::	74	:: :: :: :: ::	99	:: :: :: :: ::	124	:: :: :: :: ::
25	:: :: :: :: ::	50	:: :: :: :: ::	75	:: :: :: :: ::	100	:: :: :: :: ::	125	:: :: :: :: ::